WTFO: The Silence Is Deafening

WTFO: The Silence Is Deafening

By Khaled Hafid

Copyright © 2012, Khaled Hafid

All rights reserved. No part of this book may be reproduced, stored, or transmitted by any means—whether auditory, graphic, mechanical, or electronic—without written permission of both publisher and author, except in the case of brief excerpts used in critical articles and reviews. Unauthorized reproduction of any part of this work is illegal and is punishable by law.

Hardback ISBN 978-1-105972-348
Paperback ISBN 978-1-105972-355

Photograph of author taken by Naomi Lara in September 2011

For my father, my children and for those who have always been there. You have shown me that the world is never too big for those you love. I thank you all from the bottom of my heart.

To my brothers-in-arms and in eternity, Semper Fi…

Prologue

Breaking the Silence

Radio check, can you read me?

It's finally over. It has been nearly nine years since we literally drove in and parked our vehicles without paying parking fees in a lot resembling a sand covered egg with oil beneath its shell. We have finally sent everyone home. My brothers and sisters from all the armed services are now home. From the Marines, sailors, and soldiers to the left and right of me, entering battle without a word, to those who hooted and hollered on their way out…

Many of you have come across service members who were "over there" because nine years covers two complete enlistments; a lot of kids came in fresh and those same kids are now war vets—nine years later, a third of their lives lived in battle. You look at them in awe and in admiration, but that lasts for a brief moment because all you see is their surface. You hear them speak and you look at them as if nothing has happened. Then later, you forget that anything took place thousands of miles away in a world that most of you would never understand.

We are all affected by what took place over there. The reactions vary from insanity, murder, and suicide to silence, denial, and isolation. We, your men and women who you're told to "support," are all back in some shape or form. Dead or alive, we've all returned. The President can now say "Mission Accomplished" and go back to his plush living conditions; but there is not a single one of us who is the same person we were before we crossed that invisible line in the sand.

The definition of who I am is not only credited to how I was raised or whom I was around. The definition of who I am is written with the blood, sweat, and tears shed. To explain it to anyone who wasn't there would be useless. Most of you reading this are reasonable and wouldn't dare compare your experiences with that of a Marine or soldier in battle; but then there are others, naïve to the human aspect, that they think you should, "Get over it. Everyone has issues." To those people I say, "Go fuck yourselves." You might as well be the one pulling the trigger, sending that round downrange at us… You might as well be the one calling that cell phone from the comfort of your home triggering the explosive device meant to send me, my brothers, and my sisters home in a body bag.

There's a reason why we have a disconnect with those who weren't there. It is there because unless you were there, you weren't there. It's as simple as that. It's either you were or you weren't. There are other layers to the onion of war. Peel them back and you'll find different wars within the war.

I didn't write a journal of what occurred; it wouldn't have mattered if I had. You can write anything; it's how you remember the story that tells the true story. I remember seeing senior Marines who saw nothing more than the inside of a vehicle or the inside of a tent writing the stories of their "experiences" in journals that were barely covered in the sand that surrounded us. I had one officer call our platoon together to read us an excerpt from his journal, as if he was showing us he cared. If anything we lost more respect for him. How could he tell the story of the Marine who was shot and killed on the front line? This officer was asleep in his vehicle when that Marine lost his life. The audacity that is war, the audacity of the ignorant…

Now that my brothers and sisters are out of harm's way, some of them flying home as I am writing this to spend Christmas with their families, I am breaking my silence.

This is my story…

Chapter 1

We're Gonna Get Wasted

The Marines I have seen around the world have the cleanest bodies, the filthiest minds, the highest morale, and the lowest morals of any group of animals I have ever seen. Thank God for the United States Marine Corps.
—First Lady Eleanor Roosevelt

Marines are a special breed; we're both lauded and scolded for our insanity. From day one we're told how awesome being a Marine is and how special the title of Marine is. We eat dirt, get physically beaten by the rigors of daily tasks, and we destroy our bodies for pay that borders the poverty line. We're told how it's an honor to be a Marine from the moment we stand on the footprints painted in yellow on sacred ground in Parris Island, South Carolina, and if we want to feel that honor, we're going to have to earn it.

Why do we join the Marine Corps? We join for an infinite number of reasons that I cannot even begin to name. I will only tell you as to why I joined the Marine Corps. It's simple; I joined because I didn't want my dad to pay for my college education. He offered to pay, but I remember standing in front of him telling him that it was his money, that he had earned it. Who was I to take it? I look back at this now and think to myself, *Wow I was some badass back then when I was sixteen, telling my dad that I was going to do it my way.* The only problem is I didn't initially want to be a Marine; I wanted to join the Navy and be a sailor.

Fate would have it that my older brother was walking by a Navy Recruiting office. He wasn't too bright and didn't notice that there was a Marine recruiter in there as well. He went into the first office and spoke to the person occupying it. He told him, "Hey, my brother wants to join the Navy." The gentleman replied, "We're not the

Navy; we're the Marines." My brother naively said, "Same difference, he wants to join."

I'm sure I speak for many when I say that we also join the Marine Corps to make a difference in a life so brief. Whether it's your life or the life of someone else, you will make a difference, good or bad, sometimes both. I was also tired of getting picked on in school for being skinny, different, and weak. I was tired of being ridiculed and doubted by the masses. I didn't like growing up in the neighborhood I grew up in, an Italian-American neighborhood mostly. My friends and I were treated like dirt by the other kids because we were Arab, raised by immigrants. I wanted a fresh start; I wanted to be someone else.

A few years later, just days after 9/11, I was a Marine Sergeant in Shanghai, China, on Embassy duty. All I could think of was reenlisting for another four years so I could get payback on those who did this to our country and to my home. It just so happened that President Bush caught wind of this, and his staff wanted my reenlistment to coincide with his visit to Shanghai. A few weeks later, there I was for the entire world to see, standing next to the President of the United States. I was the face of today's men and women going to war for our nation, and a little over a year later I would truly be the embodiment of that archetype.

I was a twenty-three-year-old staff sergeant in the Marine Corps. To those who have no idea what that signifies, it means that I was very young. My peers were in their thirties, and here I was, younger than some Privates, telling them all what to do. I was twenty-four when we got word that we were mobilizing. As the Platoon Sergeant for a Maintenance Platoon in a Light Armored Reconnaissance Battalion, I was taking my men to war. My only thoughts were of how gloriously triumphant it would be.

I was recently married and had finally lost my virginity, so yeah, I was gung ho to say the least. I had finally gotten laid after twenty-four years, and the way I saw it, I was playing with house money. I, like many others, wanted awards and medals—I wanted glory.

We put all of our equipment on flatbed trucks, which were then loaded on ships. For weeks we prepared to deploy to Kuwait, thinking we'd probably sit around in the sand for months while the UN did nothing, and then get told to go back home. We were told that we were going in, to get that thought out of our heads and forget what we were hearing from the news media. They were pretty adamant about that.

We didn't have time to go home on leave to spend time with our families. We were going to go away with the real possibility of not coming back, and they wouldn't give any of the Marines an opportunity to go home to see their loved ones for fear of deserters. So what do we do as Marines? We drink!

Our platoon met at the barracks where the single Marines lived, and we filled the balcony with rowdy, high-spirited bodies and tons of beer bottles, empty and full. We each took turns guessing how long it would be before we got back and wondering who was going to get shot in the back by another Marine for being a dick. It was always the same person, so yes, Marines do hold grudges, which could possibly have been one of the motivating factors of going to war in the first place.

I was the only Staff Non-Commissioned Officer out of this group of Marines who were drinking. They were all younger Marines, and though they were junior to me in grade, I considered them my equal. These were my brothers in arms; there was no one else I would have rather spent my last night of innocence with other than these Marines. Being a Marine is indeed an honor, and it is an honor to serve with any Marine—our common insanity binding us together.

I still look back with longing at a picture taken that night, an iconic image to signify the end of an era. Kids, all of us, on our final night of normalcy. Was there a better way to celebrate other than having a few drinks with those you're willing to die with and die for? Nope.

Chapter 2

I'm on a Boat

It's barely five in the morning, and we're already awake, getting dressed and ready. Our bags are packed, placed in a pile in front of us. Normal clothing that would be deemed "civilian attire" is tucked away in storage. All that remains are uniforms of camouflage and undergarments of olive drab. We're not out to make a fashion statement, but we're wearing desert uniforms with collars so large it looks like we're Marines from the disco era. All I need is a perm, and I am set.

Going to the armory to pick up weapons is never fun, doing it at zero-dark-thirty is even worse. It is winter, and we're cold; everyone is hung over from the night before, and most of us have said our good-byes to our families over the phone, except me. I told my mom I was going to the Philippines for some exercise and would be there for anywhere from three to eight months. My dad asked me months ago if I was going to Iraq, and I told him I would be. I didn't want to lie about it, though I did lie to him when I first enlisted and told him I would only be working with electronics. I told him I wouldn't fight; I would just work on equipment. I didn't want him to be worried.

My wife was pregnant with our first child. Months before, I told my dad my son would be born on the 19th of August 2003. He looked at me as one would look at an idiot. I picked that day because it was the day I became a Marine. I had to tempt fate and demand it also become the day I become a father. I also lied to my wife about going to Iraq; I didn't want her to watch the BBC or CNN International from Yemen and freak out, causing her to miscarriage. I wanted to be right about the August 19 date.

We're standing in line in silence. No one wants to talk to the person in front of or to the rear of him. We just want to get our weapons and get to our gear so we can get some sleep. The Marine Corps has an unadvertised motto of "hurry up and wait." We wake up at the earliest of hours, a time where God himself is still passed out, drooling from his mouth with a fifth of Jack in his right hand and his left arm around the shoulder of some chick he hooked up with the night prior…yeah it's early. We get what we need to get done in a timely fashion, and then we sit around for hours waiting to begin what we've been preparing for.

As a Staff Non-Commissioned Officer (SNCO or staff NCO), we get front-of-the-line privileges and get our weapons first. We usually get issued a pistol only, not a rifle, but since I had opened my fat mouth when I checked into the battalion about speaking some Arabic, the battalion commander assigned me as his personal interpreter. This meant I was getting both a pistol and a rifle. Great. They were taking me away from what I loved doing most, leading Marines, so I could speak to some people who didn't want me in their country. Add to this the fact that I was Muslim and would be seen as a traitor and you have the ideal situation. Yeah, not really.

My status as a translator would begin as soon as we hit the ground; but there was still the issue of getting to the sandbox first. Our battalion was spread over four ships, if I remember correctly. We would go with our equipment and would be traveling with our war machines. I was with the battalion commander, so I ended up on the USS Comstock with the Headquarters Element. The rest of the Marines in my platoon were spread across other ships. I was one of six staff sergeants from my battalion assigned to the boat, and since I was an everyday platoon sergeant, I was asked to run the day-to-day operations for the Marines while out on the water. The other staff sergeants loved this; it meant they weren't responsible for anything, but it didn't mean they wouldn't open their mouths about how things should be run in their opinion.

We got our weapons and laid on top of our gear, waiting for the buses to take us down to the port. I had already visited my berthing area the day before. I did this to bring most of what I wanted with me in Iraq ahead of time so I wouldn't have to lug it around like everyone else. Now all I had was a small bag and my weapons. I was good to go.

The buses finally arrived. The married Marines who had their wives living with them on base were saying good-bye to their women. Seeing them cry was strange to me. To clarify, most of the crying was done by the Marines themselves. Who knew what God-awful things the wives would get themselves into? Remember I mentioned before that from day one they tell you how much of an honor it is to be a Marine? Well, they also tell you from day one that you'll be drinking a six-pack each day, and while you're off at war, your wife, who they referred to as "Susie," would be having her privates occupied by some guy named "Jody." I never asked where they got the names from or why they chose them, but they tell you your wife will be unfaithful while you're out saving the world. It's not like they make this stuff up; it's been known to happen, and almost expected.

The bus ride to the ships was dull. We got to see California traffic one last time so we would remember what it was we were fighting for. We stayed in the slow lane, as if slowing down would make us miss home more. We didn't give a shit, at least I didn't. Just get us on the damn boats so we can lie down on beds resembling coffins and be fed food that Sally Struthers wouldn't steal from a starving Ethiopian.

To be honest, the ride down to the port and the conversations on the bus was a blur. There must have been a few conversations, but nothing out of the ordinary. The *ordinary* being one Marine telling another how wasted he got the night before. Another *ordinary* conversation would have a Marine fucking with another by telling him that his wife was probably fucking their neighbor right now on his bed while recording it so she could send it to him in a care package. It's always in good fun. We give each other shit all the time, but there is not one person that I wouldn't jump in front of a bullet for. And it works both ways.

We arrived and got on our ships to get a brief from the senior Marine representative onboard. They told us we had the night free to go on base and get dinner if we wanted, but that the next morning we would be pulling out and setting sail to Kuwait. Thankfully we don't *sail* anymore because it would take ages to get there. That night a couple of Marines from my platoon and I got together for a quick bite to eat and headed back to our respective ships.

Back in the berthing area I found myself as the youngest man in the room. I was the same rank as everyone else, but younger by at least five years. One of the Marines in the berthing area was a staff sergeant eighteen days before I joined the Marines. He was a still a staff sergeant and didn't really like me very much. Hey, I can't help it if he was a shitbag and I was locked on. Well, I can help the latter, but him being a shitbag? That's on him.

I bedded down for the night. I fit snugly into my coffin of a bunk and barely had room to roll over. I pulled the curtains shut to close myself off from the world outside. The world being a room the size of a closet with five other guys, two of whom I know will cause problems for me. I shut my eyes, but sleep does not consume me. I wait and wait; the lights turn out, and now I am in complete darkness. Was the way I was laying in this *bed* a sign of what I was to expect if we indeed went to war? It was too much for me to worry about right now, I thought to myself as I turned on my laptop. I put in a DVD and clicked twice on the menu screen. It was a porn gifted to me by my brother-from-another-mother over in Massachusetts.

It doesn't get any better than this.

CHAPTER 3

We're Off to See the Wizard

Sergeant, I want to thank you, as well, for your service to the country. As you all know, I committed American troops to a very important cause in the last couple of weeks. And I did so with the full confidence that our military is the best in the world. The American people have got the full confidence that our military will fulfill its mission. And one of the reasons that I've got so much confidence is, I know many of the people who wear the uniform. Sergeant Khaled represents the fine quality of the men and women who serve our country. And Sergeant, thank you very much for being here.
—President George W. Bush (19 October 2001)

I woke up with some excitement. After breakfast we're to stand on the edge of the flight deck, Marines and sailors side by side, as we pull out of port. I shit, shower, and shave (the 3 S's) before I have my first meal on board. I don't remember what it was, because it was awful. I remember thinking that I would lose a ton of weight because I wouldn't be able to eat. I had what I've always had whenever food frightened me and there was nothing else available—peanut butter sandwiches.

The Marine Corps is a public relations outfit, if I have ever seen one. Celebrities shy away from the paparazzi, but the Marine Corps looks to stage photo opportunities at any time and any place. Stand and smile Marines, you're the best recruiting tool our country has to offer the young men and women who aren't yet committed to anything.

We get to the flight deck as we're ready to leave. They actually have someone come out and tell us how they want us standing, one Marine, one sailor. It was going to be a mix to show solidarity I guess, to show everyone watching us push off that we were a team. I took my position in between two sailors and looked below. There was not one soul other than the men and women who worked that dock to see us off. Here we were standing at parade rest on the edge of a moving vessel, and no one was there to see us off? Well it was early morning, everyone else was busy having breakfast and the sun was just coming up from the horizon. God forbid we were to disrupt anyone. We put on this display just in case anyone wanted to see a show.

I thought back to October of 2001, when I was announced on stage by the U.S. Ambassador to China. I marched up there as any proud Marine would to thunderous applause, took my position, and snapped to parade rest. It was intense; the President would be announced next and he would come out to applause as well. I stood there for the world to see as the face of the new fighting generation, but all I was doing in Shanghai was representing the Marine Corps and Islam. It was soon after the September 11 attacks. What sort of message would it send to the world seeing the President and a Muslim Marine on stage together? One that everyone would eat up; it was a feel good story, except I didn't feel good about it at all. I felt guilty that I wasn't going into battle. My brothers-in-arms over in Afghanistan were, in President Bush's words, "Kicking ass!" and I was receiving cheers and praise for being Muslim and not having the urge to fly a commercial plane into a building. They were all looking at me with pride, and while I was twenty-three and a bit taken back, I was scared. My mind was wondering what other Marines would think.

Here I was now, on a flight deck with my brothers-in-arms, shoving off to fight an enemy that would either lie down or fight to the death…and there was no one there to snap photos or cheer us on. There is no glory in doing what is expected of you, there is only someone there to kick you in the ass when you're not doing it.

We hit the open waters soon after, the coast and San Diego skyline drifting away. I had a meeting with command personnel. I was going to get briefed on what our training schedule would be like and what we were going to expect the Marines to do each day. It's not like there was anywhere for them to go, if they didn't like the living conditions, they could always swim back to shore. I say "they" because it's not like I was going to swim to shore—I can't swim. Yes, a Marine who can't swim.

A majority of the Marines on board with me I did not know prior to boarding the ship. There were only a few Marines from my platoon on board because the vehicles they were assigned to were on this ship. I had a month and a half to get to know these guys and get them prepared for whatever was going to be asked of them.

I had a different leadership style than the other staff sergeants. I was still in my early twenties and these Marines were my peer group. I still remembered when I was in their position and wanted to treat them as I wanted to be treated if I were them. I spoke to them as men, not as subordinates, not as servants—as men. They were not kids, as some would like to call them. They were about to go to war, and we, as Americans, do not send kids to battle. What are we, Sierra Leone? Didn't think so.

My style upset some of the other staff sergeants I was living with because to them I was befriending the Marines instead of telling them what to do. Leadership, in my opinion, is not about being able to get someone to do something; it's about getting them to understand why something needs to get done. I had to set the example for these Marines. I have based my style of leadership on being the leader I want leading me. How does one set the example? By being the example.

Within the first few days I was having words with some of my *peers* in grade. Two of the staff sergeants were pissing me off. They were miserable and wanted everyone else to be miserable with them. They didn't agree with my style of leadership or how I was taking care of these Marines, yet when I asked them to feel free to assist, they refused. I never understood the mentality of a miserable person. If you are so miserable and things are so bad, kill yourself. It's a naval vessel, there are going to be mops readily available. Where there are mops, there is bleach. Have a drink for the Corps!

Living in confined quarters takes a toll on you. I was starting to lose my temper with the other staff sergeants, finally telling them to fuck off and stay out of it. I was still growing as a staff sergeant and was still learning the way, but these two did nothing to assist. They would rather see me fail than help me to succeed. I had support from some others, but it did get tough.

The hours became days, and the days became weeks. I couldn't stand the sight of some of these guys, so I would wander off and stand on the flight deck. I would look out at the ocean and wonder what was to become of me? Was this my destiny? If this was getting to me, what else was going to get to me? I started to doubt my inner strength, and the swagger I once had was gone. I did my job, but it wasn't easy; I just wanted to go home. I looked around on the flight deck and there were hundreds of Marines and sailors doing exactly what I was doing. I was not alone.

Marines do not want to be seen as weak. We will do some of the dumbest things to prove that we are ballsy. We, as Marines, are still human beings. You could see it in everyone else's eyes; they hated it here and wanted to go home. We missed our families, hearing from them only when we were able to get on a computer for thirty minutes a day; we wanted to be with them. We will never tell you this—we hurt.

As a kid growing up, I had always tried to be the class clown but failed miserably at it. Did it ever stop me? One thing about me that you need to know is that I am stubborn. I believe all those years of practice made me good at comic relief, so I would say and do things that no one would think of. It also helped that I was a senior Marine, because that meant I could talk shit to just about anyone and do so with utter sarcasm.

I would visit my Marines on their downtime. I would visit their berthing areas and each one of them would smile and greet me with a, "Hey, Staff Sergeant!" It felt good, and it felt sincere, which made it feel that much better. I spent evenings with them, watching movies and talking shit about one Marine or another. Did we talk shit about my fellow staff sergeants? Abso-fucking-lutely! My loyalty is to the Marines under my charge, not some douchebags that made life miserable for me and others around them.

The Marines I did not know before I boarded the ship were now men that I could trust with my life without hesitation. The same staff sergeants who gave me shit for how I treated the junior Marines were asking me if the Marines had any movies they could borrow. I told them to go fuck themselves, entitled pricks.

While on ship we received our smallpox vaccination. If you want to be sick, keep reading. We all lined up and had a miniature pitchfork with smallpox on its tip jabbed into our arms three times. They told us to relax, that it "wouldn't hurt." I'd been in the Corps for a few years, so I had this down pat. The corpsman does the jabbing and on the third jab the device went all the way in my arm. He had to yank it out to the disgust of all of those around me. I didn't even feel it.

We were in confined quarters, so if someone got sick, we all got sick. Reaction to the vaccine was different from one person to the next. Within minutes some Marines had a fever, some had a runny nose, and others were vomiting. Even after they vomited everything in their belly, they dry heaved. The sights and sounds that day were something to remember. As for me, I was fine. I guess since my family is of Yemeni decent, stuff like filth and disease doesn't get to me. I went and had some dinner; the mess hall was rather empty.

Midway through our voyage one of the ships broke down. We had to stop in Guam, and I remember thinking, "Wow, as a kid I remember seeing this in a textbook." We did not expect to stop for land until we got to Kuwait. This was a welcomed stop for us, for me especially. I needed to get off the ship and away from those who were making me go batty. A couple of the Marines and I went out and got some beers. I had never been much of a beer drinker, but fuck it, I'm with my Marines and this is an unexpected break. We drank plenty and met up at the club on base. I saw some of the Command there and spoke to the battalion executive officer. We were both a little intoxicated, but not so much that we were acting like idiots. He thanked me for what I was doing for the Marines and asked how things were going. I said they were great and even though I might be considered young by the other Staff NCOs, I was holding my own.

He stopped smiling and looked at me with all seriousness, "Staff Sergeant, if anyone gives you shit, you let me know and I will fix it. You're a good Marine and don't let anyone tell you different." That comment hit home and made me realize that I had work to do. I stopped drinking and walked back to the ship. I bedded down and continued on with my mission, leading my Marines.

After leaving Guam we would soon be nearing Kuwait. The bond I formed with those Marines while floating into harm's way is, to this day, unbreakable. I look back at it now and see that it was not only me who was there for those Marines, they were there for me, too, and we were all there for each other. We survived the initial journey together.

Night fell on the final day on board. In the morning we were to disembark and make an amphibious landing on the shores of Kuwait. That night we were able to select movies we wanted to watch. When you ask Marines who haven't been laid in over a month what they want to watch and take away porn as a choice, you're going to get anything else that resembles porn. The number one selection out of all the movies available was *Unfaithful*. Ask any Marine on board why they chose that movie and they'd tell you of the scene, "where he bends her over and starts fucking her." Hey, I was one of those who voted for it.

Morning came and reveille sounded with the gongs of AC/DC's "Hells Bells." Just as we had over a month before, we woke and prepared for the journey ahead of us. No words were spoken; the lights were still dim for some reason. A somber feeling could be felt throughout. The breakfast was really good; in fact all of the food, the final day and a half was great. I swear they treat Marines ready to go to war as if they're on Death Row.

I was on the battalion commander's vehicle, so we would be the first to disembark. The loading bay in the belly of the ship was loaded with vehicles that would soon be landing on the shores of Kuwait. Above and all around us on the catwalks were the sailors who would stay behind as we played in the sandbox. They looked at us in awe. I had never seen this look before; they feared for our lives and sincerely cared for our safety. Many of them, men and women, wept as a few of us loaded up in our vehicles and buttoned down.

The loading bay opened and filled with water; our amphibious landing vessel began to float and scream loudly as the fan blades cut through the air, gaining momentum and speed. I was now closed up in the back of a Light Armored Vehicle (LAV) and could not see what was going on outside, but I could feel the eyes of pride upon us and the cheers of praise coming from the sailors above.

We all have a purpose in the United States military. We all have a mission to accomplish. For the sailors of the USS Comstock, their mission was to get us to our objective in a safe and timely manner. The sailors had done so, and had done so well. It was now our turn to do our part of the mission. We were getting ready to make an amphibious landing on the shores of Kuwait, a short drive away from Saddam and his loyalists. This is what we, as Marines, were destined to do.

God has a hard-on for Marines because we kill everything we see. He plays His games, we play ours. To show our appreciation for so much power, we keep heaven packed with fresh souls. God was here before the Marine Corps, so you can give your heart to Jesus, but your ass belongs to the Corps! —Gunnery Sergeant Hartman, *Full Metal Jacket*

Chapter 4

This Must Be Hell

You ever watch a movie where Marines make an amphibious landing and attack the beach? Hell, have you ever seen *Troy* and watched Brad Pitt kick Trojan ass as his ship hits the shore? Quite invigorating isn't it? We dream about it as Marines, being heroic and taking on the enemy. We dream of hitting the beach and spilling blood on the sand, it's sexy.

Our craft hit the beach, and our vehicle started up and drove onto the shore. It was sandy as a beach would be; it's Kuwait…everything was sandy. There was no enemy, I even half expected CNN to be on the scene and reveal to my naïve family that I was part of this soon to be invasion. There was nothing—no enemy, no press, but I was not complaining.

Sure, being heroic is one thing, but wanting to be heroic means you want to die. You don't just wake up and become a hero; you have to do something crazy. It takes a lot of work, and no one really wants to know what it takes to get that stamp of heroism. Give me the parade and the glory, but don't make me work to achieve it.

Off to our right in the distance was a Hardee's—a symbol of American influence, but I had to look no further than the tip of my nose. I was a symbol of American influence in the region; we all were.

I had heard about the riches of Kuwait. My family in Yemen spoke of Kuwaitis as they did the people of other Arab nations such as Saudi Arabia and Egypt—they spoke of hatred for them. Sour grapes I thought. Kuwait had oil and their people lived well, Yemen has…well, Yemen has…I'm still thinking about that one.

I expected to see palaces and a few oil wells to be honest with you, but it was bare and desolate. After the rest of the battalion washed ashore, we lined our vehicles on the road and drove off. We were escorted by the Kuwaiti police, running through traffic lights and barriers. We were getting the VIP treatment, if you take away the fact that we were driving in military war machines and the police were in BMW's.

Within moments we saw a huge billboard with a picture of a United States Marine. It was from the Kuwaiti people, thanking us for our help and support. Kuwaitis are rich; they have oil, so they live in luxury. There's no reason for them to get their hands dirty and fight a war, they could just pay someone else to do it for them. They have enough money.

Cars would pass us and their passengers would be waving and giving us a thumbs up. Women in burkas would even look at us from their seats and wave. A few of them would lift their veils and stick their tongues out at us. I later told my platoon commander when he mentioned it happened to him that, "Sir, it's like she just flashed you—girls gone wild, sir!"

We got to our staging area; Life Support Area (LSA) 5 would be our home for the coming weeks or months. We were still unsure how long we would be there. By now the drive had taken me as a casualty, and I was asleep in the back of the LAV. As soon as we stopped I hear from outside the vehicle our battalion commander asking, "Where's Staff Sergeant Hafid?" I popped up and said, "Here I am, sir."

Our battalion commander was a good man; he had welcomed me to the battalion months before. He sat me down and asked about my career to date. I was initially assigned to the battalion as a sergeant, but due to my meritorious promotion, I was now a staff sergeant. I believe this unsettled him because I was only twenty-three years old, by far the youngest staff NCO or even officer in the battalion.

A few months later he caught wind that I was trying to get an arranged marriage to a girl in Yemen. At the time we were mobilizing and leave was infrequently granted for fear of desertion. Leave was only given in emergency situations such as death of an immediate family member. I was not going to complain; I called my dad and told him to call off the wedding, I could not go to Yemen. He was depressed by this; he wanted to see me married for some reason, but this was a directive from my battalion commander and everyone above him.

I was called into the battalion commander's office one day and there stood General Mattis, a warrior if I have ever seen one. He was the division commander and the type of leader that you put in a glass case that reads, "Break in case of war." He would always tell us how we were going to strap Saddam to the hood of his vehicle and bring him back with us. He'd start and begin every sentence with, "My fine young men," and you couldn't help but pay full attention to him.

General Mattis greeted me and said, "Staff Sergeant Hafid, you're the most famous staff sergeant in the Corps at the moment." He started to explain how word had gotten to my battalion commander, and how he had filtered information about my wedding up through the chain of command. They were going to let me go to Yemen and had already contacted personnel about my wedding. The embassy in Sanaa was informed and all of Defense Attaché in Yemen was informed. I was stunned; my battalion commander had come through when I hadn't even asked. Though I was skeptical about being an interpreter, I was honored when he asked me to be his.

When I got to LSA-5, my battalion commander greeted me and said, "We don't need you anymore; Division is sending each of us Kuwaiti interpreters. You can go back to your platoon."

I was fired before I even had a chance. I felt a little let down to be honest. For the past few months I had an idea of what war was going to be like for me and all of a sudden that was taken away. The positive of it all was that I was going to be back with my Marines, all eighty-plus of them, directly under my charge.

It had been a few months since I had been with my platoon. I had a couple of Marines with me on the USS Comstock, but not the rest of my crew. I was greeted by my platoon commander, a Chief Warrant Officer. A Chief Warrant Officer is a Marine who was once enlisted like me but had made the switch to being an officer. This usually means you get someone with common sense, but sometimes it's a crapshoot. Well, this man was the greatest officer I have had the pleasure to work for; I looked up to him.

One by one, our platoon was getting back together. I greeted them and showed them where we were staying. We were told there would be a group coming later that night and they would be put in a separate tent. The next morning we got an idea of what we were facing.

At five in the morning, reveille sounded. It was freezing in the tent! This was supposed to be the Middle East, not Antarctica! Our tent was flimsy and barely stayed upright. The lights were fluorescent and flickered. All you heard were the grunts and groans of tired men, and all you saw was one Marine already dressed walking up and down the floor of the tent telling everyone to wake up. Have you tried waking up and getting dressed when you're cold and tired? It's not a good feeling, I'll tell you that.

We held a platoon formation to get a count of who was there and who wasn't. We were all accounted for; all of my men were in front of me. I loved being a platoon sergeant, especially to this group of men. I loved being in front of these Marines with their eyes and ears opened and directed my way. I had been in their position and most of the time I was disappointed with who was in front of me giving orders and directives. Now I was the man standing alone in front of these men. I cracked a few jokes and told them all how great it was to be with them and how life on a ship sucked. They agreed with moans with groans.

We broke formation for breakfast, if you want to call it that. The cooks assigned to our battalion had to go get the food from somewhere else and bring it to us. There were no tables, no chairs, not even a designated area where we could eat because they didn't want rats in any of the tents. I looked around and said, "Have you seen this place? Why would any rat want to come here?"

The food arrived in containers, your basic gruel and slop breakfast for the men and women who defend our great nation. We were given disposable forks that looked like they were not disposable because they had already been used, and we were given foam plates where we could place our slop. Guys who looked like me were serving us breakfast. When I say they looked like me, I mean I got a lot of, "Hey Staff Sergeant, are those guys related to you?" They were local contractors who had won the meal contract by being the lowest bidder. We definitely saw why they were the winners.

We got our food and within moments Kuwait gave us a great "fuck you" in the form of wind. In a dry and sandy region, if you add wind, you get what I like to call, "some fucking bullshit!" For those of you keeping score at home, it's another way to say sandstorm. So now our slop is sandy; I could barely eat it before, so now I was definitely not going to eat it.

I shouldn't complain though; these were the spoils of war or what leads to war. The men and women who served in wars prior probably didn't even have the opportunity to eat sandy slop. I should be thankful to my God; the God that most Marines felt was the God of a terrorist religion. I don't know how many times I heard, "I can't wait to send those guys back to their Allah." I'd have to tell them, "Umm, hey idiot, you know Allah is just the Arabic translation of the word God right? We believe in the same God, you moron."

After breakfast our battalion was called together in a mass formation. We were briefed on what we were going to do. We were all getting vehicles that were stored on ships afloat for this very purpose, to be used in combat operations. It was a way to get equipment to a war zone quickly and expensively. What they don't tell you is that there is no one taking care of these vehicles while they float around on the water. By the time we get them they're in such bad shape that North Korea would turn them away. We're Marines though, we adapt and overcome. We made it work.

Think smarter not harder is what I was told to expect. In all actuality, it was that we thought less because we are the best. It was freezing, so we wore beanies. It's a smart thing to keep your head warm; I mean it doesn't take a doctor to figure that out, right? Well, maybe it does because by 9:00 a.m. if you were caught wearing a beanie, you'd be NJP'd. NJP stands for non-judicial punishment. Basically that's being tried by someone without a law degree and you basically give away your right to a trial and any other rights you think you might have. Were we really worried about beanies?

We all started growing mustaches as a show of solidarity. There were actual douchebags out there making sure the mustaches were within regulations. I am talking about measuring with rulers. This place had nothing, there was terrible food, we would find sand in places on our body that we didn't know existed, and we were given vehicles that are supposed to take us into combat against an enemy that was going to come at us with everything they had…or so they said. This really sucked.

I left LSA-5 one fine Kuwaiti day because my buddy told me about "Camp New York" that had an Army sergeant who was hooking him up with parts for vehicles. He knew my vehicle needed two doors; (yes I had no doors on my vehicle, your tax dollars at work) so he took me to see this sergeant. When we got to Camp New York my jaw dropped. Their camp was clean; it had tents that were fortified. The camp had a tent designated for food consumption and they had a store! *What the fuck, over?* Why didn't we have these amenities? The answer, "Marines don't need all that shit," was not going to be enough, but that's all I was going to get. By the way, their food was great!

I picked up some doors for my vehicle and some supplies from the store (supplies consisted of Pringles and Combos), and we headed home. Of course, on the way back we got caught in a sandstorm, and it wasn't your normal storm that lasted for a few minutes—it lasted for hours and we were stuck! I did not want to stay outside and sleep in a vehicle when I could be in my tent sleeping under cover. We pushed on and got to our tent. It was worse inside than it was outside. I dug my sleeping bag out from the pile of sand that lay on top of it and slithered into my bag a broken and miserable man. My lungs were filled with sand and it hurt to breathe. I just wanted to go to bed; it couldn't get worse than this.

The next morning we got up to clean up the mess. Our tent had collapsed—it was held together with hollow tent poles that must have been made of plastic given by the lowest bidder, only the best for our men and women of the military. One of the Marines from Texas came in and said, "Holy shit! J-Lo was killed in a car accident!" That was only confirmed by everyone around us—we had no television, no radio, and no telephone. The media personnel who were with us would not speak with us; we were beneath them, so they wouldn't tell us if it was true or not. We had no contact with anyone. If the entire camp was saying it, then it must be true. This was an odd moment; we already hated life, and then this happens.

J-Lo was dead. It did get worse…

CHAPTER 5

Special Delivery

Before social media, before Blackberry, and way before email there was something called a letter. A letter is something you write on another thing called paper. As soon as the J-Lo news hit, everyone got out their pens and paper to write home. There was no, "Hey Mom/Dad, it's me...." It was more like, "Hey did J-Lo really die?"

When deployed, mail is gold. Mail reminds you that someone far away loves you and for that moment it took to write that letter, seal that envelope, place a stamp on it, and then send it out, someone on the other side of it was thinking of you. It was also our only contact with the outside world. We hadn't received mail on ship; it was hard for the United States Postal Service to find us for some reason, and I understand. It's not like we worked for the same government.

In Kuwait though, they brought us bags upon bags of mail. Care packages were the best. They are called care packages for a reason—someone cares. I didn't get a care package while in Kuwait; I did receive a letter though, and it was from Discover Card telling me my account was delinquent. Others received things like pictures, beef jerky, Pringles, and so forth.

There were a few married Marines who hadn't received care packages, and it was starting to upset them. Senior Marines and junior Marines alike had the same look of excitement when the mail arrived, and utter disappointment when everyone around them received something and they did not. They would openly ask why their wives hadn't sent them what they had previously agreed to send. Every relationship starts out with promises that are intended to be kept but are begging to be broken.

The lack of mail along with the sheer boredom and frustration of sitting there waiting for the command to think of ways to keep us busy had taken a mental toll on every Marine. I remember first coming into the Corps and looking at senior Marines as being immortals. They achieved their high rank because they were badass and could digest steel and gunpowder and shoot rounds from their ass without blinking an eye. I had this feeling about all senior Marines, and now that I was one, it sure didn't feel like I could do that, especially since our diet consisted of Meals Ready to Eat (MRE) and that clogged you up more than hair does to a shower drain.

I did what I could to keep the Marines going, which would, in turn, keep me going. I would joke with them, talk shit, anything. Sometimes I did things that were hilarious that were not meant to be funny. One time I was in a container that was being used as a technical equipment repair shop on the back of a flatbed trailer. A couple of Marines and I were watching some DVD's I had them store in the container for me. It was getting late so I decided to leave the container and get back to my tent. It was dark, and when the moon is not out, it's very dark. Have you ever taken a step down when there was no step there? Well I opened the door of the container and walked out. Unlike Elmer Fudd, I did not walk a few steps on air before realizing there was nothing beneath me. I fell seven feet from the back of the flatbed and landed on my head. I saw a white light but got up quickly, raised my arms up and said, "I'm Okay!" I then collapsed to the ground. Yes it was hilarious but unintended.

By now everyone had a routine—get up, dust off, get some sandy slop, get back to the tent, clean up, get some MREs from me (I was the one rationing food, so you know I got the good stuff), and try not to get into trouble. Some just couldn't stay out of it; I guess I was one of them. There will always be moments in life when you will be questioned, measured, weighed, and challenged by someone. It's how you react to those moments that will define you as whatever you are at that instant. At that time I was a Marine staff sergeant, twenty-four years of age, and leading eighty-plus men as a platoon sergeant. My predecessor was a Marine gunnery sergeant who had to be in his forties. My Marines did not enjoy his tenure as the platoon sergeant. He was loud, obnoxious, and didn't lead by the example he wanted others to set. He was a dick, and there was a reason his name was always mentioned on the balcony the night before we boarded the buses. He took every opportunity to make himself look better than the next guy. If that meant throwing you under the bus, he'd stab you in the back, shoot you in the knees, and then throw you under the bus…just to be sure.

I didn't baby my Marines; I didn't hold their hands so they could go pee. I didn't tell them to go to sleep when it was late. I didn't go to their beds to make sure they were awake in the morning. If you're a Marine and you're about to go into harm's way and you need someone to hold your hand and give you directions on simple tasks, then you might need to seek a different career path. The old "Gunny" came to my area (which consisted of a sleeping bag and my gear) where I was distributing that day's MREs. He asked me why I hadn't come to wake him and the other Marines in his tent when it was time to get up. I told him that it wasn't my job. If he wanted to be woken up, he should go to Camp New York and invest in an alarm clock. He was visibly upset, and I didn't give a shit. The tent got quiet; everyone knew what was next…

"Are you the platoon sergeant?" he screamed as he grabbed my collar and flipped out. My natural reaction was to knock the fuck out of the guy, but that would have only given me a slight bit of satisfaction. Pain is weakness leaving the body, and that's all a punch to the jaw would have done for him. I wanted to inject weakness *into* his body. This is a Marine senior to me in grade and in age…

"Yes I'm the fucking platoon sergeant, and who the fuck are you?" I yelled back at him. I held my arms out to the side so everyone could see that I would not physically retaliate. He removed his hands from my collar and I let him have it. I started cursing him out and talking down to him while pointing my finger in his face. I unleashed hell on this Marine, and I had every right to. He had crossed the line by questioning me in front of junior Marines, even if he was senior to me, and he took it a step further by grabbing me.

I didn't back down, and I wasn't going to let this bully get the best of me. This was not high school; this was not Brooklyn in the early 90s. This was Kuwait in 2003, and we were about to go invade a nation where it didn't matter who I or anyone else was before this very moment. This was the kid in me, frustrated for all the shit I had dealt with growing up. This was the man who was afraid to tell his family that he was going to war for fear of retaliation, and/or disownment. This was a Marine who remembered what it was like to be junior and not be able to speak his mind. This was the moment that my Marines would know what to expect from now on. They were led by a warrior with emotion, not a robot that could be programmed.

Word spread around camp quickly. You could hear whispers of, "Hey did you hear what Staff Sergeant Hafid did to Gunny...?" It got to my platoon commander and a senior enlisted man who was a master gunnery sergeant. We called him, Master Gunz. They called us both into their tent and held a meeting with the rest of the staff NCOs. I was expecting to receive a warning and an ass chewing, possibly even have the title "Platoon Sergeant" removed. It turned out quite differently.

Master Gunz looked at all the staff NCOs and pointed to me. As he looked over at the Gunny he said, "Staff Sergeant Hafid is the Platoon Sergeant. What he says is coming directly from me and from the chief warrant officer. You are not to question Staff Sergeant Hafid, and you are not to lay a hand on him. He is a better man than me because if it were me, I would have knocked you the fuck out." He continued, "You're very lucky he didn't press charges on you. You are very lucky he's the man he is."

Remember how I wanted to inject weakness into his body? Well there it was. He was brought down to earth, his actions exposed and balloon deflated. That afternoon he asked me as I was in front of the platoon if he could address the Marines. I told him he could, and I turned them over to him. He stood there with his tail between his legs apologizing to the Marines and admitting he was wrong. You want to castrate a Marine? Have him admit he was wrong and take away his aura of invincibility.

This incident actually increased morale. Marines would walk by me shouting, "OOHRAH Staff Sergeant!" It felt great for those few days. We all had smiles on our faces, life was good…and then the mail came.

It had started to happen; Marines who hadn't gotten mail were now getting letters from their wives and/or girlfriends. There were a few who still received nothing, and they were in panic mode by now. The letters were not what you would think. Time is a healer, but it is also a destroyer of things. Time has eroded the earth for millions of years and left scars behind like the Grand Canyon. Time destroys relationships and marriages that have been strong for decades. Time allows someone who is gutless enough the ability to convince themselves they are doing what's right.

When you turn your television on, you hear about casualties of war from enemy fire. You hear about accidents and friendly fire caused by human error. What you don't hear about is the nineteen-year-old kid who shot himself in the head because his girlfriend was leaving him for someone else. You don't hear about the Marines who received videos of their wives fucking their neighbor, as if that were enough payback for him being away from her. Imagine the audacity of that Marine to represent his nation in a time of war.

Moral started to plummet; Marines were sulking, looking down and reading letters with tears dripping onto the pages below, the words smudged and they dared not to look up. They continued reading. I sat in silence thinking of the nineteen-year-old kid who shot himself in the head and how it must have felt for him to even consider that an option. Suicide is a permanent solution to a temporary problem.

I could only speak to my Marines as a human being. I tell them that there is no one on this planet who loves them more than I do at this very moment, and they don't need to worry; I won't be fucking their neighbors. A few smiles can be seen; I give the command to fallout and have the Marines surround me. I put my hand out with my palms facing the ground. The Marines pile on and I say, "It's only us gents, you and me. Who gives a shit what's going on out there where we can't control it? Give a shit about each other, and we will never let each other down. When I say I love you, I mean it; you're my brothers and will always be that. Maintenance on three…one…two…three…."

"MAINTENANCE!" We barked out loud for all to hear. We were Devil Dogs, and we'd just experienced our first fight. The fight to stay focused and stay true to each other. I say we won that round.

Chapter 6

The Father, the Son, and the… HOLY SHIT!

Who's the man behind the chevrons? Who and why is this guy trusted by all these Marines and how did he get to his position in a way that less than 1 percent of the Marine Corps have experienced? How did he get to be this way, and what did others see in him to give him this opportunity?

I'd be lying if I said I knew I would do what I had done in the Corps up to this point. I didn't grow up playing with G.I. Joe action figures and have posters in my room idolizing anyone in particular. In fact, I have never to this day watched a complete episode of *G.I. Joe*.

My parents immigrated to the United States from Yemen. Yemen was initially made famous when Chandler Bing of *Friends* decided the only way he could escape the clutches of Janice was to say he was going there. I was born the fourth child out of eight. We made the Brady Bunch look like amateurs.

A first generation Arab kid growing up in Brooklyn, New York, is not what you would call ideal. I had no idea what the hell was going on and it wasn't like I could ask my mom and dad. I didn't understand how to communicate with others. Oh, I spoke English and spoke it well, but I didn't know how to communicate with people and didn't know the difference between what was normal and what was excessive.

I was a timid kid. I was deathly afraid of my dad, but I respected him very much. I would literally start crying when he talked to me about life. He was very vocal but was away for most of my life. No he wasn't a deadbeat dad, quite the contrary. He worked as a Merchant Marine and was out on the water trying to earn a decent wage to feed his family. I'd say the longest time I spent with my dad was a year, other times were sporadic.

My father loved me, that was quite obvious. He saw something in me that I couldn't see because I was so young. This caused my older brother to dislike me. My dad had a different relationship with me than he had with my older brother. It's as if he could relate to me. Coincidentally, my mother and I didn't get along too well, and she absolutely *adored* my older brother. There's something about Arab women and their first sons.

I was brilliant, a nerd by anyone's standards. The only problem with me was that I couldn't relate to anyone around me. I dressed and lived differently, and I followed a different religion; everything about me was different. I had to balance two separate lives—one that I had in school and the one I had at home. I wasn't even allowed to give anyone my phone number because my parents didn't want me to mingle with the Americans, we were Arabs first and foremost.

I don't know if I had a disadvantage growing up Arab, but it sure felt like it. My third grade teacher mentally tortured me, causing me to react in a way that justified his actions. Was it because I was an Arab kid? Who knows, but to this day I hate him. And yes, I know hate is a strong word.

At a young age, I was also more aware of my surroundings. I questioned things in my head but was afraid to share it with others because of what it might mean. For instance, I had affection for a girl and couldn't explain it. I was young, but it made sense to me. I also wondered to myself about God and how anyone could be sure he existed. If God created everything, who created God?

My childhood can be summed up with one word—awkward. My teeth were huge, and I smelled like syrup. Don't ask me, it's what I came to find out later in life. I was picked on and rebelled in the only way I knew how, by subjecting myself to the norm. I wasn't normal, I knew that already, but I wanted to be normal. I just didn't know how.

I never had a girlfriend. Everyone else around me was growing up and living the way any normal American would. I never thought I would have a girlfriend because my mother reminded me whenever I had a picture taken that I should never smile. She would simply say, "You're ugly." Confidence was not my strong point.

Puberty and the teenage years did not help me at all, but surprisingly my father did. My brother had run away from home and my father, being the proud man that he was, refused to let him come back. So my dad and I formed a bond; we talked a lot, and he valued my opinion. He would get up on a Saturday or Sunday morning at six and wake me up for a drive. He would use the excuse of teaching me how to drive to get to know me better.

I was scared of my dad because I wanted to be like him so much. He was my hero, and I looked at him as someone who could accomplish the impossible. I didn't want to disappoint him. He was upset that I couldn't speak Arabic well enough, but after a while he let that go and accepted me for who I was. My dad would take me on a drive, ask me to turn right, turn left, and then pull over. We were far from home, somewhere in Brooklyn and he would ask me to shut the car off. My dad started to speak like I had never heard him speak before. He would ask me how I felt about my brother running away. He would ask me about my relationship with my mom. He sat there and listened to what I said, and for the first time in my life, I had someone actually hearing my thoughts. It wasn't a friend or my brother, it was my dad. I promised him that I wouldn't let him down because I knew how much it hurt him when my brother left.

My parents didn't let me get into sports because it was "too American." To this day it makes no sense to me. I was athletic and surprisingly good at different sports. In basketball, I was called "Air-abian" for my shooting and jumping ability. I am sure the name would have stuck had they let me try out for the team. I wanted to go to college but didn't want my dad to pay for it. That was my option, but of course, it was "too American." How about joining the military? Sure, that doesn't seem too American...

I can't even make this stuff up.

When I finally joined the Marine Corps, I realized I had to face some fears. I didn't like speaking in front of a large audience. I didn't like raising my voice, and I was afraid of exerting strength because I was only skin and bones at 130 pounds. When I took the oath to join the Delayed Entry Program (DEP), I was excited. When I was brought into the recruiter's office after I joined, the first thing I was expected to do was yell from the top of my lungs, "Marine Corps! OOHRAH!" Yeah, my first one was pathetic to say the least. For my effort, I received a, "We need to work on that," from my recruiter.

Word of me joining the Marines drew skepticism from a lot of people. They already knew what I was and who I was. When I asked about how it was going to be when I became a Marine, the recruiter himself said, "I don't even know if you'll make it through boot camp yet." It wasn't the only form of doubt I received; I heard it from teachers, from students, and from my older brother. I even started to hear it in my thoughts. My dad on the other hand, he could not have been more proud.

Boot Camp was intense. For the first time in my life, I was away from home and put in a situation in which there was no escape. I couldn't lay in bed or on the floor behind the bed in silence like I used to so I could get a thought to myself. I had no one to talk to and no one to rely on. But I made it through boot camp and my father and mother came down for my graduation. My dad wasn't around for a lot of the things I did growing up. It wasn't his fault though, he was a busy man. He wasn't around when I won an award from the *New York Daily News* for my artwork. He wasn't around when I was asked to provide the artwork for a poetry book cover. Because he was not around meant I couldn't go to those events to receive my awards. My mother didn't care about them; it didn't mean anything to her. My dad knew what becoming a Marine meant, so he brought my mother down with him, he wasn't going to miss it for the world.

Becoming a Marine was a great moment for me, but I was still confused. I was confused because I thought I lacked the intestinal fortitude required to be a Marine. I struggled the first year; I was what you would call a shitbag. My uniform was lacking the sharpness of a Marine. The intensity wasn't there as well. I was falling along the wayside, and I wasn't living up to the title, "Marine." Two Marines who I consider dear friends gave me a tongue lashing to get me straightened out. I had disappointed them, which in turn made me feel as if I would disappoint my dad. It was time to change, and boy did I.

I looked good, felt good…and damn it, I wasn't good—I was great! I started to get recognized by my superiors and they put me in front of a meritorious promotion board panel. I didn't think I was going to win the first time, and I was right. But it's what I got from the panel afterwards that told me something about me that I had never seen. It must have been something my father saw in me as well, because I wanted to tell him all about it. They told me that I was exceptional, and that I would be back for the next one.

On December 1, 1998, I was a lance corporal in the United States Marine Corps; on December 2, 1998, I was a corporal; on August 2, 1999, I was a sergeant; and on January 2, 2002, I became a staff sergeant...all meritoriously, I was a Staff Non-Commissioned Officer in the United States Marine Corps at age twenty-three. In three years, one month, and one day I had accomplished what it takes eight to ten years for some Marines to accomplish, and all I wanted to do was tell my dad.

I never changed from the person I was growing up. I was just older and wiser. The Marine Corps trusted me with more responsibility, and they gave it to me. I applied all that I had learned and molded myself into what I was at that moment. The turning point had to have been when my father spoke to me in his car. It was at that moment when I was finally able to communicate with someone. It was at that very moment when I realized I was not alone, that there were many like me who thought the way I did, but like me, they didn't know how to express it. I wanted to be a voice for my Marines, for all Marines, to let them know that I was no different than them, even though I had initially done things no one thought I could do.

I never wanted to go to war; I mean who really wants to? I didn't find it to be glamorous or defining. I could have cared less. I joined the Marine Corps for an education, and then the towers came down and so did my heart. I wasn't going to Afghanistan, but I wanted to do something productive for the Corps, so I re-enlisted for another four years and seven months.

There I was in Kuwait with more than eighty Marines under my care and the test of a lifetime. My childhood was behind me. The doubt was gone because I was in a position where there could be no more doubt. I went to sleep as we all did on the night of the 19th of March 2003. Hours later I was woken up and told to get the Marines up and ready. President Bush was going to address the nation, exactly fifteen months from the day I met him, when he addressed a small contingent of Americans in Shanghai, China. On March 19, 2003, this is what the world heard:

> My fellow citizens, at this hour, American and coalition forces are in the early stages of military operations to disarm Iraq, to free its people, and to defend the world from grave danger. On my orders, coalition forces have begun striking selected targets of military importance to undermine Saddam Hussein's ability to wage war. These are opening stages of what will be a broad and concerted

campaign. More than thirty-five countries are giving crucial support— from the use of naval and air bases, to help with intelligence and logistics, to the deployment of combat units. Every nation in this coalition has chosen to bear the duty and share the honor of serving in our common defense.

To all the men and women of the United States Armed Forces now in the Middle East, the peace of a troubled world and the hopes of an oppressed people now depend on you. That trust is well placed. The enemies you confront will come to know your skill and bravery. The people you liberate will witness the honorable and decent spirit of the American military. In this conflict, America faces an enemy who has no regard for conventions of war or rules of morality. Saddam Hussein has placed Iraqi troops and equipment in civilian areas, attempting to use innocent men, women, and children as shields for his own military—a final atrocity against his people.

I want Americans and all the world to know that coalition forces will make every effort to spare innocent civilians from harm. A campaign on the harsh terrain of a nation as large as California could be longer and more difficult than some predict. And helping Iraqis achieve a united, stable, and free country will require our sustained commitment. We come to Iraq with respect for its citizens, for their great civilization, and for the religious faiths they practice. We have no ambition in Iraq, except to remove a threat and restore control of that country to its own people.

I know that the families of our military are praying that all those who serve will return safely and soon. Millions of Americans are praying with you for the safety of your loved ones and for the protection of the innocent. For your sacrifice, you have the gratitude and respect of the American people. And you can know that our forces will be coming home as soon as their work is done.

Our nation enters this conflict reluctantly—yet, our purpose is sure. The people of the United States and our friends and allies will not live at the mercy of an outlaw regime that threatens the peace with weapons of mass murder. We will meet that threat now, with our Army, Air

Force, Navy, Coast Guard and Marines, so that we do not have to meet it later with armies of fire fighters and police and doctors on the streets of our cities.

Now that conflict has come, the only way to limit its duration is to apply decisive force. And I assure you, this will not be a campaign of half measures, and we will accept no outcome but victory.

My fellow citizens, the dangers to our country and the world will be overcome. We will pass through this time of peril and carry on the work of peace. We will defend our freedom. We will bring freedom to others and we will prevail.

May God bless our country and all who defend her.
—President George W. Bush (19 March 2003)

So much for sleep, it was time to get our hands dirty.

Chapter 7

Motherfucker

It was so early in the morning; I mean hours before the sun would even come up. We weren't told what the President had said in his address to the nation, but it was summed up with, "We're going to bomb them first, and then we're going in." I hadn't even known what the President said in his address until I attached it to the previous chapter. It might sound surprising, but ask anyone who was there at the time, I would wager that more than half have never heard or read his address to this day.

That night it was cold, freezing even, but adrenaline was flowing. I was somewhat excited; I had this idea that we'd go in there with little to no resistance. I succumbed to the notion that this would be a quick campaign, we'd get our medals, and we'd go home. Marines don't occupy; we go in, fuck shit up, and then we leave. The Army takes care of the mess after the fact. They have the builders and the engineers; we have the war fighters and the riflemen.

We received our ammunition; I had about three hundred rounds of 5.56mm for my rifle and thirty rounds of 9mm for my pistol. In training, we account for every single round, and if we're one short, we comb the grass looking for it. In this situation they were quite liberal with any and every piece of ammunition. It was like Christmas. The company gunnery sergeant handed out ammo like presents. He did so with a smile. He would ask a Marine, "Do you want a grenade?" The Marine would nod, so he'd give him a crate. Remember the look you had when you received that gift you always wanted for Christmas? That was the look on the faces of these Marines. Hell, even I was happy to have all this ammo. The only thing lacking was snow, but sand could serve in its place.

We had the media with us—they pissed us off by the way—so we had to play the public relations game. We were given humanitarian rations to give the Iraqis when we drove by them. Our intelligence reports told us to expect little to no resistance and we were going to have a ton of refugees walking south to the Kuwaiti border as we pushed north to Baghdad. Each vehicle received a box of these rations. They looked like MREs, except they were yellow and had the American flag printed on them. Because I was the platoon sergeant, I received extra boxes of these rations along with extra boxes of MREs. I packed them in my vehicle with every intention of putting smiles on the poor and impoverished people of Iraq.

Our gear was packed away, our weapons were loaded, and we had our Mission Oriented Protective Posture (MOPP) suits on. Its intent was to protect us against any chemical or biological attack we were certain Saddam would throw our way. Even I was so sure of it that I was already thinking of how much it would cost to get a new laptop since I had mine out there. Anything that was contaminated was going to be destroyed. It was my first laptop and it came in *handy* on ship and in the desert. If it became a casualty of war, I'd give it a military burial.

Before we deployed, the Marine Corps was adamant about issuing us desert uniforms so we could…I don't know…blend in with the sand? The MOPP suits were jungle camouflage, which kind of defeated the purpose. I wish I had taken a picture of us lined up ready to move toward the Iraqi border. The greatest and best equipped fighting force in history and we were invading a desert country with uniforms and equipment meant for use in the jungle. It was comical, and I had to laugh. Who knew? Maybe we were taking the scenic route.

We got a final brief; everyone wants to be the William Wallace of a battle. The fact of the matter is we were a support element to a combat battalion. We were going to be in harm's way, but by the time we would get to any area, it should be cleared and secured. Our company commander was an infantry officer put in command of said support unit. His peers were leading men into a fight; he wanted a piece of the action, and you could see it in his eyes and hear it in his voice.

This was the first time I would hear a Marine officer volunteer his men for missions out of their means so they could receive glory and rewards. I remember that brief vividly; I listened in as the company commander discussed clearing homes on the way to Baghdad. These were homes that would have already been passed by forward elements and deemed clear and secure. He wanted to assemble teams from each platoon and kick in doors. That's a great plan; let's piss people off even further. When this was brought up to the staff NCOs and the officers of the company, my platoon commander had the best comment out of everyone. I'm usually the smart ass, but he stole the show. When told we would be clearing homes, my platoon commander told the company commander outright, "You mean when *you* and your company gunny clear them."

That put a halt to that idea. Classic.

I don't know where the saying "curses like a sailor" comes from, but I know for a fact that no one curses more than a Marine. I could be in a meeting with the President of the United States and the word "fuck" would be placed in a sentence at least once. In fact, a Marine can use the word in a sentence at least five times. For example, "Motherfucking fucker fucked me in the fucking ass with that fucking bullshit!" I cursed in school as a kid, but I never cursed at home. After boot camp though I was in my dad's car with my mom and every other word out of my mouth was "fuck" and she got upset with me. Oh fucking well. I bring this up because you could sum up the motivational speech I gave my Marines with a "motherfuck." They huddled around me and it went something like this, "Okay motherfuckers, we're about to fucking go over there and kick some motherfucking ass. If you motherfuckers want to go home soon, then watch each motherfucker's back. If any motherfucker tries to end you, you motherfuckers better end that motherfucker's life."

Now I am paraphrasing, but I am sure it went something like that. I didn't even know I had diarrhea of the mouth until my platoon commander made a comment like, "What if the motherfuckers need ammo?" I had a quick remark for that one, don't mind me. I was in the moment.

I told my Marines to get to their vehicles and be ready for the silent count. This would be when a count is given from five to zero and all of the vehicles in the convoy would start at once. At night this is beneficial because it prevents your enemy from knowing how many vehicles you have in the convoy. The count began and a feeling of excitement hit me. When this vehicle starts it would be the beginning of this war for me. I was already thinking of what it would be like coming home as a combat veteran—the naivety of the young and inexperienced.

The vehicles started, but not all at once. *We need a little more practice*, I thought to myself. Our convoy is lengthy; I know I'm in the middle of it with my driver, and I'm fine just where I am. It took a few minutes for the domino effect of rolling steel and fiberglass to reach us. It was dark out and it was now considered a combat situation, so we turned our lights out and left just enough illumination to see the vehicle in front. One by one, we roll out until the company executive officer radios in telling us he's the last vehicle, and he's "Oscar Mike," meaning on the move. We're headed just ahead of the border with Iraq where we would set up.

Kuwait is not a large country by any stretch, and it's not like we were hundreds of miles outside of Iraq. We were within a few miles of the border initially, so where we were going to be staging ourselves for the invasion was right down the road. It was dark when we left, but when we arrived at our destination it was bright out, damn near lunchtime. We formed a perimeter with our vehicles and counted down so we could shut them all off at the same time, but once again, that didn't happen. *We're really gonna have to work on that*, I thought to myself.

It was quiet now; we had patrols set up, walking the perimeter. All of a sudden in the distance we heard explosions. We started cheering, "It's on! Bombs over Baghdad, motherfuckers!" We're so close we could see mini-mushroom clouds forming. We had a front row seat to the "shock and awe" promised by our Commander-in-Chief. Over the radio we got word from our company commander that our mission was no longer named "Operation Enduring Freedom." I felt sort of cheated; I wanted to be a part of the response to September 11. The new name for our mission? Operation Iraqi Freedom.

I could imagine a war room somewhere in the Pentagon where the Joint Chiefs were sitting and arguing amongst themselves…"What are we going to call this?"

"How about we name it Operation Blue Falcon?"

"What about Look Ma, No Sands?"

"I know; what about we take the enduring out of the equation and insert Iraqi?"

I could envision them all in my head in stunned silence because of the sheer simplicity of it, and each of them raising a bottle of Guinness beer toasting and shouting, "Brilliant!"

We were told to dig in; we were going to dig a hole to seek refuge and sleep in if need be. It's so if a mortar or scud hit nearby, you'd be protected from the fragments hitting you since you'd be under the impact zone. I looked at it as a convenience; I was digging my grave so when I got killed they could just kick the dirt over me and fight over who got the Skittles from the MREs I'd left behind.

The sun began to shine brighter, if that was even possible. It was warm, and by golly it was spring break; I couldn't wait to see the beauty of an Iraqi spring! The Company first sergeant came out of the tent where the command post was set up and yelled, "Scud!" We donned and cleared our gas masks and hopped into our graves…I mean fighting holes. Obviously, it didn't hit us; otherwise you wouldn't be reading about the Guinness beer toasting. Like the last war, Saddam attempted to hit targets in Kuwait but missed terribly. I almost felt sorry for him, but then realized he was a douchebag and he needed to go. The sooner he got gone, the sooner I got to go home.

The command "All clear" was given and we unmasked. They gave us an idea of how far off Saddam was with his aim and we got back to sitting by our vehicles, listening to the music of terror around us. I joked with some of the Marines about how the Iraqi troops were probably running around in circles with their arms and hands in the air screaming. It was believable at the time; I expected they would provide our superior air strength with ample target practice.

Another "Scud!" command was shouted, another miss. This went on for the rest of the day. I was getting pissed off, but what else was someone like Saddam going to do? Sit there and let the goal to an Outkast hit single play out?

Nightfall arrived and we bedded down as much as we could. Across the border, bombings continued. Marine, Navy, and Air Force fighter jets screamed over our position. Luckily, and for a reason, we have orange and pink tarps on top of each vehicle. This is so we don't get bombed by someone who doesn't know what a Marine LAV looks like. We were told that thirteen Marines from our Battalion in the 90s version of this war were killed because someone from the Air Force didn't know what an LAV was. Sometimes an enemy's greatest ally is the enemy himself.

Morning came and I half expected a surrender to come from Iraq and Saddam to flee. This did not happen. The Iraqis expected the ground war to take place later rather than sooner; but we were going to throw a curveball at them, and they were going to strikeout looking. We covered up our fighting holes and formed the convoy. Over the radio the company commander described how Iraqi forces had obtained US military uniforms and would be wearing them to trick us. To avoid being mistaken for an Iraqi, we were to shave our mustaches of unity. The company commander was going to make sure of this, so just in case one of us did not understand the language of *English*, he drove around and made a hand gesture to his face, symbolizing a man (or a gnarly woman) shaving his mustache. As he drove by my vehicle I said to him, "Ooohhhhh, that's what you meant when you said 'shave your mustaches' over the radio, sir." With freshly shaved faces we moved out, creeping closer to the border. By now the forward elements had crossed into Iraq. We started out in the morning, and by nightfall we still hadn't crossed into Iraq. It resembled a Wal-Mart on Black Friday, or so I had been told. It was getting late, but finally the company commander got on the radio and told us we were about to cross over. I could see it ahead of me, a sign made by the Army Corps of Engineers welcoming us into Iraq. We sped up and before I knew it we were coming up to a pile of sand dug away to allow us into Iraq. In the United States we have trouble with our border with Mexico and can't seem to build a fence; the Iraqis piled sand up to separate themselves from the Kuwaitis. It was simple but effective.

I'm through, and I am officially in Iraq. A feeling of, *Man if they could see me now*, came over me. Then I felt the effects of fear course through my body as I heard explosions all around me and just ahead there were oil wells ablaze. My friends and family, wherever they might be, were watching. Did they know I was going through a layer of sand that separated me from safety? I lost my train of thought; I began to think of everyone I knew, past and present. I wondered what they were doing, what they were thinking. I was thinking about how at that very moment I was doing something I never thought I would do, something I was too afraid to commit to as a timid and frightened child. I wondered if all of those who doubted me, who said I wouldn't be able to make it through boot camp were watching their television screens from the comfort of their own homes. I drifted further into this new thought, this lack of focus consumed me and I thought about my child who was yet to be born—would I ever see him or her?

The heat from a nearby burning oil well burned me and snapped me out of my daze. I looked around and gazed upon the chaos around me. I said in a whisper so that only I could hear, "Motherfucker…this shit is real."

CHAPTER 8

The Fog of War

Artillery fire is heard in the distance. I couldn't tell if it was coming or going. Our convoy was moving slowly, sometimes not at all. It's late and we're human beings, and we've been awake for more than twenty-four hours. There were at least two Marines in each vehicle, a driver and an "A-Driver" to keep him awake. We came across a pack of camels, real camels not the cigarettes, crossing the road in front of us and we stopped. Off to the right I could hear an explosion. The company gunnery sergeant, sounding quite shaken up gets on the radio and described what took place. Apparently, a camel had stepped on a landmine and was sent cartwheeling in the opposite direction. I chuckle, picturing it in my head.

The last camel passes by the first vehicle and we're "Oscar Mike." I wait for the domino effect to hit us, but after about five minutes, we're still not moving. The Marines two vehicles in front of us had fallen asleep; the Marines directly in front of us get out of their vehicle to wake them up. I call out to the company commander over the radio and tell him what happened and that we were now on the move. He wanted us to catch up to them and we eventually do. Had enough time elapsed, we would have been stranded in the middle of nowhere with no idea of where to go. That would have been fun. Behind me, I hear more explosions. I look over to my driver as we both wondered what it was. After a few minutes, I realize that the pack of camels that had caused us to slow down and stop had just hit a minefield and were probably all dead. We were surrounded by landmines on either side of the road.

Our company commander was given the coordinates to where we would stop for the night. We stop in an area surrounded by oil fires; it looked like what was described as Hell to me as a child. The company commander calls all the staff NCOs and officers to his vehicle and we get briefed. Everything from this guy was described in a way that was meant to keep us aware, but you don't keep someone aware by telling them that artillery rounds are being fired over their position and they're in an impact area. What is being aware of that going to do for any of us? We're also told that each driver was to sleep while the other person in the vehicle was to stay awake. I happened to be that other person, so it appeared that I wouldn't be getting much sleep this war.

When I got back in my vehicle, I told my driver to go to sleep. A few Marines in our convoy brought over their Night Vision Goggles (NVG's) for me to look at; half of them didn't work or didn't work well enough. This is what we're given to utilize in combat. My occupational specialty in the Marine Corps was an electro-optics technician, and I had a familiarity with NVG's so I offered to take a look at them. Don't ask me how or why, but switching parts from one NVG to another would get both of them to work. I spent the rest of the night doing this. I had to stay awake, might as well be productive. This is my first night inside enemy lines. A majority of us had never seen combat before, so it's not like we knew how to react to it. In between the repairs of two NVG's I found myself wondering if this was normal. Was it normal to feel safe? I felt like all was well and besides the initial fear when crossing over, it felt no different than a training exercise. Sure there were explosions, but I'd heard plenty in training.

Morning came and we got briefed again by the company commander. We're told of advancement of Regimental Combat Teams (RCT) to the east and west of us. RCT-1 was to the west and RCT-7 was to the east. We were with RCT-5 and were going up the middle between them both. The 3rd Infantry Division (ID) of the United States Army was going through the vacant desert and would attack Baghdad from the west; the Marine Corps was tasked with going through populated areas on the way to Baghdad

There was little to no resistance, as I had expected. I checked up on some of my Marines in the convoy to see how they were doing. We talked about the advancement and how the war would be over in no time. Optimism was heard throughout. I even thought to myself that this would be awesome, having been in Iraq during the invasion and not gotten in real harm's way. My friends and anyone else who would ask me about it wouldn't know I was in a convoy the entire time. All they would know was that I was in Iraq and was part of a fighting force that liberated a nation from a tyrant. I'd be a hero.

We got in our vehicles and prepared to move out again. It was now daylight, the vehicle startup count is not as important since the enemy can see us, but we might as well keep doing it. We startup and we're on the move. The fires do not blind us anymore; we can see all that is around us. We got on the road, a main strip that resembled a freeway, and pick up speed, and I started to doze off.

Crossing into Iraq was like crossing into a parallel existence. Looking around and seeing the fires you forget that it's a country to millions of people. It's not just an objective; it's a place that many call home. Where were the Iraqis? With the ability to see all around us, I begin to observe our surroundings. I notice that this place is no different than anywhere else. We're on a three-lane highway with off ramps and exits. There are signs in Arabic and English detailing the distance to our final objective—Baghdad. Over the radio we heard there were civilians ahead. There were families, men, women, and children. I reached back for those yellow humanitarian meals and got them ready, but I still had my weapon at the ready, just in case. I saw them in the distance; Marines were tossing them meals. The people were stopping to collect the meals and were cheering us. I was smiling ear to ear; it felt amazing. I felt legitimately heroic. I was tossing over some meals and would greet them with a "Salam Alaikum" that Muslims say to one another. I felt like I was doing what I was meant to do, making a difference in this world to people less fortunate. I was overwhelmed with joy and giving. I ran out of humanitarian meals and started giving them MREs that were meant to sustain me for a week. I didn't want to pass anyone without giving them something.

We drove for a couple of hours. Our morale was high, more talk between my driver and I about going home and what it would be like. We had just gotten there, and we were already booking our tickets home. We got to our position and set up a perimeter. I set up a duty schedule for fire watch. There were going to be Marines patrolling the perimeter for any breach. I was still overwhelmed with positive emotion, smiling and telling the Marines that if they need me, they should not hesitate to call me. I could still be utilized as an interpreter, if need be. The Marines were pretty motivated themselves; we were doing good things. I bed down for the night, the plan was to stay in the area for three days and then push forward to the next objective—the final being Baghdad. I was filled with joy, my mind wandering, thinking of going home soon; we were going to free people who were living in fear, and we were going to do so with the same honor and dignity of the Marines before us in history. These people were genuinely happy to see us there; their cheers can still be heard in my head. Their smiles can still be seen in my mind with thumbs up given our way. I tried to sleep, but I was full of energy until finally the sandman consumed me. Just as I am finally able to get to sleep, I hear someone barking at me, "Staff Sergeant, they need you and the other staff NCOs over at the company commander's tent. We are going to Baghdad."

I wake up and get my gear on. I go over for the meeting, and I hear the company gunnery sergeant speaking freely about how we'd be in Baghdad in two or three days and we'd be home in a few weeks. Due to the lack of resistance, we've been told to push forward. The war was advancing at a quicker than anticipated pace. I get excited and say, "Tell us what you need us to get done, sir, and we'll get it done." We were going to push north, over one hundred miles in a day, and we need to get moving now. We all leave and get the Marines to work.

No one wanted to be anywhere but home, so any way we could get the job done and get it done right the first time would mean we'd get home sooner rather than later. The Marines had broken down the perimeter, and our vehicles were staged and ready for the road. We got the word to move out and we hit the road like bank robbers leaving a crime scene. We had been in Iraq for less than forty-eight hours, but for some reason it felt like we had been there for weeks. A second felt like a minute, a minute an hour, an hour a day, and a day felt like a week. Time had slowed down, and had done so dramatically. Time is relative to where you are and what you're doing. As a youngster you want time to slow down when you're having fun and speed up when you're bored. When you're older it seems as if you don't have enough time. Time is in constant flux and the older you get, the faster time seems to travel. This is due to the amount of time already spent in comparison to the amount of time that lies ahead. The same applies to space, the distance traveled in comparison to the distance remaining. They are intertwined; one cannot exist without the other, hence the name space-time.

We were now going to occupy space by covering a lot of it. A few hours in we hear, "Gas! Gas! Gas!" over the radio, and we have to don and clear our gas masks while driving. We all pull over, put on our masks, and then we move out. *This doesn't seem right*, I thought to myself. *Why are we still moving north if we've been gassed?* At least now the world would know we were right about the weapons Saddam had, except it was another false alarm and we unmask. The drive north bottlenecks and we stop. Marine units not attached to our battalion are on the road with us, pulled over looking ahead, just like the rest of us. Word is not being passed down to the rest of us, and when that happens the only thing you can do is speculate. It looks like the I-5 in California after an accident—everyone is standing around looking, no movement.

We're sitting ducks, just sitting there with no idea of what's going on. We had traveled twenty or so miles—far less than we had originally planned—and confusion consumed every person not wearing the rank of lieutenant colonel or above. All of a sudden the radio goes crazy with reports of a counter-attack. We are sitting on the side of the road with nowhere to go. More reports come in; this time of tanks headed our way…Iraqi tanks, and they're coming to kill us.

The road we've been on for a majority of the day resembled a pipeline about to burst with the amount of military vehicles crammed onto it. With the threat of Iraqi tanks imminent, Marines to the rear of us start yelling forward to clear the road, howitzers were going to provide protection. All vehicles veer off to the right and left, clearing the road. Trucks towing howitzers scream by us; they pass us and are no longer within sound or sight. Darkness covers us as the sun sets. Reports continue coming in about these Iraqi tanks. The darker it gets, the darker I begin to feel. I felt idiotic. Hours before I was on top of the world, feeling invincible. We were a number one ranked college football team overlooking our opponent; I now felt that we hadn't taken them seriously. We still hadn't moved from this bottleneck of vehicles. I am frightened but hold it in. I lean my head forward and close my eyes. I hope that when I open them, I am still alive.

My eyes open, and I look around; we're all intact. A few Marines are walking around their vehicles, some are brushing their teeth. We had survived the night. What happened with those tanks I kept hearing about? I hear over the radio that we're on the move in five minutes. We get on the road and drive for about thirty minutes. We pull off onto a field to form a vehicular perimeter. I don't even wait for anyone to call me; I get out of my vehicle and head directly for the company commander. Everyone else is there waiting for the company commander. I ask, "What the fuck happened last night?" He told me. It seemed the Iraqis were fighting back, and they were fighting dirty. Iraqi civilians, waving white flags were to be left alone, helped if need be, and sent south away from the chaos. We were not to engage. The enemy had traded their uniforms for civilian garb and their weapons for white flags. More than twenty Marines had been murdered by those same people. We let our guard down in more ways than one, and it was costing lives. Time was warped, we were overconfident, and the laws of war, if there could be such things as laws in war, were not being followed by anyone not wearing "US MARINES" or "US ARMY" over their left breast pocket.. The outlook was foggy; this was not going to be easy. This was indeed a war, but who were we fighting?

I'm not smiling anymore.

Chapter 9

Adventures in Parenting

Our company commander's mouth was moving but his words were muffled. As soon as I heard of the casualties from the night before, my mind fled, leaving my body behind and taking cover under insecurity. I have different personalities depending on the situation. I live three lives, which, in turn, require three different personalities: the Marine who comes first and foremost is in complete control, the Khaled or "K" that my friends see as carefree and have come to love, and finally the Khaled my family gets to see, the timid, quiet man who keeps to himself. In an instant, they huddle together in my mind's safe haven arguing over what they are going to do next. The Marine stands up and tries to talk some sense into the two other versions of me, but they sit there silently. They have abandoned him, and, in turn, they have abandoned me. This is not a place for a person with compassion; this is not a place for a person who can rationalize insanity. This is a cluster-fuck, and Marines deal with them accordingly. What I was going to say to my Marines next was going to be critical, and I didn't have time to debate it any further; I had to speak with them.

After I received the brief, I walked over to my platoon commander and explained to him that I didn't want to tell our Marines how many casualties there were, but I had to tell them what the Iraqis were now using as tactics. He agreed. Too much information is not always good information, but keeping them informed is important. You don't want to cover the eyes of your men; you will lose their respect if you do things like that. Treat them as men, give them the respect they are due as men, but remember they are also human.

I huddle them around me. I look at their faces and their wondering eyes. They are looking to me for guidance; they're looking at me as if...I was a father figure. I begin to think of the Marines and soldiers who were lost to us the night before, and I am devastated. I do not show my Marines this feeling of weakness that has consumed me. I have to be strong, even though it was killing me inside. These were men, but they were children to worried families, each of them. I hadn't met their families, but all of a sudden I felt them with me. The Marines were relying on me to get them home. Their families were relying on me to get them home alive. Every Marine in front of me had someone who loved them, and all I could do was imagine them with a family member behind each of their shoulders, looking right at me.

I never plan out what I am going to say, it just comes to me. While we were staging in Kuwait, ready to cross into Iraq, my mouth was firing "motherfuckers" out at a rapid rate. A few days later—though it felt like months—I am wiser to what was going on. I say, "Okay guys, last night Marines from other units were killed, but I am not sure how many. They were killed while trying to help Iraqis dressed as civilians. The Iraqis wore civilian garb and were waving white flags. As soon as they saw the Marines let their guard down, they fired upon them and killed them. These fuckers are playing dirty, and things have changed!"

I survey the Marines, looking at their reaction to the news. They looked as I felt inside, worried and afraid. I continue, "So here's what I want you to do. It's either us or them, and I don't know about you, but fuck 'em! It's not my job to make sure they get to go home to their families. They're already home. It's my job to make sure you, every single last one of you, get home. Fuck this place!"

Their eyes get big, and their chests swell with pride...

"If you feel the need to defend yourself and your fellow Marine, then do so accordingly. If you make a mistake and shoot someone who wasn't meant to be shot, then I'd rather you make that mistake than be afraid to take the shot later on and be killed by some scumbag who doesn't give two fucks about you or me. If you get questioned, you tell them that, 'Staff Sergeant Hafid told me so,' and I will accept full responsibility. I'd rather you and me go home with handcuffs than in a body bag. Any questions?"

There were no questions. You don't have to tell a Marine he has the freedom to kill someone more than once. I sent them back to their vehicles as we waited for word to hit the road again. I told them to get some food in them and rest up while they can. I went back to my vehicle and took a seat, the weight of the world on my chest. I wasn't hungry or sleepy. I was fighting to not think of anything, but my mind was still racing.

We got back on the road, and I looked at the result of last night's chaos: Iraqi dead bodies on the side of the road and blood stains painting the path red. A few hundred or so meters ahead I see one of my Marines on top of his vehicle traversing to the left with his .50 cal machine gun. There's a shepherd with a flock of sheep to the left of us, seeing this, my Marine reacts just as I had told him earlier. Shots were not fired, but I am sure the sheepherder had seen what one of these weapons could do. By the sheer movement of that weapon pointed his way, he turned around and went the opposite direction, keeping a distance from the road. Due to the actions of the few, the Iraqi people have now lost the right to come near us. "It's either us or them," I had told the Marines earlier, and this applied to the humanitarian effort as well. There were no meals handed out that day. Iraqis on the side of the road were cheering and giving us a thumbs up, waiting for a handout. Some of them were even signaling for food, and we would not oblige. The rations that were yellow with *our* flag on the front were not going to be feeding the people who would be shooting at us when we had our backs turned.

I still hadn't seen any uniformed personnel; the bodies on the side of the road were all dressed as civilians, except they weren't. They were Iraqi soldiers, but they were camouflaged to blend in with their surroundings. Our compassion for civilians was taken as a weakness, so they exploited it, even if it cost the lives of women and children. Hate filled me as I looked at some of these people. The generosity I had was gone. I didn't like them, and I didn't want to help them. They were responsible for the deaths of Marines…my fellow Marines. More information was coming over the radio about the prior night. We were told that Al Jazeera was broadcasting American bodies being dragged in the streets. They were parading dead Marines or soldiers—I didn't know who it was at the time— around and disrespecting their bodies. We would never desecrate the bodies of their fallen, but in their eyes, it was okay to do that to us. My anger turned to rage; I now wanted to do more than just sit here with a thumb up my ass. I wanted to be where the shit was going down. I wanted payback for my fallen brothers and sisters.

I hated having the media with us for a specific reason: the spin they would create. A picture is worth a thousand words, but video is worth an infinite amount more. The video of the bodies of those Marines or soldiers being paraded around for all to see, what were they thinking? Was it considered a victory to be showing this? What purpose did it serve? I could only imagine what the parents of those who were just lost were thinking while seeing this. Little did I know that as this was being broadcast to the world, watching it over in Yemen...

My mother was screaming, pointing at the television. She cried hysterically and said, "That's Khaled! Look it's Khaled!" My father shut the television off and told her she wouldn't be allowed to watch TV anymore, and that I was nowhere near Iraq. My pregnant wife looked on in silence, tears running down her face. My father knew I was there and that I could very well be on television being dragged through the streets for all to see. This pained him, but like me over in Iraq, he had to keep it bottled up inside and show strength. My family was looking to him for guidance. My Marines were looking to me.

We pushed north a few kilometers. I have lost track of distance, time, anything that can be measured. I don't know where we are, but I know that all around us are people who want us dead. We are to stay the night in an empty field off the road. I shut my eyes for a moment, drifting into darkness. I hear noise, the air around me wailing and screaming. I try to open my eyes, but they are sealed shut. Sand has gotten into my eyelashes, and with them being moist it has caked. It takes me a few minutes, but I finally get my eyes cleared and open them. I can see nothing. The war has come to a screeching halt; the sand of a "Mother of all sandstorms" is thick and engulfs everything in its path. We cannot move; we cannot see; we cannot communicate. War was not meant to be fought in such conditions. It was not a thousand years ago, and it certainly was not now.

I hold my hand out in front of me and lose it in the dust. It's that thick. I am still seated inside my vehicle, the doors are closed and everything strapped shut, but the sand and dust still gets in. There is nothing preventing it from doing so. I get out of my vehicle and try to walk to the one behind me, but there is no way. If I walk away too far from my vehicle, I could lose sense of direction and get lost in the storm. I go back inside and sit there. My face is pounded with sand and dust. My lungs burn as they fill with sand. This is misery. Before

I can say anything sarcastic like, "At least it's not raining," it does just that. Rain comes down and comes down hard. The sand and dust now become mud and we're covered in it. Wet, cold and muddy…I am more miserable than I have ever been in my life before. I pray to God and say, "If you could find it in you, please kill me. I can't take this anymore." God does not listen. The winds continue and the rain still pounds us. To survive this would be a battle in itself. I put on my goggles and close my eyes, this time hoping that they would not open again, but if they did, it would be to end this nightmare, serving as reality. The storm ends and my eyes open.

I am still a part of the living, but wishing I had crossed over to the other side.

Chapter 10

Lost in Translation

How does someone keep themselves from going insane when everything and everyone around them is a complete mess? By laughing at the situation. I didn't communicate how I was feeling with anyone. I didn't want them to know, and frankly, they didn't need to know. My staff NCO peers were all doing what was expected of them. I never asked, "Hey man, are you as miserable as I am?" I don't know why I never asked; maybe it was because I didn't want to know if they were as miserable, thus making me more miserable.

I talk shit, it's in my nature to do so, but I do it in a manner that is playful. When I am upset and want to forget what's going on around me, I start talking shit to make me feel better. I don't bully, that's wrong and in a time like this, it would be twice as wrong. I'm a Marine staff sergeant and every Marine below me in grade gives me respect, but I don't demand it because of my rank, I earn it. When Marines respect you, they will learn to love you, and when those emotions are involved it goes a long way. If we were pulled over for a few hours, I would talk to some of the Marines, ask them if they needed a hug, and tell them if they did, they could go over to the company commander; he's looking to give out hugs and kisses. I "don't do that gay shit," I would say. They would laugh and say, "Roger that, Staff Sergeant."

I ran out of food because a few days prior I was happy and in love with the Iraqis so I gave them some of my own. What a difference a few days can make. I refused to be taken for a fool by these people anymore; I wasn't going to give to those who were biting the hands that fed them. I went to the back of my vehicle and opened up the humanitarian rations. Unlike the MREs, these rations do not tell you what's in them; it's a roll of the dice. These things had

Pop-Tarts! Growing up my parents *never* bought us Pop-Tarts. I'd see them during commercials, when my brothers were watching cartoons, and wonder what the craze about them was. I'd ask friends in school about them, and they would say they were delicious. But I found sliced cheese delicious, so it wasn't telling me anything was special about them. Now was the perfect time to "pop my cherry" so to speak, and lo and behold...I had cherry flavored Pop-Tarts.

They were fucking *delicious*! Looks like I had me some snacks!

We were running low on fuel. Before crossing the Euphrates River we were stopped on the side of the road like every other vehicle that I could see. There was a bridge we were trying to clear, and the word on it was that it was rigged with explosives. It was being investigated by Explosive Ordnance Disposal (EOD), and I was worried because we were running out of fuel and hadn't been told that we were getting a resupply. The company gunnery sergeant is in one of the lead vehicles, and his soul responsibility is supplying the three B's—beans, bullets, and bandages. He should have at least had a few five-gallon jugs with fuel for this situation, right? But, this is the same guy who sounded shaken up when he saw a camel do cartwheels when we crossed over a few days back. I go up to his vehicle; he's looking toward the bridge with worry painted on his face. I begin to ask him for fuel. He looks over at me and freaks out...

"People are dying!" he yells.

I look at him with confusion, tilt my head to the left, turn around, and walk back to my vehicle without another word. What just happened there? Some people have different reactions to war, but this was a little...uh, crazy? He did not supply me with one of the three B's, but he added a fourth one, "bitchy." When I get back to my vehicle my driver asks me if I got any fuel, and before he could finish I raise my hands in the air, shake them wildly, and yell, "People are dying!" My driver looks at me as I did the company gunny.

I say, "Dude, you had to have been there."

In the distance dust clouds form, vehicles are crossing back over the bridge and headed toward us. They are Marine tanks and other vehicles moving south to our position, and they're doing so with a purpose. I am called for over the radio and asked to meet with the officers and staff NCOs at the company commander's vehicle. Something had happened, and I didn't like the sight of seeing war machines resembling those of retreating vehicles. Apparently, those who planned the war didn't do it so well. We were advancing so quickly (in reality, not perception) that we had put too much distance between us and our supply line. We had to call a "timeout" and regroup. This was crazy. How long were we going to stay? A day? Two days? How about a week? We had to put a halt to everything because we had no food, water, or ammo to replenish what we would use. I was glad I had those humanitarian rations.

The gunnery sergeant who was my predecessor speaks up in this meeting. He is upset that "some Marines" were eating the humanitarian rations themselves. He knows I'm one of them, but after the tongue-lashing I gave him in Kuwait, he was careful how he was going to talk to or about me. I openly say in front of him and the rest of those in the meeting, "If Marines are out of food and they need to choose between feeding themselves and feeding the Iraqi's, I think it's a no-brainer." Now this sentiment wasn't shared by everyone, due to political correctness, but the company commander tells us to just be "mindful" of what we were doing. He isn't telling us to stop, but he isn't telling us to keep doing it either.

I get the Marines together and give them the news. They aren't happy we had to stop our movement, but they understood why. I gave them a different spin. We could use this time to recover, get some sleep, and try to watch some movies (kept the latter to myself). This could be a good break, if utilized properly. Also, some of us hadn't gone "number 2" in a few weeks. It had been three weeks for me; I had been eating only peanut butter and the powder from the hot cocoa packets. A personal trainer would be proud. I like to be clean, and I like my privacy. Having to take a shit in the middle of nowhere in combat is the epitome of being vulnerable. I didn't want to be pinching one off and get capped in the head. It would be embarrassing. What a way to go, who was I, Elvis? So I thought of a way to keep me from going to the bathroom more than I needed to—peanut butter and cocoa powder, constipation express. I'd resemble our push north—backed up.

We dug in and set up fighting positions. We were going to be here for a while, so we had to be prepared for any attack from the enemy. I came up with a duty schedule and put myself on it, every Marine is to stand duty regardless of rank or position; we all have to pitch in. As the positions are being set up, I take a few minutes to myself so that I could shed a few pounds. I don't know what it's like to give birth, but after three weeks without a bowel movement, I assumed it would be the same—consisting of blood, sweat, and tears. After a few minutes, I was done. I buried the newborn and went back to the makeshift camp.

MREs are full of different types of things you can mix and match with, trade with someone else, or just discard altogether. For instance, a pack of "Charms" was forbidden. If you had it, you better throw it as far away from you as possible—something about it being bad luck. I didn't get it, but okay. Cheese, peanut butter, cocoa, powdered fruit drinks, cookies, cakes, and so forth—these were baseball trading cards in our world. I would take the peanut butter, cocoa, and fruit drinks. I'd give a main meal for some of those things; I didn't care. I only liked the chicken tetrazzini main meal anyway. I also didn't need to mix the fruit drinks or cocoa with water. The cocoa I'd eat directly out of the packet. The fruit drinks would be poured into my mouth, and then I'd wash it down with water. That's good...no, *great* eating!

Now that we had some time, I was able to heat up some water and have myself some actual hot cocoa. I had to stay awake, so I thought I'd add some coffee to it as well. It smelled really good. I couldn't wait for it to be done. It was delicious; I drank it down and all my worries went away with the warmth that filled my body. I sat back and looked up at the stars. I was feeling ok.

Then my stomach made an interesting gurgling noise.

Apparently the mix of cocoa and coffee is a formula for a super-laxative. Only hours before I had just given birth to something that should not have come out of a human being, and now my intestines were about to burst. We need look no further. I had found the biological and chemical weapons...they were in my gut.

We used this time to get settled down and to get our minds in order. Sadly, one of the Marines in our battalion was killed from unexploded ordnance. Word got out and the reality of war set back in. By now the Marines knew how to deal with death, and so did I. It's sad to say, but when we now heard of Marines or soldiers dying, we reacted like everyone else did back home...we moved on.

We received word that we were moving out in another day, and also told that a few of the high profile Iraqi targets were captured and that Iraqis had captured United States Army POWs of their own. There would be no Marine POWs because a Marine usually keeps a 5.56mm and a 7.62mm round in his left breast pocket. If the enemy was going to take any one of us, we wouldn't give them the satisfaction of torture. I had already told my Marines that if I was ever captured, they had the go ahead to try to kill my captors even if I was with them. I'd rather be dead than to be used as an example to promote their ideology. These POWs had someone special among them, a pretty blonde haired girl the media and administration would use as the face of this war. Forget that her convoy was massacred; this Barbie doll was a hero, even before the real story came out. Marines didn't need to wait for what we would come to find out later on, we already knew what had happened...and it would *never* happen with any of us.

We got resupplied and were ready for the final day of rest before we moved out. I met with the other staff NCOs and officers and we were told what to expect in the next few days. I went back to brief the Marines and ask if they'd tried the cookies in the humanitarian meals. It was like baseball in the late 90s with steroid use, everyone was eating the humanitarian meals, even though it was considered cheating. You have to do what you have to do, and you're not going to pass up Pop-Tarts, I am sorry. We had been in Iraq for over a week. It really felt like we had been there for years. Our faces were grizzled and war-torn. Our emotions were no longer that of normal human beings. Death was comical, mistakes were expected, and starving Iraqis were not our problem. We were focused on getting the job done; we'd fix our emotions later.

My worry now was crossing the Euphrates River. We were told that if the bridge was deemed unsafe, we would cross the water itself. I did *not* want to do this. I can't swim, and I freak out in water. This was the only thing on my mind at the time, and I was not a happy camper. As we neared the bridge I shouted to my driver, "People are dying!" He laughed and we drove across. I had dodged a bullet so to speak. North of the Euphrates and south of the Tigris is land you would never think of when you first hear of Iraq. It is quite fertile, the soil is black and there is vegetation everywhere—the cradle of civilization, and I could see why. I guess the jungle pattern uniforms would finally come in handy.

I was bored now; one of the things you need to avoid during the "fog of war" is boredom. War is not a constant battle. It's not what you see in the movies. A fight lasts a few seconds to a few minutes and then there is the aftermath of blood and bodies. Hollywood has it wrong. We stopped again, and I received a call over the radio. There were people ahead, and they needed someone to speak with them. *Holy shit, I am going to be speaking with someone.* I get driven up to the position where there are Marines with a group of people who want to cross into our territory. I go up to them and speak in the little amount of Arabic that I know. Luckily I am also able to read body language, and I can take their speech and body language and interpret it. Among the Marines I was interpreting for was a lieutenant, more on him later. They were complaining about their sheep getting killed by an apparent airstrike. I tell them that it wasn't us; it must be Saddam who was targeting his people and blaming us. They accepted that answer and left. They wouldn't put it past Saddam to target his own people; he'd been doing it for decades.

We would stay in that area that day, but digging in was painful this time. The soil was thick, black, and was not giving way. Hours would be spent digging our sleeping holes; luckily I got called away again, this time to a house, south of my position. A house was cleared by Marines. Three Iraqi men were detained, and I would be the one who would interrogate them. We brought them back to our position and spoke with them. They were farmers, so they said, and they weren't doing anything. Their women and children had fled and they weren't sure if they were safe. We let them go; they walked back to where they came from. A few minutes later one of them returned with a complaint. See? Democracy and freedom of speech was already kicking in. Apparently some money was taken from their home, and they wanted us to give it back to them. We had no money, and I told them to just go home and be happy that they weren't going somewhere to be questioned further.

Word got back to our battalion commander of me being utilized as an interpreter with positive results. I get called to his position ahead, and he tells me that I will be leaving my platoon and that I will be attaching myself to the battalion headquarters for the remainder of this conflict. I understood his orders; our battalion was known as the "tip of the spear" because we were the first to go into conflict and we lead the way. I was now being asked to be the tip of the tip of the spear. I was being called up to the big leagues. I now knew that I would be where the fight was and that I would be a lone entity. I would travel in a convoy but be wherever I was needed. I always knew that one day my mouth would get me into trouble, but I didn't know that it would be because of the language coming out of it.

I got my gear and said good-bye to my Marines. I would be relinquishing my platoon sergeant duties for the remainder. Before I left, I told my platoon commander and those around him a quick story of my skills as an interpreter earlier in the day.

"So there I was talking to this Iraqi guy and translating what he was saying to this first lieutenant. He asks me to ask the Iraqi a few questions, so I go ahead and do so. When the Iraqi responds the lieutenant looks over at me for the translation. When the lieutenant asks me to ask the Iraqi if he knows how many Iraqi Republican Guard are waiting for us up north the Iraqi literally says, 'No,' to me in English. The lieutenant actually looks over at me for a translation. I say, 'What the fuck sir, he said no. It means the same fucking thing in English!'" They all laughed and even though I was more frustrated about it than anything, I couldn't help but find the humor in it

As I walked away and headed to my new assignment, I thought of my dad and what he felt about me and my language skills. He would get disappointed because they were not great, and I would refuse to speak it. My dad had told me for years that I would need it, but me being stubborn, I never thought I would. I thought to myself, *Man if my dad knew this was going on, he'd laugh his ass off and tell me, "Told you so."*

I was imagining the conversation with my dad, it never took place; it only happened in my head. Still, he didn't need to be an ass about it.

Chapter 11

The Twenty-Four-Year-Old Virgin

I hated speaking Arabic. I mean really hated it. If you would have asked me while growing up if I would rather take up knitting or had to speak Arabic to others, I would have taken up knitting with the knowledge that I would have to jab myself in the eye with a needle at least once. It's not that I couldn't speak it, well I couldn't, not well enough at least. It was that my parents wanted my siblings and me to speak only Arabic. We wouldn't talk for days at times. This didn't bode too well for my linguistic skills. You get better with practice, and I was never practicing. My mother would speak to me in Arabic, and I'd reply in English. My dad would mix the two together until he finally gave up and only spoke to me in English. My mom and dad moved back to Yemen in 1997 and took my younger siblings with them. They were forced to learn the language then; I just missed out, darn.

When I get nervous I stumble and stammer my words. Sometimes I have a hard time even getting a word out. It's almost a stutter; but I wouldn't call it that because when I am not nervous, I can roll off words like a stock ticker. When I went to Yemen for the first time in the early 90s, I spoke to no one. I barely knew the language, and I felt like a fool when I spoke. It didn't help that my mom and dad gave me shit for it. This is the sole reason why my family has no idea of my regular personality. It's a language barrier that still exists to this date. The interesting part of it all is that I understand them just fine; it's the replying that I want nothing to do with. Now I was going to have to communicate with people that may or may not have critical information. Funny thing though, I wasn't worried about that. I was more worried that if my dad found out, he would want to speak with me in Arabic when I saw him again

Arabic has about a million different dialects. Each country has a different way of saying things; each thinking their way is better. The Egyptians lay claim to the "Modern Standard" form of Arabic. This is what they use in newscasts, much like international news agencies such as CNN or the BBC do with English. Now what about people from Yemen? Have you ever seen an Arabian redneck? Now Yemen is a small country, about the size of Florida, except lacking a city like Miami and everything else you might think of that would make you want you to visit Florida. There are about four or five different dialects in Yemen alone, each laying claim as the proper way of speaking…well all except the area of Yemen my parents are from. My family speaks the most basic form of Arabic known to man. The words are simplified, the grammar adjusted to suit the uneducated, and the accent is course, very loud, and overbearing. If there was a type of Arabic not to use in Iraq, this was it.

I was now assigned to the battalion sergeant major's vehicle. This pissed him off because it meant he had to shift some of his equipment around. To appease him, I gave away most of the things I had brought with me. I was packing light, and any uniform item that I had brought with me would be burned anyway. None of us had showered for weeks; we were still in the same uniform we had when we crossed over.

Just because I was assigned to a vehicle didn't mean I would end up with that vehicle for the day. It was just where I was keeping my pack, my sleeping gear, and my rations. I was now a roving entity, all over the place. I would often hear, "Get the translator," and being the proud Marine staff non-commissioned officer that I was, I would say, "That's Staff Sergeant to you."

I was being utilized by everyone. What about those Kuwaiti interpreters that division promised everyone? Well they either didn't come through, or the Kuwaitis realized this was shit work, and they could be at home watching television while looking at the time pass by ever so slowly on their Rolex watches that were bought by funds provided through the Kuwaiti National Welfare system. We were sent into combat without a way to communicate with the local population…how was this in any way a good idea?

By now I had forgotten where we were in relation to Baghdad. I had accepted that we would be here forever, and I wasn't ever going to leave. We had only been in Iraq for weeks, but once again, it felt like years. I would go on missions to small objectives, clearing homes and speaking to those occupying these homes. There was one compound we walked into; it was the weirdest thing I had ever experienced to that point. We walked in, Marines flanking each side of me. I went in with some captain and asked to speak to whoever was in charge. A few men came out with their hands up. I checked them, and we had a little chat with their leader.

I don't remember what was said in specifics, but I remember that I put together some of his words and his mannerisms to formulate what he was saying. He explained that he was in charge of a few families that had fled and was protecting them. He brought us further inside and he wasn't kidding. The women and children came out, they were frightened but he yelled out to them that they were safe. They came out one by one; they shook my hand and started talking to me. Then they brought food and sodas out. I hadn't had a Pepsi in what seemed like a lifetime; it was cold too...they had ice! It was the kindest display I had seen in this war. I was smiling again and thanking them. These were good people, and they were avoiding the conflict. They were also very smart; they had planned for this and were prepared. The Marines who were providing fire support stood down and had a few sodas. The kids were beautiful. They were happy, and we smiled at them. It was heartwarming.

We left and thanked them for their hospitality. We just wanted to know what was in that area before we received any bad intelligence or false reports. The unit I was attached to at that moment dropped me off at a checkpoint. This is where I met with the battalion commander and a few others. The battalion commander was waiting for the Army Psy-Ops (Psychological Operations) team who had their very own Kuwaiti with them. He needed their interpreter, and since the Kuwaiti hadn't arrived in time, I would have to do. There was a pickup truck stopped off to the side of the road and being detained with it was a man and his daughter. She had to have been about two years old. I have a weak spot in my heart for kids; even when I was a kid I loved children. I loved little girls, too, because they were always cuter and dressed better than boys. I once saved $600 when I was twelve years old. I told my mom that if she ever had a baby girl—I had no younger sisters at the time—I would give all of that money to her. My baby sister was later born, and I was the happiest big brother on the planet. This girl reminded me of my little sister. Yes, my mother took the money from me.

The battalion commander wanted to know where the man was going and what he was saying. I asked him. He just said he was going south, that his house was nearby. We let him go but before he left, I go up to him and tell him that I think his daughter is adorable and that he needed to give her a good life in this soon-to-be new country. I give him forty US dollars, all the money I had with me at the time, and tell him that it's from me to her. He thanks me and drives off.

Just after they left, the Psy-Ops team arrived—an Army staff sergeant, two Army specialists, and a Kuwaiti guy wearing tacky sunglasses. One thing I had learned being in the Middle East, these guys love tacky things. The Kuwaiti was tall and looked fresh; did he have a shower available to him? They introduced us and he nodded his head and said, "Oh, you're the Yemeni?" What the fuck? Was word getting around? He offered me a Marlboro Light, and I declined. I didn't smoke. Since I had already done their job for them, the Psy-Ops team departed. The battalion commander told me that I was done for the day. I got back to the sergeant major's vehicle and opened up the canvas covering in the back of it. I took out a packet of cocoa from my pack; this was the first time I had eaten all day. I scarfed it down and jumped into the vehicle; we were on the move to our position for the night. I forgot to button up the canvas in the back; I would find that out later.

We get to our position, rocky and dusty. The vehicle had tossed us around a good bit. We stop and get ready to bed down for the night. I pull out my bag and see the sergeant major struggling, looking for something. His sleeping bag was missing, and I knew exactly why. I felt like shit, and I went to look for it. It was now dark, and I could barely see. I retraced the path we had taken. I found myself outside of our lines but found the bag. I was excited, grabbed the bag, and headed back to the vehicle. It was at that time I found myself looking at the muzzle of an M-16A2 service rifle with a Marine's finger pulling slowly on the trigger.

"Whoa! Whoa! Whoa! Whoa! Whoa! Whoa! It's me, Staff Sergeant Hafid!"

"Holy shit Staff Sergeant. I almost fucking shot you."

"Yeah, I had to get this," I said, as I lifted up the sleeping bag. The Marine was shaken. He and I got to know each other on the USS Comstock. He was a good kid; he had been scouted by the San Diego Padres to play for third base for them. He wanted to take part in this war and then play for them. We all have a story of sacrifice, and that was his. Surprisingly, I didn't care that I was almost shot. I was more excited that I had found the sergeant major's sleeping bag.

"Ok, well thanks for not killing me dude," I said as I walked away, but I could feel him staring at me as I left.

That night I heard gunfire. There was a firefight nearby. My eyes had adjusted to the dark, and I saw a Marine running toward me. I hadn't even gotten out of my boots to go to sleep; I knew I would be called on again. Three Iraqi men were hurt. They had been shot and were bleeding. I couldn't see them but could only speak with them, except there was someone else already there. It was a Marine gunnery sergeant who was of Egyptian ethnicity. I finally got to see what it was like to watch someone interpret…it was not as glamorous as they made it out to be. He gets information from them and they are MedEvac'd to a position south of us to be treated for their wounds. I meet the gunny and introduce myself, and he says, "Oh, you're the Yemeni!" Seriously, who's telling these guys about me and why haven't I heard about any of them? Is there a club that I am not a member of?

I go back to the vehicle, unutilized but confused. Why were they talking about me as if they knew who I was? What was being said that designated me, "The Yemeni"? I lie down and look at the stars above. I close my eyes and try to block out the chaos around me. I sleep.

Morning came and we were given orders to remove our MOPP suits. Apparently we were too close to Baghdad for Saddam to deploy his weapons on us. That didn't sound right to me. It wouldn't have stopped him before, but I was excited to get the thing off of me. We had been wearing them for weeks without the availability of a shower or the means to clean them. We all stunk, but we had grown accustomed to the smell. Your corn-chip-smelling feet were the same as my corn-chip-smelling feet. We all reeked. I peeled off the suit and threw it in a pile. I burned it and the smoke coming from the suit was either from the material it was made of or the stench of three to four weeks of body odor and sweat. It was yellow in color; I stared at it for a little while.

I pulled out a new pack of baby wipes. I had brought three packs with me, and this was the first time I was going to use them. I got undressed behind the vehicle, my ass bare for all of Iraq to see. I had to peel everything off—my whitey-tighties (which were no longer white), my t-shirt, and my socks. They were thrown into the pile of MOPP suits, more yellow smoke. I took a baby wipe bath and got dressed. I felt fresh though I know I was not. I got called to the command post and was told that I would be attached to the reserve unit that was assisting us. When I heard this, I got pissed off. These were Marines, but they were reservists! That's like being a part-time Marine, and the Marine Corps is *not* a part-time job.

I start to openly complain for the first time. I didn't like how I was being utilized. "Sir, I don't mean to bitch, but I feel like I am just another piece of equipment that gets passed around." I said this to the battalion executive officer, the same guy who stuck up for me when we were in Guam having a few drinks. He assured me that I wasn't a piece of gear and sent me off to the reserve unit's position.

They were holding a position north of the rest of the RCT. They were the northern most element. I would be with them for a few days. I met with the company first sergeant. It was odd to meet these Marines because I felt like they were civilians who played Marine. I didn't feel safe, but the first sergeant was respectful and courteous. He earned my respect.

I was to assist with checkpoints. Word of the Kuwaiti who was part of the Psy-Ops team quitting and heading home got to our position, and I was pissed! This fucking asshole could just up and leave? He'd probably go back to Kuwait City, go to a bar, and tell some random flight attendant that he just came back from the war. He'd surely get laid. I was angry, but it was only because I was envious. I would have done the same thing if I were in his position.

It was midday now, and I was getting to know some of the Marines. They were good to go, regular men like anyone else. They just wanted to help, and hell, they were better than being with the Army or Air Force. The team leader tells me, "Don't worry Staff Sergeant. We'll protect you. You're the most important person here." That upset me. I know he meant well by it, but I was a Marine too. I told him, "Nah bro, I'm a Marine too. I *got* you."

As I'm saying this, I look up the road ahead of us and see a flash and think, *What the fuck?*

Twenty meters behind me there's an explosion. Something that lay dormant inside me that I had no idea existed kicked into action.

"They're fucking shooting at us! Get down!" I yell to everyone around me.

I look around and realize I am the senior Marine. I bark out commands and tell the Marines to seek cover and have their weapons pointed downrange. We are positioned, ready to annihilate whatever is going to come at us. A motorcycle comes screaming toward us, but he is still out of range.

"Get ready to kill this motherfucker!" I yell to the men.

Whoever was on that motorcycle must have realized we were dug in and had enough cover that we would be able to kill him while protecting ourselves as well. The motorcycle screeches to a stop and turns back around. Our vehicles scream down the road toward their location, but they had fled.

You never know how you're going to react to being shot at or engaged by the enemy until it happens. Earlier in the war I was scared for my life when I thought I was going to die at the hand of Iraqi tanks. The day before I wasn't even worried about getting shot by a fellow Marine, and now today someone actually took a shot at me and my instincts had kicked in. I had never been so angry.

Those few days spent with the reserve Marines was a turning point in the war for me. I was no longer a virgin in the sense of wartime and near death experiences. The natural reaction I had put me more at ease. I didn't want to be the type of person that balls up in the fetal position and cries without putting up a fight. I didn't want to be all talk and no action like I had seen from others.

I was an electro-optics technician by trade, but I was a Marine rifleman by virtue.

I was worried about the reservist Marines earning my respect, but it was I who had to earn theirs. One morning, a few miles south of Baghdad, I woke up on the side of the road with these Marines. Waiting for me was a cup of hot chocolate that one of them had made for me. I thanked the Marine and took a sip, but this called for something more. The Marine who made me this cup of cocoa knew what I was referring to. The day before, an Iraqi had stopped and offered us bottles and bottles of Saddam's very own whiskey. We had taken them and kept them for a moment we would deem worthy. Reports of 3rd ID attacking the Baghdad Airport had been heard over the BBC—these guys brought a shortwave radio with them, smarter than us active duty guys. We were closer to our objective, and I had brothers-in-arms with me along for the ride. This was as worthy a time if I had ever seen any. A bottle was pulled out of the pristine looking box. This was good whiskey, fit for Saddam's consumption. The cap was removed and the bottle tipped over our glasses and cups to pour out today's reward. We raised our hands in unison and toasted.

Cheers.

Chapter 12

The Hidden Faces of Terror

Throughout history there have been events that have changed the world. Each of those moments, especially with the dawn of the Internet age, has required a question of, "Where were you when...?"

It was late evening in Shanghai, China. I was standing post as the Marine security guard on duty at the American Consulate. It was afterhours, so it was quiet. I don't know what I did to get over the boredom back then; this was a time before I owned a laptop. I was preparing for my relief to come in, and I was planning to go back to my room and watch a DVD before I slept for the night.

The phone rang like it would any other time. I answered it in an unusual—but not for me—way saying, "Semper Fi! American Consulate Shanghai, Marine Guard Post One, how may I help you?"

"Dude, two planes just hit the Twin Towers!" a voice says to me.

I was sure it was nothing larger than crop duster type planes and said so to the Marine on the other end of the phone.

"No man, these are real planes," as if he were trying to convince me.

I hung up the phone and went into one of the meeting rooms in the Consulate office building. It was an old building once used as a home before it was made into a consulate. The building was constructed of wood and after all these years was starting to show its wear and tear. I opened the door and turned on the television with the lone CNN feed. Watching television is not something we normally do. What would be the purpose of having a Marine on duty if he's only going to be watching television all day? The pictures on the screen confirmed that planes had indeed struck the World Trade Center, buildings I had seen all my life growing up in Brooklyn but had never set foot in. They were smoking, looking as if they were already dead. Alarms sounded in Post One, I had to make some phone calls to certain people, there was something coming in from Washington, DC, via message traffic. I also made some calls so that I could account for all the Marines under my charge; I was the senior Marine at the time.

My actions were nothing more than reactions, anything a Marine would do in my position. With more attacks being reported, I got geared up; it looked like the end of the world to me. My relief for the evening came in but I did not leave. I searched the entire compound for anything that could be planted—explosive devices, anything. I spent hours searching alone and found nothing. I watched in disbelief as the towers collapsed. Nothing would ever be the same again.

I didn't go home that night; I spent it patrolling the compound. The consul general arrived; everyone else showed up to work with a look of sadness, confusion, and fear. One of the Americans held up a local newspaper to me that read, "Was America at Fault for These Attacks?" She shook the paper and said, "That's why I hate these fucking people!" I had a blank look on my face. The regional security officer told me to go home and get some sleep; they were going to need me rested if anything were to come up. Nothing did, and I wouldn't sleep for five days. It would be nearly six months after the attacks before I made it back home to New York. My father and younger brother came to pick me up. As my dad drove me home I looked to my right to catch a glimpse of the city skyline. This was not New York, this was someplace else; where was the defining skyline that everyone had become accustomed to?

On the night of September 11, I tried to make phone calls to many of my friends, and even those who weren't my friends to see if they were okay. I couldn't get through to most of them, but I kept trying, even after months had passed. It was the first week of March when I contacted a high school friend who had lived across the street from me. We were catching up when she told me that her boyfriend was killed in one of the towers; she began to cry over the phone and asked if I would go with her to the site on the six month anniversary. I promised her I would be there for her; I wouldn't miss it for the world. On that morning everything around me felt…different. The local morning newscast began with the anchor saying, "Good morning New York. It's September 11…" She paused, visibly shaken while her co-anchor reached out and held her hand in a show of support. On the subway ride into the city a lady spoke out and asked that we use God as a guide to get us through this day and the days ahead. Before she had spoken there was silence and blank stares from everyone, but her voice garnered their attention and mine. This doesn't ever happen in New York. Today, though, was an exception. The pain I saw in my friend's face, the tears rolling down her cheeks broke my heart. I felt helpless but made her a promise that I would get the bastards that had done this. I would find a way, and I would get them for her and for her fallen boyfriend. From the ashes we would rise...

After spending a few days with the reservists and surviving a small attack, the war had a different flavor to it. It wasn't from the whiskey; it was just something else about the environment. We were miles outside of our main objective and 3rd Infantry Division had already been making advancements on the international airport. It would only be a matter of time, but I wasn't going to assume anything. I was given a few moments of "downtime" to go south where my platoon was positioned. They were as happy to see me as I was to see them. They asked me how things were going and I told them things were just fine. I didn't tell them about the attack, but I did tell them about the whiskey. They envied me, and rightfully so; I was doing some things that sounded like fun, but boy was it stressful.

As this was going on, a few of the Marines lit up and smoked. I had always wondered why they smoked, especially when I would hear some of them coughing up a lung after a long run. I figured that if I had already had a drink, I might as well see what the big deal with cigarettes was. I asked for a cigarette, a Marlboro Light since smoking a Camel Light would seem wrong, being Arab and all. In the past, I had taken a puff and hadn't done it right apparently. This time I did what President Clinton said he didn't do, I inhaled. Laughter filled the air. I spoke no words, but my face said everything. This stuff was awesome! The first drag filled my lungs and took the edge off. I looked back at the cigarette and looked at the Marines who were laughing like they already knew. "It's good isn't it? Now you see why we smoke," said one of the Marines. "Wait until you try Marlboro Reds."

"Nah dude, I hear these things can kill you," I said to him drawing laughs. "Hey can I get a pack off you?"

The Marines were more than willing to hook me up. I knew I would need a cigarette every now and then—with little sleep and food, the addition of stress would not be healthy for my psyche. They knew this as well, a happy staff sergeant is a good staff sergeant.

Our supply line was cut off once again. We were all told to be careful with our food and water rations. By now, there were no more humanitarian rations, they were delicious I might add. We were down to one meal a day and one bottle of water a day; we really had to be careful. As this was being discussed with a couple of Marines, we look over to the right and see a Marine Captain washing his clothes with the water we were told to ration, rank has its privileges…and stupidity.

I am called to the battalion command post, and I meet with the battalion executive officer (XO). I basically answer to him whenever the battalion commander (CO) is not around. He asked if I had heard about the Kuwaiti interpreter leaving and I answer that I had. I should have known what was next.

"You're going to be attached to the Psy-Ops team. You'll be traveling in their vehicle," he said.

I had my reservations about the Marine reservists and they had proved me wrong, but this was the Army. I did not want to be all that I could be; I joined the Corps because I wanted to be one of the few and the proud—a Marine damn it! The uniforms didn't hurt either.

As he's telling me this, their vehicle pulls up and my gear is being loaded onto it by one of the Army specialists. I didn't even know my gear had already been taken off of the sergeant major's vehicle. When did this happen? I could have said no, but it wouldn't have changed anything. I was going to be with the Army Psy-Ops team, like it or not. I did not like it; but hey, this is war. You have to be flexible, Semper Gumby.

There was a benefit to being with the Psy-Ops team. They were Army, which meant they had more money than the Marines. This meant that they would have better vehicles, better equipment, and more toys than Marines had. This meant a lot of other things, one of them being that I would be speaking into a microphone for my voice to be heard by all. Where a .50 cal would normally be on top of a vehicle, my vehicle had speakers. I am sure Bose made a killing off that deal with the Government. I was barely able to communicate in the first place, now they were going to make me stutter and stammer with a live audience to critique me? The soldiers were welcoming though. They offered me water, MREs of my choosing, and even a shortwave radio that had its own built-in generator. They were giving these radios out to the local population so they could tune-in to the BBC or any other international radio station. I now realized that the Iraqis knew more about what was going on than those fighting the war knew.

We hit the road; we were going to occupy an abandoned Iraqi army barracks on the outskirts of Baghdad. This was the first time I was with these guys so I got a feel for them. I asked the senior soldier, who was a staff sergeant himself, "Hey dude, you mind if I smoke in your vehicle?" I asked him because you couldn't smoke in Marine vehicles, but hey, this is Army, they didn't have many rules—look at their weight standards. He answered, "Yeah, can I bum one off ya?"

On the way to our next position we saw the streets were filled with people. They were celebrating and looting. They came up to us cheering us on and asking us if we needed anything. A vehicle came up to where I was standing and four guys exited and opened the trunk. They pulled out cartons of cigarettes, tons of them. They gave them out to the Marines, telling me to tell the Marines that they need us fully rested and fed so we can topple Saddam. This brought a lot of Iraqis over to where I was. Instead of being the one who asked the questions, I was now the one being asked. They asked my name and where I was from. I told them from Yemen and once again, "Ah, you're the Yemeni?" Okay, this was scary; how the fuck did *they* know about me? I asked them how they knew of me and their response was something like, "We heard the Marines had a Yemeni with them and they would be coming to free us from Saddam." Great, my name was folklore now.

All around us people were looting, stealing whatever they could. We were not there to police them; we were only there to fight an enemy and to free them. A few others, some of them men of my age and in good shape, walked by us carrying duffle bags. They were not looting; they just looked at us with scowls on their faces. "Those guys look like Iraqi Soldiers," I say to the soldiers with me and to the Marines of my command, but no one pays any attention. They were happy to take pictures for their albums with these Iraqis and happy to take their cigarettes. Oh, I took the most, of course; I was a new smoker and wanted to have enough for the duration.

I tell the Iraqis we have to leave. They thank me and shake my hand. Before we get into our vehicles one last photo is taken. I jump into this one; I might as well have something to prove I was here. I light up a cigarette and drive away, waving to our new friends. We drive up the road just outside the city and get to our new position. We pull in and relax for a bit. I open the box that contains the new radio my soldier buddies gave me; I wind up the radio and turn on the BBC. I finally get to hear what's going on. Not even a minute passes before I get called away. A "Special Team" is coming in and they're bringing in high value prisoners. I am told I would be needed.

"Are these terrorists?" I ask.

"Well, they aren't Iraqi..." is the reply.

American men with bearded faces covered in filth bring in five prisoners with them, their faces hidden and hands tied behind their backs. They will be placed in a room where Marines will be standing watch over them. These were not Marines or soldiers who were bringing these guys over to us, they were a "Special Team," and I knew what that meant.

I am in the room with the terrorists. They are placed on their knees and told to stay that way. They are not allowed to speak to each other. These are enemy combatants. The articles and laws governing the Geneva Conventions do not apply to them, and I intend to take full advantage of that. A Marine lieutenant who I've never met walks in and whispers in one of the terrorist's ear, "Remember the other night when you fuckers killed one of my men? We're gonna make you pay for that..." Before he could finish, the battalion XO, who was also nearby, tells him, "Hey, get the fuck out of here!" All I could think of was the promise I made to my friend a year before about getting the guys who killed her boyfriend and thousands of others. I knew these were the type of men who were responsible for what had transpired a year and a half earlier. They were big and bad, boasting for all to hear, carrying lighters that showed bin Laden's face with a picture of a plane going into the World Trade Center. These were bad guys, and they now belonged to me.

Every war involves a certain race or religion. If you have someone on your team of that same race or religion, you might question them out of instinct. I never thought this to be an issue. I never questioned anyone's feelings toward me as an Arab; I never questioned anyone's feelings toward me as a Muslim. I only saw myself as a Marine, but what I saw from my battalion commander next made me wonder what he had thought of me before. I inform the Marines who would be watching the detainees that night that I would be sleeping right outside the room. If they needed me, I would be right there. I roll out my sleeping bag and look up to see the battalion commander standing next to me. He looks at me with a sense of relief and says, "So what do you think, Staff Sergeant?"

"Fuck 'em, sir. They're fucking pussies now that we have them. I'm staying right here, just in case any of them has the balls to say something."

He looks at me with a smile and thanks me for the job I am doing. He pats me on the shoulder and walks away. Then it dawns on me, before this very moment he wasn't sure what my stance on this war was. I didn't blame him, like I didn't blame the *random* searches at the airport. As soon as those towers fell, I knew it was a different world; I was just living it.

The next morning I was called into a room to respond to one of the terrorists crying and screaming. In the room was the one terrorist and all around him were senior Marines from my battalion, including the master gunnery sergeant from my platoon. I don't know why they were all in there, but they saw me go in and talk to this guy. It went something like this:

"So you and your bad asses aren't so bad now? You're not men. You're not even women. You're dirt. You're the biggest joke I've ever seen. Look at you crying, feeling big and bad now…?"

I was overcome with emotion, yelling at the top of my lungs in a language I was not comfortable speaking, but speaking with the command I had as a Marine. The confidence in my ability to speak Arabic grew; I didn't care about how I sounded or even if I stuttered. There was no room for the stroking of egos, certainly not mine. This man who was crying understood everything I said to him. I spoke with the voice of those who will never be forgotten. I rambled on and on. I was grabbed by the arm so I could stop and was taken back to my vehicle. Everyone had seen how I had taken this personally, how this affected me as much as it did anyone else, if not more. I got back to my vehicle, visibly shaken. I lit up a cigarette and looked at the sky. I exhaled a plume of smoke. I kissed my fingertips and pointed to the heavens. I flicked away the cigarette and got inside the vehicle. We rolled out as I lit up another cigarette. I make eye contact with the soldier driving our vehicle through his rear-view mirror and speak…

"Let's go to Baghdad."

CHAPTER 13

Chicken Tetrazzini

Getting emotional about things is a peacetime luxury. In wartime, it's much too painful.
—Edmund H. North

I was the battalion's only interpreter and now that I was serving as the Army Psy-Ops Team's mascot, I mean interpreter, I had no time for anything else. Before getting to Baghdad we were unsure what we were going to get from the enemy. They hadn't put up a fight when we crossed over, but then they fought dirty and tirelessly when we had gotten to the Euphrates River. What were we to expect now? The fighting was sporadic—our military might was seen by the entire world and now the people of Baghdad were seeing it. The airport was under the control of 3rd ID, and we were patrolling in and out of the city. The traffic going in and out of Baghdad was intense. There were more cars than there were people and without a police force to control things, there was anarchy.

Baghdad had fallen; there was no fighting to be had for us. We drove in as victors, hailed by the people of Baghdad as their saviors. "Good Bush!" could be heard shouted from the crowds. I couldn't help but say, "I like it shaved or trimmed." Our battalion had no real mission, so the Army staff sergeant I was with wanted to start doing what his job called for, talking to the local people and getting all the information he needed to help support them now that their supply lines were non-existent. We set up a position, just the two of us, and local leaders came to talk to us one by one. This was my greatest fear, speaking to dignitaries when it required someone with far more knowledge and experience with the language than I had.

I was tired, for days we had set up shop and everyone who had something to gain by winning our favor was coming to talk to us. I was grumpy, hungry, dirty, unshaved, and you could name just about anything else and I was feeling it. I remember one man coming up to me and speaking so eloquently that I just stared at him slack jawed. I looked over at the Army staff sergeant and said, "Dude, I have no fucking idea what he's saying."

The kids were out; they were having a good time. Marines would give the kids Skittles and the Charms candy that we weren't allowed to keep for fear of bad luck. Children would come out each day and stay with us. It was safe for them. They knew this, we knew this, and everyone else knew this. Time was winding down; we were already discussing how to rebuild the nation with the people of Baghdad. I could sense home was near, but I still felt like I wasn't going anywhere anytime soon. Time was winding down for the night as well, there was a curfew put in place. This was to prevent anyone from being mistaken for pockets of resistance, popping up and shooting at us.

I announce over the speakers that everyone should go back to their homes. It was dangerous at night and a curfew would be in effect soon. The crowd disperses; the kids say they would be coming back in the morning to say hello. I stop them and tell the little girl with them, who the older kids would not share their candy with, to come over to me. I give her a $20 bill and tell the other kids that if they try taking it from her, I'll shoot them. She was so happy. The beautiful children, they will make the future of this nation a bright one.

I am starving, so I grab an MRE from the back of the vehicle, Meal Number 21–Chicken Tetrazzini, my favorite! Some of the Marines back at our staging area had some seasoning. I am already salivating at the thought of a warm meal and all the flavors I would taste, once I drown it with seasoning. We get to the staging area, a compound that was once used to make all sorts of chemicals. The battalion had just gotten there, so we missed out on picking a spot to park. It didn't matter; we parked our vehicle in the center of the compound near the building where the command post was set up. I pull out my meal and am ready to prepare it. Just as I am about to rip open the package I am called to the command post. One of the forward companies had someone and they needed an interpreter. The Psy-Ops team isn't needed, so I go alone. One of their vehicles comes to pick me up and take me to their position. By the time I get there, the person had been let go. He wasn't a person of interest. They were just wondering who he was and what he wanted.

Time for me to go back I guess.

"Oh, we were told you would be staying here tonight Staff Sergeant," says the company commander. "We're not sending anymore vehicles out on the road because of the curfew."

"Well that's great, sir. If that had been communicated to me earlier, I could have been better prepared," I say with sarcasm and anger.

It was dark; the weather was cool, but not as cold as it had been previously. My pack, sleeping bag, and my meal were all with the Army Psy-Ops team, and I was forced to spend the night on the side of the road. It didn't matter, by now I could have slept on a bed of nails, as long as I could go to sleep.

I slept through the night without any issues. I was still starving; I hadn't eaten in days. I looked worn down and in need of a break; even I knew I couldn't hold on much further without food. With the coming daylight I asked to be taken back to my vehicle, but I was told that would be at around lunchtime or so. They had to do some patrols first. Yeah I was pissed off, but I know I am not more important than the mission, so I wait. I got in one of their vehicles and assisted whenever they needed me to assist.

It was lunchtime now, and, as promised, I get dropped off at the front gate of the compound/staging area. I am let in, and I go to my vehicle. I pull out my shaving gear, toothbrush, a change of underwear, and whatever else I could use to make me feel like a human being again. I look over to my chicken tetrazzini meal and it's still intact. These Army guys are honorable after all. I get called over to the command post by the battalion XO; I report to him looking ragged and sickly. He sees that I am worn out and in need of a shave. He tells me, "Okay, we'll let you get a couple of hours to shave and get some chow in you before we get you some more work to do." I nod my head and thank him.

I allow myself to smile; I feel that I am doing a pretty good job at this and begin to think about my dad and what he would think of me. He would be proud of me, but he has no idea what it is that I am doing. It didn't matter, I just wanted him to be proud of his son and know that I looked up to him. I looked up to him so much so that I told him that when my son is born in a few months, I would give him his name.

Wow! I'm gonna be a dad soon, I think to myself. Things were dying down, and I would be home in the near future and my child would be born with a war veteran as a father. I had always felt like my father's son but now I would be the father to my own son. Just a few more months and it would come to be. Thinking of something far ahead, before it would happen, had gotten me disappointed and in trouble before. This time would be no different.

I pulled a cot off of the back of the vehicle. The Army travels with cots; I set mine up and sat down on it. I pulled out the main meal and put it in its heater. By the time I finish shaving and other hygienic duties I had to attend to, my meal would be ready, and I would be able to eat for the first time in who knew how long. I turn on the electric razor I had bought from Wal-Mart months ago, by now it was rusty, dry, and filthy, but it still worked. I put the rotating blades to my face and you could hear them struggling to cut the stubble that had formed. To add to the strain was some dirt that was caked on my face. Like I said, I was filthy. Round and round I shaved in circular motions. My face had gotten used to this. The first time I used this razor, I damn near cried.

I pull out a polished steel plate; I use it as a mirror so I can trim my sideburns that have come out of hiding after seven years of Marine Corps grooming standards. I take my time; I want to do it right while I allow my meal to heat even further. I grab my fingernail clippers out of my hygiene bag. I cut my fingernails one by one, ensuring I get a good cut and for some reason I collect all the cut fingernails, so I can account for them. Don't worry, I don't save them. I just make sure I have all ten remains, and then I discard them. I don't know why I am such a stickler about having all ten nails accounted for before I throw them away.

I grab some baby wipes and start to wipe my face off, getting into every crevice I could find in my ear and near my eyes. I look at the wipe and it is nearly black. I throw it away and grab another one and continue on my face. Then I move to my arms and hands. I am saving my feet for last. Once I get done with my hands, I lift my leg to chest and lean forward so I can untie my boot, and that's when…

"Staff Sergeant, we need you at the front gate now!"

"Motherfucker! What the fuck for now?" I yell at the Marine who is only doing what he had been told to do.

"I was told to come get you, Staff Sergeant. There's someone at the gate."

I get to the front gate and it's an Iraqi man who wants to make a deal with us over something. I don't remember because it wasn't important. I tell him to go talk to someone down the road. They can help him there. I motion to the Marines to open the gate to let this man out. As they open the gate, I see a small family running toward us: two men and a woman with a baby. The Marines stop them, but the man screams, "Please help us. He's not breathing!"

My eyes open wide. I tell the Marines to let them in. I yell behind me, "Get the doc and the ambulance!"

The older man is holding the baby, his son who is barely breathing and looks near death. I ask the man what happened, and he replied, "Before we came to Baghdad, they kicked everyone out of the hospitals, even the children."

I couldn't believe this, who would do such a thing? Why would they do such a thing?

The Navy doctor came to look at the baby; I was scared, but nowhere near as scared as this family was. The boy looked to be laboring even more, struggling to breathe, turning green in color. Tears formed in my eyes as I looked on, hoping the doctor could do something. We came here to save these children, to give them a future, if not now then when?

I look on shaking, trembling with fear, and then the baby stops breathing.

The doctor takes him from his father's arms and applies CPR to him. I am nearly crying now, afraid for this family to experience the ultimate loss. The doctor stops, hands the baby back to his father who looks over at me and asks, "He died?"

The Navy doctor waves his hands in front of the family in a crossing motion as if to say "he's finished," and they burst into tears. The other man with them is his eldest son. I turn around and look away. I am not the only one as the Marines who called me to the gate also look away. I do not have strength to speak; I am overcome with heartbreak for this family. I am useless now; every one of us crying tears of pain, symbolizing everything to that moment. I escort the family out and the gate closes. Not a word is spoken. We are in mourning, and we all go our separate ways. I had just witnessed the death of a child and the worst thing that could ever happen to a parent, just moments after thinking about becoming a parent myself.

I go back to my vehicle; I look at my meal and throw it away. I felt guilty that I had been complaining that I was never given enough time to eat, while a child is now dead, never to eat again. I lie down and stare at the heavens above in silence. Word got back to the command post about what had happened at the gate. Out of compassion, I was left alone for the rest of the day and night.

I didn't even know the boy's name…RIP.

CHAPTER 14

Top of the Ninth

Whenever you're mourning or whenever your heart is broken, it is natural for you to close ranks within yourself and bottle up your emotions. This is very dangerous and, at that time, I did not understand. Seeing that little boy die in front of my eyes is a memory I knew would never leave me. I lay there on my cot in silence, staring at the heavens above. Streaks of light appeared in the sky, I knew those were just meteorites burning up in the atmosphere; I'm a sucker for science. I remember when I was a kid I would believe in things like Santa Claus, the Tooth Fairy, and wishing on shooting stars. Santa and the Tooth Fairy would come through for the years my parents gave us Christmas and for the times my teeth came out, but I had never seen a shooting star before. With all the light pollution growing up in Brooklyn there was no way you'd see one, and if you did see a shooting star, you'd better start praying. It meant something bigger than a meteorite was headed your way and you were about to be to be vaporized.

This was the first time I had ever seen a shooting star. I made a wish. I knew it wouldn't come true, but I wished anyway. I wished that what had just occurred would never happen again. I knew it wasn't going to be a wish fulfilled, but I still had to try. When you're feeling helpless, as I was at that moment, you're willing to try anything.

Baghdad was supposed to be the Marine Corps' final destination in this conflict. We had done the job up to this point and had experienced great success. We might have moved too quickly through some areas and stayed too long in others, but overall we were successful. Moral was high, and for most of the Marines, things were going our way. Three Marine regimental combat teams had swept through southern Iraq in a matter of weeks. One Army Infantry Division came in to flank Baghdad from the south and then the west, bypassing the cities, leaving them for the Corps. 4th Infantry Division's area of operation was to the north, but Turkey had refused to allow American forces to use their country as a base to attack Iraq.

North of Baghdad was an unknown; there were no American forces in that area. Tikrit, Saddam's home city, was to be the next objective for 4th Infantry Division, but they were out of the picture now with no direct access to the north. They would have to regroup and come from the south, like the rest of us; but it would take weeks, if not months, to get them and their equipment to where they needed to be. Who would be responsible for Tikrit now?

A mission to take Tikrit was being planned, known as Task Force Tripoli, a task force that would make Marine Corps history. It would be the first task force consisting entirely of Light Armored Vehicle elements and would mark the furthest inland Marine forces had ever traveled. We're amphibious, there is no beach landing in the middle of the desert, but there is plenty of sand. Tripoli is a city in Libya known to most Marines from a verse in the Marines' Hymn— "From the Halls of Montezuma, to the shores of Tripoli..." We now gathered our things and prepared to head out, but first we were addressed by our battalion commander, the first time we had been addressed by him since leaving Kuwait. We were told that we were doing a great job, that we were setting records and making history. It was indeed true. We were making history. Our story would be told and remembered throughout time itself, but in what way would it be remembered?

We left the compound as a battalion ready to begin our next mission. I had barely spoken to anyone since the death of that boy and it was to stay that way for the time being. I just wanted to get this war over with and as far away from my thoughts as possible. We staged to the east of Baghdad on deserted farmland. We were to spend half the day there and move north at night. Christmas came early that day, two trucks stopped by the staging area with mail. It took a few hours to sort it out, but eventually it was distributed, and yes, even I received a few letters. The simplest things in life can go the furthest, and these letters meant everything to me. I sat there and read each one, word for word. I looked at the penmanship, the color of the ink, and the smell of the paper. Each one of these letters was once in the hands of someone who had been thinking of me. Where for a fleeting moment, I was the one person on their mind.

It was as if electricity was running through the rows of vehicles and each one of us was a light being turned on, shining bright for all to see. I was probably the brightest because I needed something to pick me up, and letters from home meant more to me than food or water. It gave me more sustenance. I walked around with a glow, visiting Marines from my platoon and sitting with them. We talked and discussed many things, but nothing about the war. We talked about the letters we'd gotten and about news from back home, though there was still nothing about J-Lo being killed in an accident.

We noticed an Iraqi man approaching our position, an older man, possibly in his sixties. He walked over to us and told us that this area used to be his land and that Saddam took it from him.

"Well Saddam's not here anymore now is he?" I said, smiling at the man.

He smiled back and nodded, and then he asked if he could get us anything.

I asked him if there was any food nearby, and if there was, if he could bring us some bread, something hot and fresh. He said he would try, so I gave him some money that I had left over. He took it and went on his way. One of the Marines tells me he doesn't think the guy will come back, but I knew he would. The man brought back some bread, not much, but enough to make me happy. I thanked him and gave him a couple of bottles of water. He left us and I brought the bread over to the Marines.

This was the first time I had eaten in a few days, and it was great. The letters I had received breathed new life and purpose into my mind and body. It was getting dark now; I would have to head back to my vehicle to talk about our purpose in Tikrit with the Psy-Ops team. When I arrived, the staff sergeant was asleep with the BBC on the radio in the background, detailing our mission—so much for surprising the enemy.

The next morning, before we take off, the staff sergeant of the Psy-Ops team hooks up his CD player to the speakers on top of the vehicle. He tells the driver to move the vehicle and park it in an area facing the convoy. When we get there he hits play and over the speakers plays one of my all-time favorite songs. It is "Enter Sandman" by Metallica, the song that is played in Yankee Stadium whenever Mariano Rivera would come to the mound. Mariano would enter the game to close it out for a Yankee win. How fitting that this song would play; the Marines were needed to close out this war.

I look at the Marines in their vehicles, shaking their heads in unison, absorbing the music, taking in the moment. The drivers of each vehicle tap their steering wheels, and in my mind I drift away. I find myself in Yankee Stadium, the crowd on their feet clapping and singing along, Mariano Rivera running to the pitcher's mound to grab the ball. Around Mariano, the Yankee infield is tossing the ball around, and by now they were indeed playing because baseball season had started. Mariano Rivera starts to warm up, the crowd chants louder and louder with the anticipation of another Yankee victory. Music has always had a place in war, why not now?

Warm-up pitches are over; a batter enters the batter's box to face Mariano. The song dies down and becomes the start of our silent count. All the vehicles start at once. We have perfected what was once a problem; it comes with practice and with dedication. We sound as one, and we move out—hell on wheels.

The Sand*men* are coming, and we're looking to close it out for a win.

CHAPTER 15

The Mayor of Tikrit

Traveling at night, without the help of streetlights illuminating the way, gives you a different idea of where you are and what's around you. Objects look different, and what is benign during sunlight is threatening in darkness. Shadows in the dark resemble the creatures of the night. This isn't childhood, when you can turn on a nightlight and call out to your parents. You're alone in this one, so you do what you can to keep focused on the mission at hand. I'm a little tired from all that's gone on, but I cannot help but stay awake. We've done all that's been asked of us and now we've been tasked even further. I could have been upset by having to take on another mission, but being a part of history really means something to me. The Marine Corps is full of tradition and history. In boot camp they spend a week feeding you Marine Corps history. The Corps is the only branch of service that does this. History is a part of every Marine, and it is our history that drives us to seek a better future.

I love a good sales pitch, and my recruiter sold me on the Marine Corps. Had it been any other guy in his shoes, I don't know if they would have convinced me to join the Marines over the Navy. He asked why I wanted to be a Marine. This was a great question because I didn't want to be a Marine. He was smart; he knew I wanted to be someone special, someone who wanted to make a difference. President Reagan once said, "Some people spend an entire lifetime wondering if they've made a difference. The Marines don't have that problem." Had he used that quote from Reagan, a President I respected, I would have been sold, but he got me with something else.

He said, "When sailors or soldiers get out of the service and return home they're known as 'ex-Navy' or 'ex-Army.' Marines though, when they get out and go home they are 'former Marines,' because once you're a Marine, you're always a Marine."

Well sign me up! I knew I wanted to be a part of something bigger than me, and part of something that would give me the opportunity to make a difference, one way or another. So flash forward eight years, and I am being told that we're going to take part in a historic march up north to finish off this war. Had this been another contract, I'd sign it. I believe our mortality gets the best of us at times. We know our fate is certain death, but we all want to leave a mark somehow on eternity. This was my chance at immortality, to be a part of this mission. You'll do anything to lend a helping hand in history. The drive was long and boring, so I helped drive. The conversation was dull, so I spiced it up with some talk about my bizarre life to date. Eventually I ran out of stories to tell and silence was followed by snores from the rest of the guys in the vehicle. I fight to stay awake and do so barely.

Tikrit is Saddam's hometown, so when morning comes and we see our surroundings, we aren't surprised by what we see. There are photographs of Saddam everywhere, the infrastructure is well kept, and those entering Tikrit are greeted by a gateway of Saddam's arms holding crossed swords. The guy loves himself, that is a given, but he really believed he was something he was not...a warrior. We're staged on the side of the road, and so far we have encountered no resistance from any loyalists. There were no shots fired, no reports of casualties, but we have yet to go into the city. Later that morning forward elements of the task force would enter and face small arms fire. Those who attacked were quickly killed, and the forward elements would continue moving in. There was no need for me, so I stayed put, sitting outside my vehicle trying to open up an MRE.

A Marine from my platoon comes over and asks if he could sit down and eat with me. I moved over to my right and welcomed him to sit. He sat down and asked how I was doing; we made small talk and sat there for a good hour, just talking. There are thousands of personalities, men and women with different histories that are brought together to achieve an ultimate goal, victory. Very few care to dig into the human factor of what it takes to make it this far. Is it because no one cares, or is it because they are afraid to find out what insanity it takes to do this, to get through this? I don't know; all I know, at this moment, is that I am having breakfast with a Marine who looks up to me, and for each of us, it's a break from reality we could both use.

We enter Tikrit in the evening, the fighting, for the most part, is over. The city is different than what we'd experienced before. There is no looting. The people aren't too excited to see us, but they're relatively peaceful. Our battalion moves into place in one of Saddam's palaces. His property covers much ground, so we're able to pick and choose where we will be spending our time. It's over; we know it is; we can feel it with every mission they give us because each mission is a joke. The first night the Psy-Ops team and I take full advantage of the new atmosphere and find a vacant house with running water. We decide that each of us would get a chance to shower while the rest of us wait outside standing guard.

When it's my turn, I walk in to a dirty bathroom that seems unfinished. There are no tiles on the floor or wall, just bare concrete. The shower is nothing more than a leaky pipe, the showerhead having been broken off and the water pressure gone. Still, I get undressed and get under this slow and barely steady stream of water. After a month without showering, this would be more than enough to satisfy us. I lather up and wash away a month of filth and stench. I get dressed and feel fresh. After we all get a shower, we go to where the battalion is staged and bed down for the night.

Morning comes and we see people from the media walking out of the buildings with rugs and anything they can carry with them. They are looting and getting the good stuff too! I bet they didn't mention that on the nightly news. All I managed to take with me was a doorbell that was battery operated and some postcards from Iraqi Airways. I planned on taking the doorbell to Yemen and giving it to my wife. That way she would be the first person in her village with a doorbell, she would be famous!

We were told to tag along with the battalion commander on a visit to the local hospital. When we get there, we find the Iraqis were using the hospital to store weapons. We find tons, and I mean tons of weapons at the hospital. Saddam would kick dying children out but leave his weapons in these hospitals? This man is a coward, definitely not a warrior. We met with the hospital caretakers and had some tea. Initially intimidated by us, the caretakers were kind and welcoming, offering us cigarettes and tea. I had informed the battalion leadership before getting there that if the Iraqis offered us anything such as tea, we should take it. The tea comes and they each look at me. I've had this sort of tea before while visiting family in Yemen. It is some good stuff, and I don't hesitate while I drink the first cup. After seeing that it wasn't poisoned and didn't kill me, they each have some tea. I'm glad I could assist in being the taste tester.

Our meetings were to discuss what we could do to assist in getting Tikrit up and running again. It wouldn't be so difficult because it was already functioning without issue. Because there was little resistance, there was little damage done to the infrastructure. I also assumed it was because Saddam was in town and God forbid he was unable to watch his television programs. I remember our first meeting with this group specifically because they offered a lieutenant and me cigarettes that I will never forget. By now I had been smoking for a few weeks so I was used to the nicotine rush, but this cigarette was different. A few puffs into it and the lieutenant and I look at each other and back at the cigarette; it was laced with something else. For the first time in my life I was high, and it was awesome!

A few times I would get attached with another Marine unit to patrol north of Tikrit, near the border with the Kurds. A few scuffles broke out between the Iraqis and the Kurds, with the Kurds taking advantage of the lawlessness. I had to put myself in the middle of these skirmishes and tell them all to cool it and that things would be different now. To get to the north of Tikrit, we had to cross a bridge that had nearly collapsed. It looked as if King Kong had taken a bite out of it. There was once a bomb scare on the bridge, and I had to make an announcement over the speakers to get the people out of harm's way. I said what I thought to be the right thing to say. However, an Iraqi man comes up to me and says in broken English, "You speak Arabic very bad." I hand him the microphone and he announces the possibility of a bomb on the bridge correctly, getting the proper response—people fleeing the bridge. Before he had spoken, anything I said had received blank stares. I'm glad he was there to help.

Reporters from Fox News and the *LA Times* were there. They ask me a few questions before the Fox News reporter stands in front of the bridge holding up a microphone while looking into his camera saying dramatically, "Behind me the threat of a bomb looms. Is this the new Iraq?" I wanted to kick his teeth in. There was no bomb. I don't even think they aired the story, or the fact that there was no bomb. The French media was also there. The gentleman knew we didn't care for his countrymen too much so he says in his accented voice, "I know. I know. Where are the tanks?" Referring to the lack of support we received from France.

We had found a house on Saddam's compound and moved in, just the four of us. The road was above us, and anyone could look down. Whenever I would come out, Iraqis would point at me and call my name. By now everyone knew who I was; I was the Yemeni Marine who came to free them from Saddam. They liked Yemen. The Iraqis never forgot that Yemen voted against the use of force to remove Iraq from the occupation of Kuwait while Yemen served as a non-permanent member of the UN Security Council in November of 1990. So, if I were someone else, say a Saudi, they would not have cared for me too much.

We would set up roadblocks, and I would assist in interpreting. A Fox News team was nearby and I asked them, "Hey did J-Lo really die?" They looked at me with confusion and said "No." I asked if I could use their phone and the cameraman says, "Yeah sure, dude. Take your time. Call whoever you want." I called the house of a childhood friend in Brooklyn; his mom answered the phone and was happy to hear from me. She started to cry, which made me feel awkward. I didn't like the attention. I asked if she had my sister's phone number in Detroit. I call my sister who screams over the phone with excitement. This told me that she knew I was in Iraq. She begs me to call my mom who was "going crazy" over in Yemen, worrying about me. I asked her, "How do you know I'm in Iraq?"

She replied, "Everyone knows."

So much for discretion.

I call my mom and she answers the phone. She sounds tired and sickly. The weeks in Iraq, the constant watching of the news had taken a major toll on her, and I could hear it in her voice. She asked how I was, not where I was because she knew I didn't want to say where I was. She asked me if I was okay, and I said I was fine and that I would be going home soon. She gave the phone to my dad and says, "Here, it's Khaled. He's still in Iraq."

My dad sounded happy to hear from me, unafraid and unscathed by the chaos of the last few weeks. He was very calm, which I knew was a show of strength to my mother and every other family member there. He offered the phone to my pregnant wife and it cut off. I try frantically to call her back and I finally get through. She's hysterically crying over the phone, crying and sniffling. I tell her to relax, that no one could kill me; I tell her that she is married to someone invincible by simply saying, "Do you know who I am?" She laughs a little, still sniffling after the tortured time she had spent the past month, bottling in her feelings. I tell her that I am coming home and would see her soon. We say good-bye and hang up. I give the phone back to the cameraman thanking him.

I go back to the roadblock I had been manning with a few Marines and let them know that J-Lo was indeed alive. They already knew. They had found out earlier in the day. I give them an earful for not telling me saying, "You know keeping your Marines informed is important right?!" A few Iraqis hovered around our position, calling me over wanting to talk to me, to joke with me. Some of them would bring me food, which I would never turn down. It was far better than the MREs we still had; I could no longer find any chicken tetrazzini meals because we had run out of them.

I became very popular in Tikrit. Whenever I would go into the town, people would welcome me into their stores and restaurants, offering me food and drink free of charge. I wouldn't accept. I offered to pay. We were told to "stimulate the Iraqi economy" by buying things from them. Wherever I would go though, people knew my name. Some joked that I should run for mayor in Tikrit, but there was no way. I didn't have enough signatures to run.

Our mission was over, the Marines had accomplished history and we would now wait for 4th ID to come from the south and assume control of Tikrit, as they were originally supposed to. I was exhausted from the patrols and the running around. I had received many tips on Saddam being in town and relayed them all to our command. I knew they were all full of shit, but sent them in anyway. Each time, based on a tip, we would go out to search for him, but nothing came from it. Eventually all tips of Saddam's whereabouts were taken as a call for attention and a possible trap from the remaining pockets of resistance.

It was on one of my patrols north of Tikrit that one man caught my attention. He said he knew of Saddam hiding nearby in a small shack with two to three other men. To me this one sounded a bit different, and I relayed the information back. But if you cry wolf too many times without a wolf present, no one is going to listen to you. The Army 4th ID was also a day or two away, and the task force was shutting down and getting ready to leave town. No one investigated the tip.

The Army staff sergeant leading the Psy-Ops team comes up to me and tells me that we're taking Sunday off. We would shut off the radio to our vehicle and ignore any calls that had anything to do with the battalion needing us. By now they were using us to go shopping for sodas and food. It wasn't glamorous, and it wasn't critical either. That day I slept in and got as much rest as I could. I then took the postcards I had "acquired" and wrote to those who had written me. I had one postcard remaining. My final postcard was written to someone from my past who had an idea of me that did not represent my true person.

I care little for what people think of me, if they are not someone under my direct charge. If they are someone I grew up with or worked with in the Corps that had no relation to me in my position of leadership, their thoughts of me meant nothing. It's happened many times before that I have had arguments with people and they've said awful things about me or to me, but it never got to me. I'd brush it off. There was one person from my awkward childhood who I made feel distain toward me, and even as adults I had tried to mend bad feelings, but to no avail. Maybe now would be different.

I grabbed the blank and dusty postcard and filled out a brief story of my time there, it was the only time I would ever speak of my time in Iraq, up until this moment of you reading this. I had hoped to use this moment to show that I was not all bad. Somewhere in me there was still a kid who hadn't received the approval from a person he cared about, and though those feelings are now gone, approval still mattered to him…to me. I sent the postcard with hope, that time does indeed heal wounds…I received no response.

The Army 4th Infantry Division arrived to take the mission over from us. I knew from the looks on their faces that they wanted to see some action. We had established a rapport with the local people—they didn't do anything to hurt us or go against us. I tell the Psy-Ops team I was with that, "Your people are going to fuck shit up. I can see it." They didn't know what I was talking about. We had a day or two of turnover with 4th ID; we even head back to the hospital to introduce them to the caretakers there. Now comfortable with us, the caretakers spoke freely with me…this time about our occupation of their city. I do not translate what this man says to me to my battalion commander because it felt personally directed at me, the head caretaker says, "So you come here and tell us that Saddam is a bad man and that you're helping us by getting rid of him. Why don't you tell them about Yemen and your President there? Why won't they go into Yemen? I will tell you why, it's because there is no oil."

I assure him that it's not the case, but he had made a valid point. If not Yemen, what about Libya, Iran, North Korea, and other nations with dictators who rule their people with an iron fist? I drink my final glass of sugar with tea and bid them farewell. As we leave the hospital there is a fire pit with the weapons we had found earlier, they were being destroyed.

On our final night in Tikrit we celebrated with grilled chicken and soda purchased from the local population. I was able to get these items with my linguistic skills and by forming a personal friendship with the local people. We left in good terms with the people…the Marines left in good terms that is. We heard what the newly in charge Army forces were doing; they were kicking in doors and tearing apart homes searching for anything that would get them awarded a medal of some sort. There was nothing we could do. We were no longer in charge of the operation and in the morning we were headed to Al Diwaniyah where we would regroup with the other units of the 1st Marine Division. From there we would go home. As I tried to sleep that night I could hear the screams and the cries of the people, in one day the Army had fucked up what we had established over a week's time. "Oh well, I won't be coming back here any time soon," I would say to myself as I shut my eyes.

"This war is over; it's not my problem anymore."

CHAPTER 16

What Now?

Leaving Tikrit was somewhat odd, at least for me it was. Our battalion, along with other units that made up the task force, was packed up and ready to head south. We would go through Baghdad and park our asses in Al Diwaniyah for an undisclosed amount of time. We would either be sent home or we would wait for another mission, in case someone felt the need to start some shit. As we pulled away, it felt as if we were handing Tikrit over to people who didn't care about their purpose, but cared for personal gain. I could only imagine what the Iraqis felt, but to me I felt like these guys were...occupiers, the irony of it all. These were my fellow brothers-in-arms, but there was something about these soldiers that I couldn't put my finger on. Was it because they could give a shit about the people they were watching over? Was it because they'd rather be home? Was it because I could sense a bit of envy in their eyes? They knew we would be going home soon, while they would have to stay and clean up the mess.

Like I mentioned earlier, Marines do not occupy, we go in, we fuck shit up, and then we go home. The Army is trained to assist with the handover of control back to the people, but from what I saw in the short time spent with these guys, it seemed as if we were the ones who knew what we were doing. These 4th ID guys, well I couldn't vouch for them.

On our way south through Baghdad, we see hundreds to thousands of Iraqis marching and chanting. Apparently the Shia Muslims were doing a ceremony or ritual they hadn't done since before the rule of Saddam Hussein. I don't know what was being reported back to the United States, but in the month we had been in

Iraq, we had made significant changes, positive changes, but time would be the ultimate judge of what we had done.

The drive south was long but relatively quiet. There were no incidents to report, no shots fired, no ambushes—there was nothing. We pulled into this compound of sorts, Marine vehicles were everywhere. Every Marine unit that took part in the war was already there, most of them had already picked out their turf and unpacked. Our vehicle stopped and I got out. I looked for a familiar face and found a few. The Army staff sergeant told me that they, the Psy-Ops team, had to report to division headquarters just ahead and they would be back.

I found my platoon; they were already in place and had made themselves comfortable. They found a hangar and set up two-man tents and had folding chairs out. They hadn't been there for more than a day, but they had moved in for the long haul. I greeted my platoon commander and we talked for a short while. I was still unsure of what I would be doing next, so I did not know when I would be returning to the platoon. Behind me I hear a vehicle pull up; it's the Army Psy-Ops team vehicle. The staff sergeant steps out and tells me they've been reassigned. He extends his hand out, and I extend mine; we shake hands and give each other a small embrace. The other soldiers come out and say good-bye and thanks to me. I give them my contact information and ask that they contact me in the States upon their return. I was sad to see them go, but excited that I wasn't going with them. I stood and watched as they drove away.

I go back to my platoon commander and say, "Sir, looks like I'm all yours again!"

With everyone back now, we gather our Marines together and the platoon commander informs us that I will be their platoon sergeant again. Combat missions for our battalion were no longer necessary, so we would wait in Al Diwaniyah until division says otherwise. The platoon would set up shop and function as it would if back in the States. We would repair equipment, vehicles, and weapons; we were a maintenance platoon, and our job had just started.

There were showers set up, and there was even a store. This compound of sorts was going to be our home, but not a single one of us knew for how long that would be. I walked around to see for myself what we had to our disposal, and I came across the sergeant major. He hadn't seen me much since the Army Psy-Ops team had taken me, so he asked me to sit down and talk with him. We catch up and he says, "You should be getting a Navy Com for this." A "Navy Com" is a Navy and Marine Corps Commendation Medal, an award presented for sustained acts of heroism or meritorious service, for valorous actions in direct contact with an enemy force, but of a lesser degree than required for the Bronze Star. This was a legitimate award, and when the sergeant major told me that I should be getting one, I have to admit I got excited and said, "You think so Sergeant Major?"

Before the war and even during, there were many Marines talking about awards, ribbons, and anything they could decorate themselves with so they looked like wartime heroes. Officers wanted to get awards that would distinguish themselves above other officers, and staff NCOs wanted to get awards so it would look good on their next promotion board. I wanted an award only if I rated it, and everyone around me was sure telling me I did. The Army Psy-Ops staff sergeant also asked for my information. They were putting me in for an Army Commendation Medal as well. For not doing much in my own opinion, I was sure going to get recognized. Meeting with the battalion executive officer later on, he also confirmed that he would be writing up my award. This is where things got a little stupid.

Marine commanders of all types—platoon, company, battalion—were all told to submit their Marines for awards. It was my platoon commander who didn't take this as a chance to reward anyone who set foot in Iraq; he saw it as a chance to reward those who rated awards. There were other commanders who submitted awards for their Marines for standing watch, for driving, for handing out meals, for shit that was their job. I respected my platoon commander for going against the grain and for doing things the right way. There were hundreds of awards submitted for a battalion of a few hundred in numbers. It became so ridiculous that three Marines in the battalion who were enlisted grade E-9—the Master Gunz being one of them—had to sit down and go through every award recommendation and pick out the ones they deemed unworthy out of the hundreds that were submitted. It took them a few days.

I heard about this, and, out of curiosity, I asked the Master Gunz if my award was in the pile of submissions he went through. He says to me, "You know your name came up. We were wondering who was going to be the one to write up your award. It should be the battalion XO." I was told that I should ask the battalion XO about the award again and I did.

"Yes, Staff Sergeant, I've been meaning to do that. Don't worry. I'll take care of you."

I took him for his word; I knew he would "take care" of me. I thanked him and went about my business.

It had been over a month since we had crossed over and now the battalion was back together. Companies had re-formed and gone back to their original structure. Platoons were back in order, and everyone was where they should be. We took this time to repair, regroup, clean up, and unwind, which basically meant there was nothing for us to do. It was warm now, by afternoon each day it would be scorching. Walking around the camp, you'd see Marines looking half-dead sitting in chairs as time passed by ever so slowly, or you'd see Marines waiting in line for up to four hours to purchase items from the makeshift store they had set up for us. There were thousands of Marines around, but it was quiet. We were in a world separated from the outside, a world that was separated from that world as well.

Our days consisted of waking up, waiting in line for three to four hours to pick up some Pringles, French Onion dip (greatest thing with the word "French" in it), beef jerky, cigarettes, opening up care packages with items we could have used *during* the war, not after, and sitting around all day trying to find some shade so we didn't swim around in a puddle of our own sweat. We had showers now, but by the time you showered and walked back to your tent, you were sweating and covered in sand all over again. What seemed like years while in combat operations made the time we were now experiencing seem like decades…time came to a screeching halt.

There were Marines with us whose contracts with the Corps had expired, but due to Stop-Loss, they were extended until they were no longer needed. Stop-Loss is the involuntary extension of a service member's active duty service under the enlistment contract in order to retain them beyond their initial end of term service and up to their contractually agreed end of obligated service. The Marine Corps had put an end to Stop-Loss, so plans were put into place to get these Marines out of Iraq and back home so they could process themselves out of the Corps. In peacetime, the Marine Corps sends replacements for anyone checking out of a unit to go to another one or to get out of the Corps completely. What happened to the replacements that were supposed to come to us while we were in combat operations? Now, you would think that if we were sending people home, it would mean we would be going home soon too, right? You wouldn't need to bring in replacements, right? Well that's exactly what was done. New Marines were brought to Iraq to sit around and do nothing—hurry up and wait.

I did everything I could to keep myself busy. I read and re-read magazines that were relatively new to us. I talked about baseball with a few of the Marines and how I was going to go to Yankee games when I went home for leave and to games up in Anaheim. Each of us had a story of what we were going to do when we got home. It was in our eyes, the glimmer of hope.

Then *it* happened.

A sickness spread through the camp. Enough Marines were sick that if we had to move out, we wouldn't be combat ready. It was called the "it" virus because someone would ask, "Oh you haven't had *it* yet?" Marines would have to excuse themselves about fifteen times a day to go to the toilet. I don't know what happens to someone's body that can cause them to go fifteen times in one day, but it was certainly something to behold. I didn't get sick. I was around everyone else, and it wasn't like I was cleaner than anyone else. We were all living in the same shit. My explanation was simple and went something like this…

"See, what you guys don't understand is that I am Arab. There isn't a sickness on Earth that I am not genetically prepared for. What you would think is the plague, I would probably get the sniffles from. If I get sick, stay far away, because you'd probably be dead."

What I didn't tell them was that in 1992, when I was in Yemen for the first time in my life, I had the same symptoms they had. So whatever *it* was, *it* sure wasn't going to get me again. Toilet paper was now more valuable than Pringles, and when that happens, the shit has hit the fan, in the literal sense.

With nothing for our Marines to do, a mission was made up so Task Force Tripoli would reform and patrol the border with Saudi Arabia. This was around the first week of May, so somewhere on a ship in an undisclosed location, our Commander-in-Chief was announcing that combat operations were now over and "Mission Accomplished." I wish he was telling our command that, because early one morning I got packed up and headed out with another unit. It never ends!

There were reports of Wahhabis coming into Iraq from Saudi Arabia, attacking civilians along the border. This was never confirmed, but due to the fact that we'd been sitting around for so long, I think someone got antsy. Someone wanted to add more fluff to their award recommendation. It was to be a seven-day mission. The night before we departed for this mission I walked into razor wire that for some reason was set up in our compound. Why was it set up, to keep me away? Well it worked because it stopped me dead in my tracks. I pulled out the wire and a chunk of flesh from my knee and bandage it up with a single Band-Aid—it never ends!

On the way to the border we go into the desert—no roads, just sand and rocks. Our vehicles were breaking down left and right; the rocks were puncturing tires. We get to our positions and wait. One day passes and we see nothing. Two days pass and we see nothing. On the third day we are told to return, our mission was over. Holy shit, apparently it does end!

Advance elements of Marines from our battalion were sent home to prepare for our return. I was part of this group initially but after careful deliberation, only one Marine per platoon would be sent back, and I was considered too valuable to be sent home early. We were now being told that we would be going back to Kuwait in a week or so, and then back home a week after that. With things winding down and with news that we would be going home, morale was at an all-time high. Marines had already started to get their awards and ceremonies were held for them. I wondered about mine, and was told I wouldn't be forgotten. I still believed it.

A few days before we would leave, a stage was set up and fliers were handed out. It was for a talent show, but more of a *Gong Show*, time for Marines to unwind and have a good time. I volunteered to get up there and make a fool out of myself. I did a standup routine that had some of the guys laughing, but overall I bombed. I didn't care; I wasn't as bad as the Recon Marines who were booed off the stage. Their response was typical of Recon Marines, "Take the fucking indoc!" A collective laugh could be heard throughout, these guys were taking things way too seriously; I mean we're going home. After all we've been through, lighten up.

A day before departing, the battalion is called together for the last time in Iraq to thank the reserve unit attached to us for their time and assistance and to bid them farewell; they were not going home with us. As they drive away, I wave to them. I had spent time with them, and I grew with them in the short time I had known them. They would never be forgotten. A meeting with all the staff NCOs and officers is held and we're briefed on our route back to Kuwait. The intelligence report we receive is that there is no enemy in the vicinity, combat is over; we should get to Kuwait with no issues. We all leave to go to our respective vehicles, all packed and ready to go. As a last "fuck you" from Iraq, wind and rain appear from nowhere and pounds us throughout the night. We weren't going home without a last good-bye from the nation we had just liberated.

Morning came and we pulled out of the compound, waving to Marines left behind to serve a few more months. We headed south, a trek that would take most of the day. The entire time during the ride I thought to myself about all of those I had met, all of those I had come to know. I thought about how I would feel when I crossed over into Kuwait and all of it hits me at once. In combat, brotherhood is forged in blood, sweat, and tears. You will never forget the people you spent your most vulnerable moments with. They will be in your heart, and you will love them forever. You might never see them again, but the bond is infinitely strong. I thought of every Marine, soldier, and sailor I came across during this time. I thought of every Iraqi that I had ever spoken to.

I see the British up ahead; they wave and shout, "Welcome back Marines!" and we wave back at them. What had seemed like years spent in a chaotic atmosphere was now in the past. What had seemed like something that would never end was now indeed over. I crossed over into Kuwait with my Marines, something I had been dreaming of months before, leaving a country, a war that I'd never miss, except I was wrong.

I did miss it, and I didn't understand why.

CHAPTER 17

The Desert Jewel Known as Kuwait

"This is it?" I say to know one in particular. I look around and see that we were back where we had started. LSA-5 in Kuwait, the place where J-Lo was dead to us and the place where we dined on sandy slop. Just outside of our tents newly installed air conditioning units could be seen, and a generator was not too far away. It wouldn't be too bad from the looks of it. We would have cool air, and I'm sure we'd be able to have some form of decent food. As soon as we stage our vehicles a call comes over the radio for all of the remaining MREs to be collected. For some reason, eating MREs for more than a certain amount of time could do some damage to you internally. What gave them that idea, the weeks of constipation or the six pound petrified turds that were birthed? Either way we unloaded our vehicles and threw the MREs in a nice pile.

Most of the men were excited; we were going home, and what's not to be excited about? They gave us a date—the 27th of May, which would be perfect because we'd be home for the summer. I, on the other hand, felt like something was missing, instead of finding out what it was that was missing, I decided to occupy my time with anything that I could find. How about focusing on the sweltering heat? We entered our tent and to our dismay the air conditioning unit outside was nothing more than a mind-fuck to appease the wandering warrior on approach. The generators were not hooked up either, so we had nothing but the lights, which could have been powered by a hamster running on its wheel. It was well over 110 degrees outside; inside was even hotter. With over a hundred Marines crammed into this tent the temperature rose even further.

"This is bullshit," I say. "Why didn't the fucking advance party do something about this? Instead it's *Semper I, fuck the other guy*?" I was pissed and openly voicing my displeasure about things. I had noticed that about me over the past few days leading to that moment. I tolerated less, became less patient in all matter of things. I didn't want to hear excuses from anyone. A few days earlier I had cursed out one of the two staff sergeants who gave me a hard time on ship months before and called him a "bitch" because he openly complained that I was using a printer for work purposes and he had awards to write up, probably his own.

I dropped my gear off and get undressed; our consolation prize for losing out on air conditioning was the ability to walk around in a t-shirt and shorts. They had to be military issue of course, anything else would be absurd. Who wears basketball shorts and a regular t-shirt in the desert? They would stick out like a sore thumb! Give me olive-drab green, at least we'd look dull when we stuck out. I lie down and put my desert cover (hat) over my face. I didn't want to speak to anyone. Within minutes I wouldn't have a choice.

We were called to a meeting; a schedule of events to take place, a layout of the land, anything that could be discussed was to be discussed. We would be staying here for a week; so we had to occupy our time properly. All the MREs were collected and you could hear in the background a forklift dumping them into a ditch in the sand. Bury them, no one would ever know. We couldn't go back home as we were. We had to clean everything we had. God forbid we bring any Iraqi sand back with us to the United States. I am being literal about that; a few Marines had once empty Tabasco bottles, the small ones, filled with sand or dirt from different areas in Iraq. It was to be a souvenir of sorts, but nope, that would not be allowed.

I had always heard stories of wars past when Marines would bring home weapons they acquired along the way. There were even stories of Marines bringing back ears, legs, and other various body parts they found on their journey through battle, but that was before we became a kinder and gentler Marine Corps. I acquired thirteen, yes count them, thirteen AK-47 rifles while I was out and about, touring the country. Ten of them were sealed in plastic and still lubricated. These were great weapons, and I wanted to bring some with me back to the United States and give them to friends and family as gifts.

I should have known something was different by my rationale. Who gives friends and family AK-47 assault rifles as gifts? Apparently I wanted to! I had planned to have one of the rifles I confiscated de-milled and bronzed. I was going to place it in a wooden shadowbox and present it to my friend who had lost her boyfriend in the towers during the September 11 attacks. It was going to show her that I had kept my promise and got some of those responsible for her boyfriend's death, but now customs was trying to take that away from me.

There were horror stories of how Marines tried to sneak weapons through customs. Yes, we went through customs. The Air Force provided Airmen (their contribution to the war) to inspect personnel leaving Kuwait, heading back home. Marines caught with weapons would face a court martial. If you want a Marine to do something, tell them they can't. If you want a Marine to not do something, make up a story as to why they can't. Like the story of a Marine master sergeant being demoted to corporal (four pay grades) for trying to sneak a weapon out by strapping it to the engine of his vehicle. Did that really happen? Probably not, but who would risk it? Most of the Marines felt the same way—there was too much to lose. I say "most" because I am almost sure that some Marines would at least try to bring some weapons back, I just don't know who would or how many would succeed in bringing some back with them.

There was an amnesty box set up, initially small in size—no one expected there to be many weapons picked up along the way. I left for lunch one day with the box overflowing. I hadn't turned my weapons in yet. I was determined to bring a few with me and had a plan. When I returned, the box was gone. In its place was an even larger box. Apparently everyone had something. I had thirteen rifles; what did everyone else have?

We had to clean the vehicles given to us for the war. They had to go back on a ship and float around for a few more months or years, until they were needed elsewhere—maybe back in Afghanistan or North Korea. Who knew? Something about the Marine Corps that is hilarious, give Marines nothing to work with, and ask them to make it workable for someone else. The vehicles we had received barely made it through the war, but we had to turn them in ready for someone else to use…in better condition. Other vehicles and equipment that we brought with us had to be cleaned and inspected so that it could go back to the United States. This would take place over a few days, luckily I was a senior Marine so I didn't have to partake in the fun; I got to go on runs to other camps in the 110 to 130 degree heat.

I gave my thirteen rifles to the Hazmat NCO. He would put them in barrels that could not be inspected, and we'd get them in the United States. I was confident I would have these weapons when I got home and from there I could give them out. Not well thought out now was it? Luckily, a day before the inspection, the Marine sergeant comes to me and says he can't do it. I found all thirteen rifles in that larger than life box that had pistols, grenades, and anything Marines thought they'd be able to take home with them. I was upset. I really wanted to make that shadowbox with a bronzed AK-47 for my friend, but that was no longer an option. Oh well.

It was relatively quiet for us that week. We prepared to leave; all mail we received now was left in a pile for anyone who wanted to scavenge for something they wanted. After all vehicles and equipment were cleaned and inspected there was not much left for us to do. I still had some DVDs from the start of the war; they were scratched up from the wear and tear of travel and abuse. I hadn't had a chance to watch them much. Fifteen to thirty of us would huddle around a thirteen-inch laptop monitor and watch a few movies until it got too hot for the laptop to operate. We'd then lie in a pool of our own sweat until it cooled down at night. The time to do anything productive was before and after sunlight. Anytime during the day was just too hot. If you wanted to drink water, drink water before and after the sun was out. If you drank water during the day, you would burn your throat; the water got too hot, hotter than a cup of tea.

Support the troops! Yeah, that's all you heard back home, but here we were, warriors returned from battle and they couldn't support us with air-conditioned tents. They couldn't support us with giving us coolers to put drinking water in. They couldn't support us by putting toilet and shower facilities nearby; they put them hundreds of meters away. Supporting your troops doesn't mean what you think; it means support the idea of supporting us. As long as you think you're supporting us by sending us smiles and a "we support you" comment in a letter, you're doing okay. You're blind to what really happens. We're cheap labor, making less than minimum wage and more than willing to jump in front of a bullet for another one of our brothers. We're crazy.

Coming back to Kuwait after what we'd been through and to have nothing to show for it besides being alive (which isn't taken for granted mind you) was really disheartening. For most of the Marines in my platoon, they were alright with this, as long as they got to go home. Then there were those of us who saw too much to forget. We needed to be reminded why we did what we did, and this was not the way to do so. It takes a toll on you. I hadn't said much about it other than the original outburst I had the first day back. I was still the platoon sergeant, and I had to set a better example. If I was letting it get to me, what about other Marines? How would they feel?

We were two days from departing, so it was time to turn in all the ammunition we had taken with us. We couldn't carry any with us; we had already gotten approval to bring our weapons on board a chartered US carrier flight. Oh yeah, no boat this time around. They stuck some other Marines who were flown out to Kuwait the first time to float on back home. It didn't seem fair to me, but fuck it. The ammo was turned in; at least we wouldn't have an incident where someone got shot accidentally before we got home.

We didn't have anyone shot *accidentally*.

A meeting with all the platoon sergeants was held outside my tent and in the middle of about three other tents. We were getting the seating arrangements for the flight home. It wasn't like we got a seat number or anything, just what class we would be in. All staff NCOs and junior officers would be in business class, all senior officers and some senior staff NCOs got to go into first class. It didn't mean we would get the first class treatment though, just the seats. The junior Marines all sat in coach—our appreciation for their hard work and sacrifice.

As this is going on we hear a distinct sound that I have come to know as a bullet passing by, greeting us saying, "I didn't get you, but one day one of my cousins will." We're told to get back to our tents, account for everyone, and stay there until we're told otherwise. My platoon was good to go; we waited and waited for word. No one was talking until we got word that a Marine was purposely shot…by another Marine. Bullies come in all different shapes and sizes. I was bullied growing up. I was a skinny little Arab kid in Brooklyn; I fully expected it. I wasn't bullied in the Corps because it was a new start for me, and I wasn't going to give anyone the opportunity to do so. Not all Marines are able to achieve this, and not all Marines are such nice guys.

A Marine from our battalion was being bullied by another Marine in the same platoon. They were both the same rank, corporals in the United States Marine Corps, non-commissioned officers, and leaders of men. They had worked together in combat and had worked together before that. Apparently the Marine being bullied had enough, walked up to the Marine in his tent and shot him in the neck from point blank range.

At that moment, I realized that this war was not over and would never be over for us. It took away our innocence and took away our rationale. What would make a Marine who was two days away from going home shoot another Marine in the neck, attempting to end his life? I didn't fully get it, but another part of me did. I don't know what scared me more, the fact that a Marine was shot by another Marine, or the idea of knowing what that Marine was thinking while doing it. Rumors started swirling, this time it wasn't about J-Lo and her fine ass dying. It was about our return home. After a Marine gets shot by a Marine in the same unit, you would think an investigation would take place. We would certainly be staying in Kuwait for a longer period of time. Sure, why not? It was only the end of May; it wasn't hot enough yet!

The next day we meet as a battalion for what was intended to be the final formation over in Kuwait for Operation Iraqi Freedom. Not a single one of us thought it would be. We were certain we would be staying longer. Our battalion commander, a man who didn't take the easy way and go home with the advance party, gets in front of us and tells us what happened. He then tells us what will happen next.

"Gents, we're going home tomorrow..."

The words were music to the ears of those smiling, but what constituted being home? I didn't know anymore.

Just get me on that fucking plane.

Chapter 18

Reality

If you're going to be traveling, especially flying internationally, you get to the airport about three hours before your flight and you go through a lengthy screening process. If you're a Marine going home after being in Iraq, you never look at security screening the same again. We packed our bags only to unpack them and then repack them again at each station of customs. Like cattle we go through lines and stations, I even "moo" a little to show my defiance, if that's what you'd call it.

Our flight was to be an evening flight, and I had been awake since dawn. I wanted to get a head start and be ready for anything, and that meant being put in charge of getting my Marines home. I had to give up a sergeant to the battalion. Marines from every platoon, including my own, had to provide a Marine sergeant to take shifts guarding the Marine who had shot the other Marine. Oh yeah, we were taking him along with us, and he was staying in business class too! In the future, if you want an upgrade, just shoot someone in the neck a day or two before your flight.

I didn't want any nonsense. My men were just through Iraq and had made it this far; there was no need to baby them. After breakfast that morning, I gathered them around me and told them where they needed to be, when they needed to be, how they needed to be, and why they needed to be there. "If you want to go home today, you'll do everything I tell you. If you want to spend more time here fucking around in the sand, then let me know now, so I can have someone fuck you up." The Marines laughed as I said this, but I meant it. I already knew who to choose to serve as the face pounder and ass kicker.

In the final weeks, as we sat in Al Diwaniyah collecting dust, we started to grow out our mustaches again. By now our company commander had bailed on us and had gone home. He had orders and was relieved of his command, so that he could execute those orders; he wouldn't stand in the way of our mustache growth, so it was a great moment for us. After I spoke to the Marines as a group for the final time in Kuwait, we took a photograph. About only 60 percent of the platoon had grown mustaches though, the other 40 percent either didn't want to grow them or hadn't gone through puberty yet. I believe it was the latter.

The sign in the photograph said it all, "Who wants a mustache ride?"

Back to the process, I go through customs and meet the rest of the senior Marines of my platoon in a small tent sectioned off to the rest of the camp. It was our very own boarding gate and we would all sit down and wait. I got hungry and in the corner of the tent I see boxes of MREs. I know we were told not to eat them anymore, but I'm sorry, chicken tetrazzini was just too good to pass up. I sat my ass down on the floor in the middle of the tent and broke open the MRE. Did I know that we would have food and beverage on the flight home? Yes I did, but I wasn't ready to be treated like a human being again. I had grown accustomed to being given sandy slop as a hot meal privilege and hot water as a needed beverage. Getting airplane food would have been like eating at a five-star restaurant. I didn't think my stomach would be able to take it. Were there chairs in the tent for me to sit on? Yes, but I was used to sitting and sleeping on the ground.

It was finally time to go; we boarded a bus that would take us to our aircraft. It was a chartered airline, I believe United or Continental. As I boarded the plane, I remember thinking to myself, "Man, I'm boarding an airplane with not one, but two weapons. Do they know I'm Arab?" The flight attendants were older, apparently they had all volunteered for this duty and to do so you had to have seniority. What they should have had was a bunch of women in bikinis handing us beer as we got on the plane. I took a seat with the staff NCOs that I had a tolerance for. A few of the others I had ignored because I had issues with some of them on the boat ride here, then more issues with a few of them in Kuwait, and then even more issues with other staff NCOs while in Iraq. It was ok though, being a nice guy only meant that more people wanted to talk to you, and some of those guys were just irritating. I placed my rifle and pistol behind my seat. We strapped in and were ready to take off, though I wasn't ready for this; it didn't seem right.

I hate flying. I have always hated flying and will always hate flying. I have seen too many movies where the plane goes down, and nothing frightens me more than the takeoff and landing of a man-made machine that defies the laws of gravity. I didn't think we would be allowed to take off. I don't mean that someone would stop us. What I mean is that I thought fate would end it right there. Iraq and Kuwait, this "theater" of operation that we had spent months in but had grown up years in experience, it wasn't going to let us go away that easy.

I grabbed onto the armrests, as I always do on takeoff, and leaned my head back. The plane sped up and the front of the plane elevated. I remember this vividly because at that moment I remember thinking, *I'm off the ground while the chumps in the back are still on Kuwaiti soil.* Once airborne, the Marines went crazy in the rear of the plane. We weren't out of the woods yet. I just had a feeling. I hadn't let go of the armrests. By now we'd leveled off and were out of Kuwaiti airspace. On the television monitors in front of us we saw where we were in relation to where we took off. Our destination would be Frankfurt, Germany, but my eyes focused on the country that had a grasp on me...a part of me was still there.

Guilt overtook me. I personally felt guilty for leaving Iraq, for leaving other Marines behind. Ever since I was a child I had always wondered what was going on somewhere else in the world at the very moment I was thinking. I knew that over in Iraq there was a Marine and there was a soldier, each of them manning a position they are told to hold for hours, days, or even weeks. They were over there doing that while I was on a plane heading home, in the plush seats that make up business class. Out of my sight, a flight attendant comes up to me and asks, "Would you like anything to drink?"

She had startled me; I hadn't spoken to an American civilian in person since before we boarded the ships in January. I gathered myself and asked for an orange juice. I would much rather have had an alcoholic beverage, but they would not trust us with alcohol, not on the ride home. Hours go by, and I settle down. The reality of leaving sets in, and I pick up the phone in front of me. If I am going to go home, I might as well tell my family that I will be home in a day. Oh yeah, I didn't tell my family because I didn't believe it was really going to happen, and I wanted to be sure. I look at the phone, and it tells me to swipe my Visa or MasterCard if I wanted to continue.

Another example of supporting the troops is displayed right here to me, and I get angry. I am on an American carrier that was paid for by taxes that I and other Marines pay (yes, we pay taxes) and all they could provide us with was orange juice, water, a meal that was unworthy of chicken tetrazzini, old flight attendants that wore American flag pins, and phones that I had to pay $10 a minute to call home. I was livid, cursing under my breath as I swiped my card. I dialed my older brother's number in New York to tell him that I was on the way home. He didn't sound excited like someone would after hearing from their brother for the first time in months, instead he asks me, "Where you calling from?" When I tell him from the airplane he tells me to hang up and call him when I get back to the United States. I hang up and decide not to call. Like the rest of my family, money comes first, being human comes third; culture comes second if you were wondering.

I fumed on the inside; anger consumed me as we arrived in Frankfurt. I don't say much to anyone; we deplaned and sat in a waiting area. I don't recall if we were offered any breakfast or any food items, so I assume that we weren't. A few unlucky Marines had to stay on the plane to watch the Marine held in handcuffs still on board. We boarded the plane again and took off soon after. By now I was not worried about crashing because we were far enough from Iraq or Kuwait for it to do any damage to us. I am now sure we would arrive safe. I started playing out scenarios of our return. Before leaving for the war, the young Marines and I would listen with ears open and eyes wide as the older and more experienced Marines spoke of how it was returning home from the Gulf War in the early 90s.

Our platoon commander told us about his experience coming back home when he was bused back to base in the early 90s. While on the freeway, cars were honking their horns for them in celebration, pizzas were handed to them through the windows of their bus, and they were all welcomed back as heroes. When they got to the base there were families waiting for them with signs and balloons. It was like nothing I had ever imagined. I began to get excited; I began to want to be home for this.

We crossed into United States airspace and an announcement was made, "Welcome home Marines."

We collectively cheered. Crashing now wouldn't be so bad because we were home. We would die at home. This was my thinking back then, I don't know why I was thinking this, but it was rational to me at the time. As we made our approach, I saw the cars on the interstate and wondered, *What are the people in the cars thinking of? Are they thinking of the troops back in Iraq? Or are they thinking about some bullshit that means nothing?* The plane touched down. There were more cheers, and I saw that outside the plane there were people I had never seen lined up to greet us. They were personnel from the Air Force base welcoming us home. We deplaned and I felt the need to kiss the ground, but I refrained from doing so, more of my brothers and sisters were not home yet. Shaking hands as we entered the waiting area for our buses, I looked around. Waiting for us are crackers, cookies, chips, and sodas. Some cell phones were set up so we could call our families. Other Marines went to them; I did not. I sat and waited for the buses.

We got on our buses and headed to Camp Pendleton. On the interstate no one noticed us; no one paid attention to their returning warriors—no horns, no pizza, what a gyp!

We drove through the gates of Camp Pendleton; most of the base was empty due to a majority of the Marines being deployed. We were only moments away from our friends and family, well, at least everyone else was. We got to our battalion, around were families from all over the country welcoming home their Marines and all Marines. There is no rank here; if you were a private or a captain it didn't matter, you were no one more than John or Brian. It's all that mattered to them, and I couldn't be happier for those Marines. Cheers could be heard. I could hear names I knew yelled out in excitement, but not my own. I try not to let it bother me as much, but it would have been nice to have my dad there. It would have been nice to have someone close to me in some way hug me and say, "It's good to have you back."

We get off the bus, and I turn my weapon in. The Marine in captivity is turned over to the Military Police and his weapon is also turned in. I get my sergeant back from babysitting duty. There is one final formation held by me. I tell the Marines to be back to work the next morning; we would be going on leave in a few days, but not today. I don't give them the command to "fallout" but a command I have not said and they have not heard in months.

"DISMISSED!"

The Marines give out a loud "OOHRAH," hug each other, and go to their families. I walk by all the joy and smiles and head for the squad-bay barracks set up for the Marines who have no place to stay. I pick out a bed for me to call home for the time being. I take off my boots, sit on the bed, and then lie down. I look up at the ceiling; for the first time in a what seemed like ages, I would be sleeping under a roof made of concrete, not a roof made of netting, tent, or clouds. I am upset for a moment, alone in thought and silence all around me. I hear myself, as if I was not in control of my own voice say, "Quit being a bitch. You're home now."

I close my eyes for a brief moment and open them up to see if I am really home. I am indeed home, it is reality, but reality is only in the mind of the one living it. The walls around me are closing in; I have to get out of here.

Welcome home.

Chapter 19

Christine

I brought the letters written to me by friends back home with me. It was the only thing that would remain unchanged, the words written in ink, the texture and smell of the paper, the dust in the envelope accumulated from all the times I had taken them out to read them while over there. I put them in order of when I received them and put them on my bed. I got up and walked back to the battalion where the families have dispersed and the party is nearly over. In the barracks to the left and to the right of me, Marines celebrate with beer, getting hammered as if they didn't have to work the next day. I catch a ride to the home of one of my married Marines so I could pick up my car that I had left with his wife. I was lucky it was still there. I had set up payments with the bank to pay for it while I was gone, but they never went through. I was ninety days delinquent; I would take care of that when I had time, now was not that time.

    I say hello to his wife, go into their garage where I had left a few items such as clothing so I could change out of what I was wearing, what I had been wearing since January. I grab what I need and head back to the barracks. I undress, but I also unpack everything I have with me. I take apart my equipment, even the CD wallet I had used to hold my DVDs. I wanted to wash away the past few months. I dump everything into three washers located on the first floor and run them through the wash cycle—yes, even the CD wallet.

    I shower; the shower is a fortress of mental solitude. My mind wanders at an uncontrollable speed. I turn up the heat to surround myself in steam and to scorch my skin. If my mind is occupied by pain and my vision obscured, then I wouldn't focus on the reality that the past is indeed behind me; that the nightmare is over. After I shower I look into the foggy mirror to look for any sign of change, but I see the same person I have seen before. I see me. I put on my patriotic boxers (I call them patriotic because they are in the pattern of an American flag), and I sit back down on the bed. I look at the letters on the bed and begin to read them one last time before I start throwing them each into a small trashcan I set in front of me. I leave only the letters that have phone numbers, details of the people I would need to contact. Among them was an invitation to a college graduation for a friend, we'll call her Christine.

With the Internet age now in full swing, you're exposed to more people. You could meet someone by searching for the common interests you each possess, or you could meet someone by chance. It was during the last week of September 2001 that I found myself in London on leave. I was staying at the Marine House after being convinced to take some time off after the terrorist attacks in the United States just weeks before. I was checking my email on a fellow Marine's computer when a window pops up through AOL Instant Messenger. It was an acquaintance of his, someone he wasn't interested in talking to, so I went ahead and chatted with her instead. This was Christine.

Apparently Christine liked this Marine in high school and would try to talk to him every now and then. I saw this as an opportunity to get to know someone new, so I introduced myself. I wrote down her screen name and would later add her to my AOL Instant Messenger account. When I went back to Shanghai a week later we continued to chat and kept a low-key friendship, nothing out of the ordinary. When I reenlisted, I was told that Camp Pendleton, California would be my next assignment; she lived in Santa Barbara. That wasn't too far in comparison to the distance between Santa Barbara and China; so we decided we would meet when I got there. We talked about various things, nothing too serious. For example, we both liked *The Powerpuff Girls*. Don't judge me, watch it for yourself. It's amazing! One of the first things we planned to do was watch the upcoming Powerpuff Girls movie, which was due to come out around the time of my arrival.

When I got back to the United States from China, I would call her and we would talk. This went on for a few weeks, and I brought up watching the movie with her in July of 2002. Eventually we lost touch, she wouldn't answer any of my calls, and I would leave voicemails for her only to be ignored. On a day that I decide to try one last time, someone else answered her phone. The person on the phone said she was her sister and that I needed to leave Christine alone, that I was scaring her. This caught me off guard to say the least, but I say to her, "Sorry if I did or said anything to her to make her feel that way," and hung up.

Before I left for Iraq she got back in touch with me, explaining that she was too afraid to meet me. I wasn't too pleased with this, but I was a forgiving person. I gave her my deployed mailing address and she said she would write me as much as she could. One of the letters she sent me contained an invite to her graduation. I was touched that she wanted to include me. She really wanted me there and hoped I'd be home for it. Well I was home now, and I needed to call her to tell her I would be able to make it. I put on civilian attire for the first time since before we left in January. It had been sitting in storage for months, and it had a strange feel and smell to it, but I didn't care.

I pulled out everything I had thrown in the washers and threw them into dryers. They would dry as I made a trip down to the mall. I honestly didn't know how I would react returning to civilization for the first time, but one thing was for sure, my sense of speed while driving was gone. After leaving base I was on the I-5 headed to the mall. I looked down to see that I was going ninety-five miles per hour, and I hadn't even realized it. Everything around me seemed slow. I felt as if I was also moving slow. The only thing moving fast was my train of thought; it was pegging out my mental speedometer.

I take out my cell phone that I had kept in a bag in the desert and call the good people of AT&T. I tell them to activate my phone; I have indeed returned. They do, but once it picks up service, the screen goes blank. I guess that's what I'll be buying at the mall, a new phone. I go into an AT&T store and ask for an upgrade. They take my phone and work on it, giving me a, "We'll be right back," to keep me appeased. They point over to the phones on display and tell me to go ahead and feel free to make phone calls anywhere in the United States. Who would be the first person I would call? It wouldn't be my family. That would be for later.

The phone rings and a woman answers, "Hello?"

"It's me Khaled. Remember me? I'm back."

It was Christine. She screams hysterically, sincerely happy to hear my voice. I smile and tell her that I would be able to make it to her graduation. She is obviously excited because her speech is littered with many, "Oh my God," remarks. I have to admit, she sounded like a typical Californian to me; like a "cheerleader" I would tell her.

Her graduation was to be on Saturday the 14th June. She invited me to come up to see her on the 13th of June, which would be a Friday. It would be the first time I would ever meet Christine.

I got my new phone and headed back to the base and the barracks. I picked up some food along the way, McDonald's double cheeseburgers with Big Mac sauce. It was my favorite because it was cheap and you can't beat the sauce. When I got back to the barracks I pulled everything out of the dryer. The gear had a tag on it that said in bold, all capital lettering, "DO NOT MACHINE WASH." But I didn't care, my stuff looked great. The CD wallet on the other hand, it didn't survive the spin cycle.

The next day we are back at work, still in our desert uniforms. We had not been given the go ahead to change back into our camouflage greens or "woodlands" as we called them. I was told to send everyone home at noon. They would come back to work on Monday. It would be a four-day weekend; I could only imagine what trouble the Marines could get themselves into, so I get them all together briefly, to give them a talk that is short and to the point.

"Gents, you made it through Iraq. You made it through all the bullshit. It would be stupid if you guys did anything to fuck that up. Understood?"

Understood. We spent that morning cleaning our weapons just to turn them back in. Whatever occurred the night prior was the talk amongst the Marines. The common theme was that most of them had gotten drunk; some of them did so off base, and the rest the same at the barracks. Others got laid—free or paid for, it didn't matter to anyone. Everyone was relatively happy. Now we weren't going to go on leave just yet. The battalion had promised the Marines they would be able to take a full thirty days of leave after we returned. The problem was we still had a few Marines in Kuwait who were getting some last minute things done before they could leave. There is an advance party, the rest of the battalion, and those we leave behind just in case. We had about ten Marines from my platoon stay behind. When they all came back, we would all be allowed to go on leave. We would wait for them.

Noon came and we were dismissed for the weekend. I remained low-key. I keep to myself. My weekend was to consist of cleaning up and settling in. I would call my family in the coming days, but I wanted to make sure I was ready to talk to them. I called a few friends and made plans with them, plans that I had every intention of executing. But promises are made out of emotion; I cannot even tell you how many times I was told I would get to see someone when I got back. I remember the letters telling me that, "when you get back, we're going to…" We're going to what? That's what I wanted to know.

I called my family in Yemen; they asked me when they would see me. I tell them that I am not allowed to go to Yemen right now, that I had to clear it with the command and that it was too late to do so. This was a lie; I didn't want to see them. I wanted to go to Christine's graduation, and I wanted to go to a few baseball games. Baseball is my vice, it's the one sport I can watch and marvel at everything that is taking place. Many say it's a boring sport, but that's because it is misunderstood. Baseball is a thinking person's game, and I am a thinker. I wanted to catch a couple of games before the graduation, and I wanted to go home to New York to spend time with my friends from high school and to watch the Yankees. One can get lost in the art of baseball. I also had another reason. Well, let's say 2,204 reasons.

A Marine Staff Sergeant with six years in-service gets paid a base salary of $2,204 a month. To my family they didn't care that I had gone from E-1 to E-6 in a little over five years. They didn't care how I did it or how rare it was to do so. After each promotion my mom or sometimes my dad would ask me, "How much are they paying you now?" Around the time I had gotten married, my brothers and I had decided to collect our money together to build a home in Yemen. This basically establishes your family name in the eyes of those around you. I never understood this; to me it was showing off to others, to people I could care less about. My brothers were Merchant Mariners; they made more money than me, but no one understood that. I had only given about $10,000 toward the construction of the house. I wasn't carrying my weight. I didn't want to hear anything about it from them when I got back. They didn't understand that my diet consisted of Ramen noodles and the occasional dinner at a restaurant to spend time with friends, just so I could save money. When they would hear about me eating at a restaurant, a look of disgust would come over their faces. It was a no win situation, and I didn't want to lose anymore. I'd see them when I was good and ready.

After the long weekend of nothing for me, the Marines had come back to work. We were in our woodland uniforms and everyone had some new toy to show off. There were new cars, new phones, sunglasses—the spoils of war in the form of saved money by going months without having to pay for bills or drinks when going out. Saved money becomes spent money. Spent money becomes no money—back to square one. There was nothing to do at work, just sitting around until noon each day. I met a friend of mine at a Dodger's game. I watch as the Dodgers defeat the White Sox two to one. I remember having a Subway sandwich and my friend looked at me awkwardly, saying, "You come to Dodger Stadium and eat Subway? You should try a Dodger Dog!" I tell her that as a Muslim I can't eat one because they contain pork, but I say this while drinking a cold beer. Perfectly logical isn't it?

I was feeling good. I was able to watch my favorite sport. I was with a good friend; life was falling back into place. In a week I would meet Christine, but I needed to watch another baseball game, so I asked my friend if she wanted to go with me to catch the Mets and Angels in Anaheim. We set the date, Friday the 13th, June of 2003.

It's Friday morning, the 13th of June. I don't baby my Marines, so I fully expected to get to their barracks and see that it was cleaned up. Thursday nights are what we call "Field Day" in the Marine Corps. It's when we get a hair up our asses and clean up the barracks— not a normal cleaning, cleaning as if you would put bleach through a shared needle. It had to be clean, white glove clean. I am appalled when I arrive. Beer bottles are everywhere. Marines are passed out and some are still drunk. The night before the rest of the Marines from the battalion had returned, and this was their way of saying, "Welcome home!" I knock on all the doors and get everyone out of their rooms. I form them up outside and give them a verbal lashing like they've never seen. I don't hold back, I even cross the line a little.

"You motherfuckers think you could just tell me to go fuck myself and I would take it up the ass smiling? You must be out of your motherfucking minds…"

A Marine sergeant speaks up, "But Staff Sergeant, they just got back from—"

"I don't give a fuck who came back, and where the fuck they came back from! Does that give you motherfuckers the excuse to live like fucking pigs? Do Marines tell their motherfucking platoon sergeant to go fuck himself? I don't fucking think so! Fix it *now*!"

The new company gunnery sergeant arrives, and I tell him that my Marines have failed inspection; there is no need for him to go check. He nods his head and says, "Okay, looks like you got a handle on it." That kind of shocked me a little. I was expecting another, "People are dying!" reaction, but this was different. It was welcomed.

The Marines get the barracks cleaned up, and I meet with them again. I explain why I was upset and why they should be upset too. I ask them to raise a hand if they thought what I was doing was bullshit; no one raised their hand in agreement, no one except me.

"I think this is bullshit," I tell them. "I shouldn't have to do this; if I were you, I would be pissed. I'm pissed that I have to do this to you, but you made me. Gents, I don't want to fuck with you, but if you fuck with me, I have no other choice."

Honesty will go a long way with Marines. I wasn't going to sugarcoat anything. I wasn't going to say they were fuckups one minute and then great the next. I was going to explain to them why what they did the night before was wrong in the most forceful way I knew possible and then reason with them after they had been emotionally drained. Rational thought is when you have less emotion involved. I knew this more than any of them. I let them go early that day. I let them loose right after I spoke to them, four hours earlier than I should have. I wasn't going to fuck with them any further. I had made my point. I also had to get ready for the game and the weekend, so it was best I do what I had to and get it over with.

This was my first trip to Anaheim to catch the Angels in action. I marveled at the massive baseball caps that greet you when you arrive. They actually have the numbered hat sizes in each of the brims. I laughed when I saw this. I was wearing my Yankee garb, t-shirt and hat. Mets fans were everywhere, about the same number as Angels fans. I greeted the New Yorkers, because if you're a Mets fan in California, you have to be from New York. There are no Mets fans raised outside of New York, that's reserved for the Yankees. I meet my friend and we go inside.

I have always loved the national anthem; I get teary eyed whenever the "bombs bursting in air" verse is played. This time I was listening to the anthem in a foreign ballpark, and I did not expect to hear the explosion of fireworks during that verse. I flinched violently when the fireworks exploded; my friend looks over at me and says, "Are you okay?" I look and nod at her signifying that I am, but in my head I'm thinking, *Oh my God. I'm like one of those war veterans that are on edge.*

The Mets won that game, I think 7-3, but I couldn't forget that moment during the anthem. I stood alone and cheered in the stadium when they showed footage of the game in New York, the Bronx; Roger Clemens pitched against the Cardinals and had won his 300th game to go along with getting his 4,000th strikeout. I said good-bye to my friend and got in my car. I had to head to the graduation, but I was shaken. I pulled into a gas station and grabbed a drink. I drove for two hours, calling Christine's phone along the way to tell her I was in route to her. She has me meet her outside a bar. She was celebrating with friends. I was not ready for this; I was in a bar with people I had never met. They were bumping into me and shoving me. I tensed up and my fists were clenched. I walked outside and stayed out there for about an hour. I waited for Christine out there. I couldn't go back inside. She came out a few times to check on me. I tell her, "I am fine, just needed some air."

She leaves the bar, and I follow her back to her place. I sit on the couch and she puts in *The Powerpuff Girls Movie* DVD. She sits in front of the television like a child would, as I sat there watching her and the movie from the couch. I lose consciousness and find myself on the same couch the next morning. I haven't moved, still in the same clothes from the night before. The day is her day, and I am to spend it with her family and friends at her graduation and then at a celebratory lunch. I take a seat and find myself completely confused and lost. I have never found anything to be as difficult as I was finding this moment to be. I was asked questions by her younger sister, as if I was being interrogated. Other family members found out that I had just gotten back from Iraq. They say a collective, "Wow," and that is it.

There was to be a dinner that evening, but I come up with an excuse as to why I can't make it. As I get in my car Christine hops in and thanks me for coming. She says to me, "I'm really glad you came. You're a really great guy." As if to say that her actions a year prior were unwarranted. I smiled; I needed to hear that from someone. I needed to hear that I was normal. She hugs me and says, "Good-bye." I pull away with a smile on my face, thinking to myself that things would be okay. I had a friend in Christine who understood me. I'm going to be just fine...

I never learn do I?

CHAPTER 20

The Pastime

Though I am from Brooklyn, I didn't get to experience the city of New York until the summer of 1999. I was a corporal in the Marine Corps and was able to get myself attached to a special event held each year in the city, Fleet Week. I knew of Fleet Week because my dad took me to one in 1996, months before I went to boot camp. On the way up the eastern seaboard of the United States, Marines who knew I was from New York would ask me about the city. They would give me the strangest look when I would tell them, "How would I know?" When I was growing up, I was never allowed to go into Manhattan or anywhere for that matter. Curfew on a school night was 3:00 p.m. Basically, as soon as I walked in the front door of our apartment, I was done for the day.

It wasn't until that week in the summer of 1999 that I was able to go out and experience the city for what it is…a city that has the most to offer. I went to bars and clubs. This was back when I didn't drink, but I still had a great time! It probably helped that we were in uniform and everywhere I went people would greet us. That was something that even I knew never happened in New York…no one would say hello just to say hello.

Another thing I was prevented from enjoying in the greatest city on Earth was following professional sports. I don't know what my father and mother had against sports, but I was forbidden from watching it on television, listening to it on the radio, and certainly never allowed to go to an event. Joining the Marine Corps gave me the freedom (yes you read that right) to do things I had never been allowed to do as a kid. I went to my first Yankee's game on Memorial Day in 1997 and couldn't believe how real everything looked. We lost that game, blew a 6-2 lead, but I now knew what I had been missing. I was hooked.

I had my bags packed and was ready to get dropped off at the airport. I moved out of the open area with all the bunks and found a room in the barracks that was once used as an office. I made it into a living room and bedroom combination. I had dialup Internet, cable TV that I spliced from the roof, a refrigerator, and my own bed. I was living pretty well, and I didn't have any bills to pay. It was from this room that I planned my trip to New York. I emailed friends to see if they would be available to hangout. I even made some phone calls to others to see if they wanted to catch a game. In letters from some of them they couldn't wait to see me and would be up for anything when I did come back. While they were excited to hear from me, they asked that I contact them when in New York. We would go from there.

It is also from this room that I bought tickets to many, many games to watch the Yankees. I was going to be in New York for my birthday, so for my birthday I would buy myself some tickets to catch them. I didn't want to go alone, so I bought tickets for my youngest brother as well. I would also be visiting a friend in Boston. Why not get tickets to Fenway and watch the hated Red Sox? I had never been to Fenway and had always wanted to go.

I felt like a kid again, to be honest with you. I waited in my room for the Marine who would drop me off and take my car for the month. All I could think about was what would happen in New York, who and what would I get to see? I was excited about the games, excited that I would only have to worry about beating the Red Sox on the Fourth of July instead of having to worry about whether or not I would live to see the next day. It's the simple worries in life that we take for granted, and I was seeing this now.

I booked a flight with JetBlue because it was $99 each way. It meant that I would have to drive to an airport named after an actor in Orange County, but I did not care. I was going to New York! The airport was small in comparison to the ones I had used previously, but once again, I did not care. I checked in and went through what I now know as being *randomly* selected to be searched. I know the process better than the people searching me. I instruct one of the security staff to ask me to raise my arms and stick them out to my sides.

He looks at me and says, "You've done this before?"

I reply with, "Oh yeah, I've been selected 'randomly' each time I go through an airport. I have the best luck."

I get to New York the next morning. It's a redeye flight, and I am already in New York City mode. I drop my bags off in my apartment, go to the bagel shop down the street from me, pick up a bagel and the paper, and head to the subway station. Could I have watched the morning news and enjoyed breakfast from my apartment? Sure, but one appreciates the simple things in life; I wanted to enjoy the sights and sounds of New York City while reading the paper.

It is on the train ride into the city that I found the perfect spot on the map, Bryant Park. It's near Times Square and it screamed "New York City" to me. I get to my destination and emerge from the underground subway. New York City has a way of hitting you in the face, and it does right then. It's a cloudy and rainy day but the buildings around provide some sort of cover. The air is brisk and not too warm. I find myself in awe of everything I see. I also find myself doing a cheesy spin around to catch all angles of the view. No one notices me and that's the part of New York I love most; everyone has their own thing to do. I find the park and sit down at an empty chair and table. I pull out the day's paper, unfold it, and put it on the table. I take out a bagel—plain with cream cheese—and unwrap it. I sip from my cup of hot chocolate and open up the paper, avoiding the front-page news, which is mostly Iraq coverage. I focus on the sports.

The Yankees had completed a sweep of the Cardinals; they'd be facing Tampa Bay the next three days. I had tickets for the last two games. I didn't think I would be able to get a game in on my first day back. As luck would have it, the drizzle that was causing my newspaper to fall apart would cause the Yankee game to be rained out.

I finish my two bagels and hot chocolate and sit there watching, listening. I look at everyone walking by at a blistering pace; I wonder what they're thinking. I hear a horn blaring as a taxi tries to get by a bus. I wonder why he is in a rush. I lean back in the wooden chair painted at least a hundred times by the Parks Department and soak in the atmosphere. I feel disconnected from everyone though. They're unchanged, unaffected with what is going on over in the desert. I envy them. I envy their ignorance. I get up and cover my ears with headphones, playing music to drown out the sounds. It feels as if I am in a dream, as if no one sees me there. You will always go unnoticed in New York City, but for some reason this was starting to bother me. I didn't know why no one would look at me.

I put my hands in my pockets and walk down the street. I walk to Toys R Us and go inside. I was never allowed to own toys past the age of eight; and now I wanted to be surrounded by them. I look at the toys, the games, all of the things American children take for granted. I wonder what simple toy would suffice for a child in Iraq, who could care less about a toy; they have adult problems to deal with. I am filled with guilt.

I leave the store and head for the subway. My day in the city is cut short, and I head home. I spend the day listening to sports radio and surfing the Internet. Most people go home to spend time with family; I spend it doing what most would consider dull. This was good enough for me though. I was content; I was out of view of anything that could possibly upset me.

The next day I had a game with my youngest brother. He was eighteen years old and looked up to me. He was a smart kid, my equivalent. He and I would have conversations about things that would cause our other brothers to look at us with blank stares and start drooling. Nothing against them, they just weren't on the same level of intellect as he and I were. I didn't want to go near the city after the day I had there. What would start out as a day of joy and tranquility, ended with me feeling guilty for being surrounded by everything that symbolized *what we fight for* as Marines. There was one thing that made me feel good, one thing that could ever calm me down...the game of baseball.

I went to the bagel shop down the street again and picked up a bagel. I got on the train and headed straight for Yankee Stadium. I didn't care that my brother and I had a game at 7:00 p.m., a full eleven hours later. I would be going to the first game of a day/night doubleheader that started at 1:00 p.m. I wouldn't be able to get into the stadium for hours, but it was just being there, seeing the stadium of the team I had always found a way to escape life with; I just wanted to see it again and know that it was real.

The train approached and I saw the stadium. A feeling comes over me that I could only imagine would be the feeling of a child going to their first game. In a sense I was a child, exposed to things never before seen, having to start anew. I walked down the steps from the elevated tracks and looked at it, marveled in its history...the home of the New York Yankees. I am simple in a sense. Within the first few moments of anyone meeting me, they would come to find out two things: the first that I am a Marine and proud of it. The second is that I am a huge Yankee fan and that I live for everything Yankees. We follow teams and idolize athletes that have no idea who we are as people, but they have a lasting and important impact on our lives. The Yankees are this to me.

I walk around the stadium for a few hours. I purchase tickets to the game and as soon as the gates open, I am inside watching batting practice. The game of baseball is hypnotic, soothing. It's the music that quiets the beast in me, the light that shines on the darkness that consumes me. The game is set to begin; the National Anthem is set to play. I take off my hat and prepare to stand at the position of attention. I look around and see a few fans with their hats on.

"Hats off. Take your hats off now!" I yell without even a thought of doing so. My subconscious is not going to allow anyone to disrespect my country.

The Yankees get hammered in the first game but win the second. What I remember from the first game was being allowed to move to the good seats because the crowd resembled a Devil Rays' crowd, scarce. I also remember seeing for the first time that Tampa Bay fans were...douches.

My brother meets me for the second game. He seemed shocked that I was there all day; it was a way for me to take a break from taking a break. For my birthday, I headed back to the stadium. I look at the giant screen and see all the birthdays being celebrated. For some reason, I thought someone would put my name up there. I was optimistic. Instead, I was treated to a pitching masterpiece by Roger Clemens. He was pitching a no-hitter only to have it broken up in the eighth inning. We won that game in extras, free baseball for me, a gift from the Yankees.

I had seen friends the first few days. Not much was discussed, and it seemed sort of awkward. There was just nothing I could talk about. Even with my brother, I had a hard time talking about anything that wasn't Yankee related. One of my friends saw this and gave me his tickets to the Subway Series. It was the first time in the six years since they started playing in games that mattered that I got to see the Mets against the Yankees. It was terrific, thanks to a 5-0 victory and bragging rights on the ride back home.

It's not a coincidence that this month of leave was a blur and that all I could remember, in detail, were the baseball games I had been to. It's all I cared about; it's the only thing that couldn't let me down. I went to Boston to pay a visit to a good friend of mine. I would take her to her first baseball game. It was the hated Red Sox against the Detroit Tigers. Pedro Martinez was pitching, and it was a show. The ballpark made me feel like I was home; even the fans where I was sitting were brilliant. The Red Sox won that game and had swept the Tigers for four straight. I was the only one cheering for the Red Sox to lose. I didn't care if the Tigers won, as long as the Red Sox didn't, but the Red Sox did indeed win.

My next game would be back in New York, a game that would be held on the Fourth of July. It was the Yankees against the Red Sox, and it started out great. Soriano hit a homerun to left field, leading off the game for the Yankees. We scored another that inning and I felt great. My feeling didn't last very long. There were fireworks that day, but they came from the Red Sox. I left the stadium after the Yankees lost, but I felt good. Baseball is a godsend. Baseball is God.

I was at the game alone. I looked at a man with his son and smiled. I wanted that. I wanted to be able to take my son to a game and teach him all I knew. I looked at this kid's dad and wished that I could share moments like that with my dad, but if he or my mother even knew I was at a Yankee game, he would shake his head in disgust. It was okay though, because on August 19 when my son is born, I will cover him with pinstripes and navy blue. It's what I had to look forward to. Five days later I tried it out by taking my nephew to a Tigers-White Sox game in Detroit. I fell asleep in that game, my final baseball game on this trip, only to be woken up by a foul ball landing at my feet. My nephew was excited; it was great to see someone enjoy the game as I did, but it was time to leave.

I got to JFK, my trip completed. I wore a cap that symbolizes loyalty to a team, a sport that without it, I don't know what that month would have been like. All I had hoped to do with friends…well that never game to fruition. It wasn't because they were busy, it was because we were nowhere close to being on the same wavelength. Everyone I had grown up with had been traveling along on the same path as me, but then I hit an oil slick and spun out of control. I was in need of a tune-up, but instead of going to see someone about it, I turned on anything that didn't speak of improvised explosive devices (IEDs), or sectarian violence. Everyone has a way of dealing with things. My way was to buy me some peanuts and cracker jacks, and I didn't care if I ever got back…

Back to reality, back to work, back to Iraq or back to anywhere else for that matter.

Chapter 21

I Called It!

Going back to work after being away from it all for a month was like watching the end of a great movie and then going back to see if everything stayed as is. For some reason while we were in Kuwait the first time, we were shown a video of Marines returning home after a deployment. It was accompanied by music and the scenes were certainly heartwarming. I caught myself shedding a tear. I was always a sucker for happy endings. What they never show is what happens after the Marines get back.

All the money that was saved on the deployment was, in one way or another, gone. Some Marines found out their wives were spending their money without discipline; others went out and bought new cars while their previous cars were still relatively new. A few Marines paid off some bills. I, on the other hand, went to baseball games and had a few thousand dollars left, but that would go to a computer and another baseball series in Anaheim when the Yankees would make a return.

It was sunny and beautiful. It's Southern California; it's pretty much a law for it to be perfect out. I greeted my Marines and the phone at my desk rang…

"All staff NCOs and officers need to meet down at the battalion classroom," said the voice on the phone.

I get them together and we head down to where all the senior Marines were. There had been quite a turnover—new faces in, old faces out. I had now been a part of the battalion for over a year. I had some sort of tenure, but there were others who had been a part of the battalion since before I joined the Marine Corps. Outside the classroom was a Marine who was having all of us sign in and put down our security clearances. This was certainly odd; we don't do that unless…

"Gentlemen, what you have in front of you are country handbooks for North Korea," says the intelligence officer standing in front of us all.

My jaw drops in shock. I look over at some of the other staff NCOs and they have the same reaction. Detailed plans on how we were to react to North Korea were laid out and a timeline of when we would do so. The last time I had been briefed like this we were headed to Iraq, and I remember what happened there.

After the meeting we talk amongst ourselves. "These aren't Iraqis. These fuckers will fight and die fighting," I would say.

"They have artillery, and they know how to use it," another Marine would say.

This was some serious shit. Our vehicles and equipment, sandblasted from the deserts of Iraq and Kuwait, were inbound and we had to get them ready. Korea is no joke. We hear about the history of the Korean War, a war that has not been declared over, and we think about the conditions Marines had out there. I remember how I felt that one day and night in Iraq when I was cold, wet, and muddy; I wanted to die. Those conditions would seem like paradise in comparison to what was waiting for us in Korea.

We were tired, just realizing that we were indeed home. The Marines were not to be briefed on what we were told, not until we were given the order to execute. All I could do to maintain sanity was do what I have always done: mingle with my Marines, talk with them, fuck with them, and make them think I had everything under control. If they saw that I was human, I don't know how they would have reacted. I just needed to be the me they had come to know.

My days at work were nothing spectacular. The job of a Marine platoon sergeant is to keep the Marines motivated, train them, and get them to where they need to be. It's like doing the same for yourself, except you do it on a much larger scale. Physical training, PT as we call it, was held every morning now, something about keeping us in shape for "future deployments." I was the only staff NCO in my platoon to PT with the Marines. The others had other things to do, like sleep in. The Master Gunz though, he would PT on his own, and if he found us running along, he'd jump in and lead from the front. All you could do is try to keep up. The key word being *try*. For a man in his forties, he ran like a gazelle.

One thing about being a platoon sergeant that I have always loved is speaking in front of the Marines, projecting my voice. I loved singing as well. During PT we would sing cadence while running, and even if I wasn't feeling well, I always asked to be called out so I could sing my cadence. When I do this a pride in me comes out for all to see, my eyes widen to the size of a crazy person's. I smile and sing; music has always given me inspiration to do or think of something. I always think back to when I was afraid to open my mouth, afraid to speak. Not anymore…

> Rolling down the road in my '42 Ford
> Got a plastic Jesus sittin' on the dashboard
> I think he's keen and I think he's cool
> He'll walk across your swimming pool
> He won't slip, nah, he won't slide
> Because his ass is a magnetized
> But the plastic Jesus he's a got to go
> Cause the magnets are fucking up the stereo

The Marines love it, barking out each verse after I do; it gives me a rush, makes me *want* to go to North Korea and show them the warriors that we are. Every time out there, singing a few different cadences, my Marines begin to look over to the left at me. They begin to smile, causing me to smile. They know what's coming next.

> My girl just turned thirteen
> The prettiest thing that I've ever seen
> And I'll do just anything
> To keep that girl of mine
> Her friends think I'm real cool
> When I pick her up from school
> And I'll do just anything
> To keep that girl of mine
> I'm just a swingin' guy
> Picking up chicks from the junior high
> And I'll do most anything
> To get laid once in a while, YEAH

We're Marines. We say disgusting things, taking solace that they are only words. Words don't hurt people; they don't kill people either; Marines do. So whenever someone gets upset and complains that they were offended by that or the Jesus cadence, I tell them what Marines before me have told others with weak hearts: "Get the fuck over it!"

Every evening I would go back to my room, turn on the computer, and watch Fox News. I was a huge fan of Fox because I felt they supported the troops in a sense. They were the ones who gave us the phones in Tikrit. They were the ones covering the positives in Iraq. CNN covered the IEDs and the bombings, anything negative. I didn't want to see anything negative about the war; I loved when Bill O'Reilly would lay the smack down on some hippie who said the war was based on lies.

Fox would cover the Iraq war and the nuclear crisis in North Korea, by now I was sure we were going there, but I had decided I would not tell my family. I could not put them through what they had gone through just a few months before. I needed a break from the news, from the base, and from anything war related. When you're a Marine, war is everywhere around you. It's in picture frames on the walls of every building. It's in the names of streets on base; and it's in the eyes of every Marine you see.

Thank God for the Yankees. They were in Anaheim for three games during the week. I went with a fellow Marine, Yankee fan, and friend. It was one of the things I said we would do together when we were sitting in the filth of Al Diwaniyah. I paid for the tickets for all three games; he paid for the parking, a fair deal in my eyes. He would also drive, so I would get to drink. The Yankees swept the series, shocking for those of you who follow baseball; the Yankees rarely beat the Angels, let alone sweep them in a series. It was at these games that I was able to eat, drink, and be merry. I cheered my team on while others heckled me, but not much. A majority of the fans in the stadium were Yankee fans, so I was in good company. There were a few Angel fans that gave me a hard time, but there was one Angel fan that I will never forget.

He was sitting in front of us, an older man, gray haired and balding. He was loud; he heckled us and said, "Fuck the Yankees!" He got up and said, "Come on Angel fans, let's show these guys." I swear there were maybe three people who cheered with him. I looked at him with pity, stood up and yelled, "Let's show them how we do this! Let's go Yankees!" I got the whole section to go crazy. He waved his hand as if to say, "Get lost," but it was he and his fickle supporters who had lost.

We begin to converse, we are rivals, but we are civil fans. He was a Marine, a fucking Marine! I could hate you for being a Red Sox fan, but if you were a Marine, you were my brother for eternity. "Semper Fi," I tell him and shake his hand. "I still don't like the Yankees," he would say. The man, no, the Marine tells us that he served in Korea, and I look at him with even greater respect. This Marine was indeed a warrior, back from a war that goes on today. There he was talking to me, a Marine of a different era.

At the end of the game we shake hands and embrace, telling each other to take care. I knew I would never see him again, but you never forget moments like that. Those three games, even to this day, are my favorite games I have ever been to.

Talk of going to Korea was dying down now. There was no chatter of anything at work; it was very subdued. The battalion was working feverishly though, trying to get everything done, get everything ready in case we were needed for war. Contact with my family had been sparse. There was nothing for me to talk to them about. I had no money to send. I barely had enough to send my wife. I was lucky though, money in Yemen went a long way; it wasn't like she was taking care of anyone but herself.

It was on the 18th of August that I found myself as the Battalion Officer of the Day, the OOD if you will. The next day would be my seven-year anniversary from the day I joined the Corps. I tell the two sergeants on duty with me that it was my anniversary; one of them was also celebrating the same date as his anniversary. He joined on the same exact day in the same year, but I out ranked him. He didn't need to know that. I felt guilty, so when he asked me what year I had joined, I didn't answer.

"I have to go on a rove," I told him and walked out, hoping he wouldn't ask me again when I returned.

I visited Marines in the barracks that night. The good thing about being OOD is that you get to spend the night with your Marines and see what it is they do. Nothing much was going on; they were boring like me. I went to the other barracks to check on the Marines that I had spent time with on ship and greeted them as well. I went there to shoot the shit, trying to will time to go by faster, ending my night of duty.

It was now midnight; I was on duty until the morning. I received a phone call; it was officially the 19th of August. I looked at the number on the caller ID and smiled. I was expecting this call. I had been expecting it for more than nine months.

I had done just about everything a man could do at a young age. I had met Presidents and leaders. I had gone to countries and had seen sights that I had never dreamed of. I have gone to hell and back, and led Marines through the thick of it.

I answer the phone; it's my father, the man who was strong and confident while speaking to me months earlier, knowing that I was in danger but showing confidence to strengthen the others around him. His voice is clear and loud, his excitement is like none I have ever heard. I had made my father a promise, I loved the man; he was the reason for my existence. I promised to name my first born son after him. You want to show someone how much they mean to you? Honor them with immortality; remember them so they will never be forgotten.

My father, openly crying and talking to me for the first time says, "You have a son!"

I had done so many things in life, but this was the one thing that dwarfed everything combined. I was full of pride, full of joy. I was alive and had made it to this very moment, the moment I told everyone would happen. "On the 19th of August, 2003, my son Mohamed will be born," I told my dad in November 2002. I was right, and what's the first thing I tell my dad when he tells me?

"I told you it would happen! I was right!"

I had to get that in.

All I could think of now was the idea of being a father, responsible for lives already; this was someone I was responsible for from day one of their existence. This wasn't someone else's child; this was my very own son. I hung up and put the phone back in my pocket. "I'm going on a rove," I tell one of the sergeants in the room with me.

I walk outside and everything looks the same. I go into the bathroom and look into the mirror, even I look the same. Though I wasn't the same; moments before I was a brother, a son, a cousin, a husband, a nephew, an uncle, a brother-in-law. I was a Marine, a leader, a warrior, and a man. The one thing I wasn't is now the most important. I am a father now, and the future is bright.

CHAPTER 22

The Dilemma

I was not around for the birth of my son, so the first thing I want to do is see him in any way possible. I ask for photos to be taken and sent, but the way things work in Yemen, I had to wait a few weeks for someone to fly back to the United States and provide film of my son. I wanted to know what my child looked like. I wanted to know that he was real. They say that seeing is believing. I must have called Yemen more times that week than any other time in my life. I never enjoyed calling because it meant I had to speak Arabic. I talked to my mom; my wife was too tired or too busy with my son to speak.

I was willing to wait for the next pay period, so I could afford a ticket to Yemen. Airfare started at about $1000…that's more than half of my paycheck…for the month! I told my mom I would be there in a few weeks and she tells me not to come just yet. She explains that my wife had just had a baby and it was going to be a month before I "could have fun" with her. This was my mom telling me this, and then I got to thinking.

I had just spent some time in Iraq and gone through that experience there. My parents and family were worried right? I mean, they wanted to see me, didn't they? I was saddened by this, I wanted to get on a plane as soon as I could afford it, but I was asked not to come by my mom so I "could have fun" with the wife later. Like I could give a shit about that? I just tell her "okay" and don't call for a while. I would plan for an October trip.

It was hard for me to talk to people I had known prior to the war. I almost had resentment toward them for no reason. I couldn't communicate with them like I had previously, so I spent most of my time on the Internet looking up people to chat with, primarily women. A couple of these people were hit and miss; I'd talk to them for a day and then never hear from them again. Others had a lasting effect.

One person, for instance, was a single mother, but also a Marine, like me. I became sort of a mentor to her. We would chat and eventually we would exchange telephone numbers. I gave her guidance and advice; it was platonic. I still cared for my wife; she just had my child. Another person came out of nowhere. She had found me through AOL, looking for another Marine. It was random, but we would talk every now and then. She would become a special person to me one day without me knowing it, her name was Nicole. All I expected from her was a meeting and maybe some coffee. That was it.

Work was monotonous, nothing was going on, just the normal routine of maintenance for the Marines, and my job was to make sure things were running smoothly. I maintained a good relationship with my Marines. We went out every now and then. We drank, but change was continuous. Marines were getting out, and new ones were coming in. Even our battalion commander was leaving, being replaced by an Italian who looked like a Mafia boss. When a battalion commander is replaced there are slight changes, but when this man took charge, we all felt it. I don't have a problem with superiors. It's when they do things that affect my Marines and their morale that it starts to bother me. Morale did in fact go south when the battalion commander was making changes, and yes, I was upset by this. Out of my own stupidity I even called him "an asshole" in an email to other staff NCOs. Something I later realized was stupid and immature. I was surprised none of them ratted me out.

Upon meeting this man though, I saw what his objectives were; he wanted us to be ready for any and everything. He wanted to set the example of leadership from on high. He demanded more from his staff NCOs and officers, so much so that many of them were looking for ways to transfer to other units. Then the bombshell hit…

It seems going to Korea was no longer an option; there were problems in Iraq still. I knew leaving Iraq, Tikrit for example, that there would be issues with the soldiers who took our place. From day one they wanted to leave their mark—a-new-sheriff-is-in-town mentality. "Hearts and minds" was our motto; you don't win over hearts and minds by kicking in doors, implementing curfews, and arresting anyone you suspect of being an insurgent or terrorist.

Marines understood this, and it's because we do keep things as simple as possible—a common sense approach. If someone is in your home and tells you how to live your life, you're going to want to punch them in the face. Iraq was not our country to conquer; it was our country to liberate. It's why we took down American flags after some Marines flew them in victory. This wasn't Iwo Jima or the surface of the moon. It's why leadership at the Pentagon grimaced when they saw the Marine put the flag on the face of Saddam's statue in Baghdad.

We were running five times a week now, PT every day. We were frantically getting our vehicles and equipment ready for something, but now we weren't going to Korea. We were called down to the same classroom where we were briefed on North Korea. We were shown numbers and percentages of casualties, and we were given country handbooks. To my dismay it read, "Iraq – Transitional Handbook."

Since the first of May, when President Bush announced "Mission Accomplished," not one Marine had been a casualty due to insurgency, and Marines had been in country until about the time of them telling us this. This was four months in country and not one Marine casualty. The Army on the other hand, they were experiencing casualties left and right.

Our battalion commander, new and definitely in charge, stands and tells us that the Marine Corps has been asked to go back to Iraq to assist. He tells us with confidence that we would not be experiencing the high number of casualties that the Army had faced each day. Marines train differently, and we would continue to train. I didn't like where this was going; we are not trained to occupy.

"Gentlemen, I have volunteered our battalion to be the first Light Armored Reconnaissance unit in Iraq when we go back. I am not the only one who's volunteered. The other two battalions have as well, but if we're in as good a shape as I think we are, I know we'll get the nod."

There is silence, or maybe it's because I was silent and everything else around me was muffled. I go to my room that evening and complain about this to my Internet friends. My favorite one, Nicole, could care less. I don't blame her; she is eighteen and doesn't really understand the whole concept. I wasn't going for sure; no one had gotten the nod just yet, though it bothered me enough for me to begin having nightmares.

I spoke more to my new Internet friends. Christine was also in the mix; she and my Internet friends were the constants in my new life. These people did not know me before the change in me. Christine knew of me, but she hadn't really known me. As for Nicole, she made me laugh; she was carefree. Her cheerleader voice made me laugh even more. They were my escape; they were new because my life was new. They never really understood what they meant to me, and I was afraid to tell them for fear of losing them.

I held onto hope as things died down at work once again, much like they had during the news of the whole Korea fiasco. I felt this meant we wouldn't get the nod, so I planned my trip to Yemen. It was now October; I would be missing the baseball postseason. It was okay though. I would get to see my wife, my dad, my mom, and my son, and I had some Yankee gear for him. So we'd be there in spirit.

For those of you who are parents, how many of you had a child born and then were not able to see them for the first month of their existence? You hear stories of a parent falling in love with their child as soon as they see them, but I wasn't sure about this. I was nervous that when I saw him, I would feel no different. Anxiety filled my chest and chaotic thoughts clouded my mind. I didn't know what Yemen had in store for me, especially now that I was coming back from Iraq. For months I had been hoping to leave Iraq, and now that I was out of there, I was heading back to the region, on vacation nonetheless. The feeling of not knowing what would happen was too much for me, so I did what I knew how to do best. I watched baseball.

My flight to Yemen would be in the evening, but I like to get to the airport early. On this day, I would not be doing that. I would watch as Johan Santana mowed down the Yankees to help the Twins take Game 1 of the division series. This is why I didn't leave for the airport on time. I wanted a Yankee victory. Oh well, I left for the airport soon after so I could be *randomly* selected for screening again.

Traveling to a place where something or someone awaits you has a special feeling to it. I was a father now, but I didn't feel like a father yet. I didn't have my son with me. I wasn't raising him. I thought all of this would change when I would get to Yemen. As soon as I would land, I would go and see my son…except that I didn't.

It had been nearly a year since they had broken ground to start building this house in Yemen, this symbol of success and, in my opinion, arrogance. I got off the plane and my father was there waiting for me. I am happy to see him for the first time since before the war. I see a new pickup truck and ask, "Whose is this?"

He says to me, "It's ours. You owe me $3,000 for your share."

It had started.

I expected to go to the hotel my dad was staying at, pick up what he needed, and then head to the village where my family stayed. It's in the truck that I hadn't realized I had purchased that my dad tells me we would be staying in Sana'a for two days to pick up supplies for the house being built. This was my dad; I still feared and respected him. I did what he said.

I call my wife, expecting her to be shocked and upset, but she wasn't. She knew about this ahead of time and tells me not to worry; it's for the house. What didn't anyone get about this? I wanted to see my son! It was at this moment that I felt a disconnect, a realization even further that it wasn't what I wanted to make me happy, it's what they wanted to do to show others we were happy. This fucking house was tearing us apart as a family, and no one cared to see, not even my wife.

For two days I stay at the hotel in Sana'a, and for two days I think about the time lost that could be spent holding my son. It is during these two days that I give my father an envelope with all the money I had to my name, approximately $1,400.

He looks at it and says, "That's it?" He looks over at my watch, a watch I had bought weeks prior and asks, "How much did you pay for that?"

It was a $95 Fossil watch, but I was afraid to tell him it was that much, so I tell him, "I got it on sale for $75."

My father was different; he didn't look at me the same way he used to. Comments were short and remarks were sarcastic. When he would watch CNN with me, he would comment about the war and say, "They're full of shit. There's nothing there," in regards to the weapons of mass destruction. Anything about the war and the United States led invasion was negative. It then dawned on me; my father was disappointed in me.

We finally left Sana'a and headed to the village where my father was raised, where his grandson who holds his name was born. It takes nine hours and all I can do is imagine what it would be like. Eleven years earlier my father made his triumphant return to Yemen to fanfare and excitement. I get to the house and have to knock on the door for them to open it for me. There was no celebration. I greet my mother and my sisters, then head to see my wife. I walk into the room and see my son laid out on the bed, waiting for me. He is silent, content, his eyes wide open. He's over a month old now. He knows not what he sees, and he knows not that I am his father. I am his father though. A father! I can't fucking believe it!

My wife comes over to me, and I kiss her on the forehead, a sign of respect and admiration that I have for all women who bare children. It is something I could never do, but women do it with such bravery.

I was to stay in Yemen for a month, that's what the plan was initially. I lie down on the bed and place my son on my chest. Within moments his eyes shut, the beating of my heart sings him to sleep. He is the reason why I did not end up dying; he is the reason why I did not give up hope after watching that little boy die. His existence gave me the want to be able to provide a future for him, a future of endless possibilities for my son. I fall asleep, tired yet content with all that surrounds me.

I am awakened the next morning by the sound of my father outside speaking to my youngest brother over the phone. My dad speaks in English, so no one else around him can understand what he is saying, but I understand him loud and clear.

"Khaled? Well I don't know about him. He lies too much. He said he was going to bring more money, but I don't know. He's a liar."

I was crushed. My father spoke to my youngest brother about his disappointment in me, about how I didn't bring enough money to give toward the building of the house. My father spoke of shame and disappointment that resembled a time when I was fifteen, when he told me that he was ashamed of me because of my tameness, and how he couldn't bring me around others. I was timid; I knew nothing at that age.

I avoided my dad that day, seeking comfort in my mother. Maybe she would understand, but instead she confronts me. "Why do you lie? Do you have another wife and family you're not telling us about?" she says while crying. I am shocked. What the fuck was going on over here? Why were they so disappointed in me? Did they not understand that I barely made enough to survive? I had no one to talk to. What about the wife?

She also did not understand. She would not stay by my side when I asked her to stay with me and just lay in bed beside me. She left my side to go to the kitchen where my mom was and told me, "I've got work to do." When I told her that I came here to see her and my son, she only tells me that she's busy and has work to do.

I stay in my room with my son each and every day. I tell my dad that I will be leaving earlier than planned. I did not want to be there anymore than I had to; I was not welcome. I use the excuse that I had to get ready for a deployment to the Philippines, and that I would be making more money so that I could send it to them for the house. He was approving of this—it made him happy. What was this house doing to us as a family?

I later confessed to my mother that I had heard what my father had said over the phone. I told her with tears in my eyes that I went through anguish just to bring them the money that I did. I pleaded with her to believe me that I don't make much money in the Corps; that my brothers are Merchant Mariners, and they make more in a few months than I did in a year. I tell her that the house would kill us. This went on deaf ears. She then told me about how it was for her and how she cried every night. How she screamed every moment the television displayed pictures and video of dead Marines. She told me how neighbors and some family would ask if I was in Iraq, and if so, it was "not a good thing." I knew what that meant; I knew what I had to do next.

My father arranged for my ticket to leave before the end of the month. I planned it this way for two reasons. The first reason I already explained, I was not welcome. The second reason, the Yankees were in the World Series, and I wanted to be there for the parade when they would win, because they just had to. I needed something good to come out of this trip.

I left Yemen; the entire trip was a trip of silence. Relationships that I had with everyone were damaged. They would never be the same from that day forward, and I knew it. I could not explain or rationalize with anyone there; it wouldn't matter to them without the dollar signs.

I arrived in New York a broken man, needing the Yankees to win for me. I watched in silence and sadness as Jorge Posada grounded out to Josh Beckett. As Beckett reaches over with his glove to tag Posada out ending the World Series, I thought of what my mother had told me, of what my dad had said, and of the people coming to my house asking them if I was serving in Iraq. As the Marlins celebrated on the field I realize then what I have to do and say to myself…

"I have to get out of the Marine Corps."

Chapter 23

Dilemma 2—The Sequel

How do you tell your boss that you have to quit? How do you tell your subordinates that you're going to have to choose family over them? I got back to California and back to work. Marines both senior and junior were happy to see me back from Yemen. I was happy to see them as well, but I didn't know what to tell them. I spoke to my platoon commander and the Master Gunz; they both heard me out. I explained my situation. I explained that my family is from Yemen and that they were questioned about me and my involvement in Iraq. As a father now, I worried for my son, and even though they didn't show me as much love as I had expected, I worried for my family. They both were surprisingly supportive. I offered to terminate my contract and pay for the difference in losses to the Corps.

I explained this to the company commander and the battalion sergeant major and they began researching what I had to do in order for me to terminate my contract. There is always a way to do something, and the Marine Corps has always put provisions in place that allowed for some flexibility. These were circumstances beyond my control.

A few years into my career as a Marine, my superiors knew I was destined for greatness in the Corps. I don't know how many times I heard, "Hafid, you're going to be Sergeant Major of the Marine Corps." That would make me the most senior enlisted Marine in the Corps. With the amount of time it took me to get to staff sergeant, I would be eligible for sergeant major before my thirty-third birthday. I had plenty of time to achieve that designation.

I loved being a Marine; it was something my family never understood. I loved being around Marines, they are as real as real can get. I wanted to stay in until the Corps told me they had enough of me and gave me the boot. I would always think of what my final thoughts would be when I retired, and what I would say to the Marines at my retirement. There was nothing else I imagined myself doing; I even put off college. I thought it was something I didn't need to do anymore.

I wasn't a shitbag Marine; I wasn't one that gave up. I gave everything I had at all times. I never wanted to give anyone anything to correct me on. I didn't want to give anyone who doubted me any ammunition. The Marines in my command knew I wasn't making this up. They knew I wasn't going to quit on them unless it was absolutely necessary. This killed me inside. What made it worse was that this was happening a few days before the Marine Corps Birthday Ball.

The Marine Corps Birthday Ball is a tradition in the Corps that everyone takes pride and part in. It's when Marines get together, put on our best uniforms, and celebrate the birth of our beloved Marine Corps. It's when you see Marines in their best uniforms, when they have their medals mounted and brass polished. It's when they have their uniforms pressed and shoes spit shined. It's when for one night, you put aside your personal differences with a Marine you may not enjoy the company of and wish him or her a "happy birthday."

I called Christine to talk about what was bugging me. I had been in contact with Christine sporadically, and we had seen each other one other time since her graduation. It was only a few days before the Ball. The person I had intended to go with had not returned my phone calls and it dawned on me during a phone call with Christine to ask her. "Hey you wanna go to the Marine Corps Ball this weekend?" I asked.

She got excited and said yes. I didn't expect her to be so excited about it. She got off the phone immediately and prepared for the Ball by going out to buy a dress, getting her hair done—whatever women do to look good for any given event. I figured she was a good friend, why not show her a good time... the Marine Corps way!

The Marine Corps Ball was to be held at a trucker's rest stop, just across the Nevada border. It would be held in a place called Laughlin, much to the dismay of the Marines who wanted to go to Las Vegas. Hell, I was one of those Marines who wanted to go to Vegas. I would pick up Christine on the way and we'd go to Laughlin together...road trip! This would be the first time Christine and I would be alone together for an extended period of time. She was nervous about it I am sure. I just wanted her to be calm and see me as the person she saw at her graduation. I expected the ride to be long, so I had a full assortment of CDs in the CD changer, just in case we ran out of something to talk about and it got awkwardly silent. The CDs were never put to use.

Christine and I talked about so many things. For the first time, I was someone who was separate from the Marine she and I both knew. I wasn't the guy she met through her Marine friend; I was her friend, period. I had other friends like that, where you meet them through other people and then the two of you become closer than you and the person you knew them from. She asked about my son, and as I talked about him I looked over at her. She was staring at me. She was observing my reaction about how much my son meant to me. She noticed that as soon as I had begun to speak of him, a glow was emitting from me. He was the only person who didn't look at me with disappointment when I went there to see him.

Christine and I talked about what I was going to do. I had told her about getting out and what it would mean to my Marines if they deployed again and what it would do to me. I explained how much they loved me and how much they meant to me as well. I also mentioned my platoon commander, we had just received word that he would leave and it bothered me. The Corps had spoiled us with a great leader, and now he was leaving.

We get to the hotel, and it was as cheesy as you would expect. It was a wannabe Las Vegas, designed for the random traveler who was just passing through. We got our bags and checked-in. I asked for a room with two beds. I was sharing the room with her, not a bed. There were none available; we got a room with a queen-sized bed. I told Christine I would sleep on the floor. She told me I would not, and I respond with, "I've slept in worse. Believe me, this is paradise." I didn't go into detail. I never did.

I got dressed quickly; it didn't take much when you've prepared your uniform like I have always done in my career. I wore my patriotic boxers; I was going to be a proud United States Marine, all the way down to my boxers. Christine on the other hand, she took a while…women.

In the bathroom for what seemed like days, she steamed, blow-dried, brushed, applied, and so forth. She did all of this as I sat on the edge of the bed, waiting. I sat there with my trousers and shoes on, my dress blue top (known as a blouse) hung on the closet door, anticipating the moment I would free it from its slumber so that it would cover me with its glory.

I looked over at my blouse. It had a few new campaign ribbons, and I wasn't the only one wearing new medals or ribbons. Marines from the battalion had received their awards. They received awards for valor, for driving, for handing out meals, for just about everything. The award I was promised? They forgot to submit it before the deadline. This would not be a day to reflect on awards earned but not given; this was a day to celebrate the Corps.

Finally, at long last, Christine shouts through the bathroom door that she's done. I get up and put on my blouse, adjusting the buttons and medals so they look pristine. I check myself in the mirror, making sure I look as good as I think I do, and I do. Christine comes out and she is stunning. I tell her she looks gorgeous. She is wearing a green dress, very classy and elegant.

We head down to the ballroom and one by one we pass Marines in their uniforms. Some are new to the battalion and this is their first Ball with us. Others are new to the Corps and are nervous to be at their first Ball. I have been to numerous Marine Corps Birthday Balls. This was cake to me, and yes, this is a birthday, there would be birthday cake, too.

Marines greet me left and right, shaking my hand, wishing me a "Happy Birthday Staff Sergeant!" I look over to Christine as if to tell her, "See, I told you they loved me." She couldn't believe the outpouring of love and admiration I got from my Marines.

The ceremony begins, the National Anthem plays and a tear rolls down my cheek. It always gets to me, that "Star Spangled Banner." Speeches are given and it's then that we're told that we've been chosen to be the first to represent the Marine Corps in our return to Iraq. The battalion commander had gotten his way.

What would they call this operation? Someone had to have some sort of plan for a better name right? Well, like in Hollywood, even operations have sequels. This would be called "Operation Iraqi Freedom 2." I waited for something else to be said, like, "Operation Iraqi Freedom 2—We're Coming for More," or "Operation Iraqi Freedom 2—We Left the Oven On." No, just that. So it was official now, we were going back to Iraq, going back to the place that I thought would never be done with us, and I was right. The only thing is, I had asked for my contract to be terminated because of the dangers my family faced in Yemen. I wouldn't be a part of this war, and I felt like shit. But I was going to put it off for one night. It was time to celebrate. "Anchors Away" plays leading up to "The Marines' Hymn" and a chill goes up my spine, also known as motivation.

After the ceremony I walk over to my platoon commander and talk his ear off about how it sucks that he's leaving. I grab a few Marines from our platoon and say to them, "Hey Corporal, Sergeant, doesn't it suck that he's leaving?" More Marines from our platoon flock over; pretty soon there are ten or more of us surrounding our platoon commander, beer and whiskey bottles in hand when someone's wife yells, "Take a picture!" I squat down to where the shortest Marine is, a junior Marine, but a good friend of mine, and I hold his head up by his chin. Cameras flash and it was a great picture…the last one we had with our platoon commander.

As the night went on Christine was busy chasing me around. I am a social butterfly. I am comfortable in this element. I am amongst my Marines. There is no one there who doesn't understand me. They are my brothers-in-arms, and they've eaten the same dirt as me. As I pass each Marine in my platoon I stop and tell them, "Hey, happy birthday, Devil. Go over to the chief warrant officer and tell him how great he is." They say, "Aye aye, Staff Sergeant," and go over to the platoon commander. I tell about twenty Marines to do this. Losing the platoon commander wasn't something I looked forward to.

Christine had a crush on one of my Marines, the Marine I mentioned earlier who was junior and a good friend of mine. When she was tired of chasing me down, she would talk to him. I didn't mind; he was a good kid, and if he was good to her, I didn't care.

I get called to the front of the ballroom over the microphone and speakers. A familiar tune begins to play, and I am thrown the mic. "Talk to me, tell me your name…" I begin to sing, the first verse of Ricky Martin's "She Bangs." I am surrounded by the Marines of my platoon. Christine laughs in the distance as we all sing and dance. The year before I had done the same but on stage, and Marines had their girlfriends stuff dollars down my belt. I made $7 that night, but this night was not about making that paper, it was about celebrating the moment, the Corps, and each other.

The night was over and we had all gone back to our rooms. Some had gone to Vegas down the road. Christine and I would call it a night, both excited and pleased that it was such a great time. The next day we went to Vegas. She wanted crepes for some reason from the Paris Hotel; I just waited for her, as she waited in line for it.

On the way back we talked non-stop about how some Marines acted, how I was acting, the things I did and said, and so forth. She was still shocked by how the Marines did indeed love me and the bond we all had with each other. I thanked her for such a great time, and she returned the thanks. I hugged her and wished her well. She called me later that night to tell me she had left her dress at the hotel. What was I supposed to do? At the end of the call she said she wanted to hang out with me some more the coming weekend, and if I could, to invite my friend. I laughed and said okay.

After the weekend we went back to work, the Marines now knowing they would be deploying yet again. This is when things started getting ugly; numerous Marines were coming up with reasons to not deploy with the battalion. Stories of how one Marine said he was having emotional problems, of how another Marine said his wife would leave him were coming out. Speaking of "coming out", a few Marines claimed to be gay so they could get kicked out of the Marine Corps. Say what you will about gays, but there were actual gay Marines serving that would never stoop to this level, they were not cowards. There was one story we heard of a Marine staff sergeant's wife calling the command to demand that her husband not deploy because he had asthma. I was angered by this, angered by the illegitimacy of these Marines and the lack of pride they displayed. We had a new platoon commander and the first thing he saw was this crap? And to add to that his platoon sergeant (me) was on the verge of getting processed out of the Marine Corps. He didn't like this; then again he didn't like many things, probably because he was short.

While going to see the sergeant major about my separation request I see written on the white erase board outside the battalion commander's office, "Today a Marine died because a staff sergeant couldn't deploy due to asthma." I don't go to see the sergeant major; I go back to my office and do work.

It's during a meeting between the staff NCOs, the new platoon commander, and me while going over the rosters of who was deploying and who wasn't that I got fed up and said something that would change my life.

It's when I am asked by the Master Gunz, "Well what's going on with you? How's your separation going?"

I look over at him with a stern look and say, "It's not. I'm going with you guys, but I can't let anyone know about it."

I was referring to my family. I knew the risks, but the greater risk was losing my Marines.

Sacrifice has been made for centuries by men and women before me. Men and women in battle, men and women who were family to those lost in battle. Who the fuck was I to be ducking out of this when my very own men were headed back to certain danger? Sure, I would be fine. Sure, I would be safe and unharmed, but I would never be able to look at myself in the mirror again. There are things in life far worse than death, and one of them is letting down your Marines…my Marines.

Chapter 24

Turn Out the Lights

Much like the 4th Infantry Division in Tikrit, a Marine who missed the war with our battalion was anxious to make a name for himself, Marines of all ranks and pay-grades, each one salivating at the opportunity to improve their career path. Newly appointed personnel tried as hard as they could to get Marines to forget their predecessors. Even our very own newly appointed platoon commander got in front of my Marines after I spoke to them and addressed them as follows…

"I saw how you guys gave your previous platoon commander a proper sendoff. I hope that when it comes time for me to leave I can get the same kind."

What he was talking about was a party we had set up for our outgoing platoon commander. I coordinated with the sergeants in my platoon and the company commander to get something done for him. Our plan was to throw him a surprise party at Hooters and the entire platoon would be there to greet and honor him. I went down to the company office and convinced the company commander to let us out of work early, so we could do this for him. He agreed to do so with the promise that I would get our platoon commander on video doing some kind of dance. It would be the chicken dance and he got to do it with about ten waitresses, lucky bastard. At least I held up my end of the bargain.

People deserve to be shown how much they are appreciated. I felt it would be an injustice to let our platoon commander go without us showing him appreciation. That day was great. The Marines had a blast, and all the love and admiration was given to the outgoing platoon commander. I like to observe things; I like to see if I can get a feel of what people are feeling.

Marines were in separate groups with pitchers of beer on each table. Waitresses were talking to and taking pictures with each one of them. I was talking to our outgoing platoon commander and our drugged up Master Gunz (he just had surgery) about some old stories. We were laughing hysterically, especially when the Master Gunz tells me his story of when he first saw my name as being inbound to the battalion. He thought I was a terrorist. We're all having a great time, but looking over at our incoming platoon commander, it looked as if he felt he was out of place. He was.

Even if he did feel out of place, you don't tell your Marines the next day that you hope to be honored by them. It means you expect it. It means you want it, and it means you aren't genuine about anything you do from that point forward because you're looking for a reward. I was disgusted and as soon as he walked away from the platoon a few of the Marines came up to me and said, "Only Jerry deserves that kind of party." They were referring to the previous platoon commander. I nodded my head in agreement.

With the upcoming deployment Marines were encouraged to make plans for Thanksgiving and Christmas and to spend time with their families. I had no family with me and I didn't want to tell anyone that I was going back. Just the thought of me going back there and not telling my family was something I did not want to think about. I had to do a few things, like find a place to store my items and find a way to get my cousin's car to someone I could trust. He had left it with me while he went out to sea.

The holidays are a time I usually enjoy most because it's the one time people act civil. It's the one time people can just get over themselves and enjoy the sights and sounds of joy and cheer. It's the time I get to watch movies that remind me of being a kid again, when the only worries I had were if I was awkward or not. These days I had real world worries, and it wasn't like I had anything in front of me to show for it. My son was in a different part of the world, and I was making minimum wage, if that.

Christine invited me over for Thanksgiving. I was honored that she invited me over to her family's place. They didn't have turkey, something about not liking it, but they did have some chicken. Christine let me spend the night on the couch and took me to my very first "Black Friday," where I got to see the insanity of Christmas shoppers. Getting up at three in the morning to wait in a line for four hours to get a $5 copy of *Porky's* is not what I would call fun, but spending time with Christine was just that, fun. I used my skills of observation and coordination to assist in the shopping. I was given three items to find when we entered the store, and I would go out and find the items. I'd come back within a few minutes to the surprise of Christine and her friend who had tagged along with us. This friend of hers later confessed after seeing that I was harmless that she was the one who had told me the year before to stop calling Christine. She felt bad about it, no harm no foul. I pointed my finger at her and said, "It was you!" in jest and we all laughed about it.

Christine bought a movie she said I would love called *Serendipity*, and she said we would watch it when we got back to her place. After about ten hours of waiting in line and pushing and shoving, all of their wish list items had been checked off. I was complimented on my shopping skills and my focus on getting what I needed to get. For a first time participant to this yearly fiasco, I held my own pretty well.

Watching this movie with Christine did something to me that I hadn't done since that baby boy died in front of me months earlier. It weakened me and let out emotions that were human in nature. *Serendipity* was a feel good love story. It was magical, but I had come to know that life was not magical for many citizens of the world. I shed some tears and Christine saw this and said out loud, "Awww!"

I told her to "shut your face," and she laughed.

Christine and I began to hangout each weekend, sometimes I would drive up after work and spend time with her. She started a new job, and I encouraged her when she was struggling. One day she called me out of the blue sounding frightened and said she had to leave work; her father was sent to the hospital experiencing chest pains. I left work as well and headed up to see her immediately. We paid a visit to her dad who was in bed at the hospital; he had a scare but was fine thankfully.

I didn't like seeing Christine vulnerable. I didn't want to see her hurt. I looked at how much she loved her father; he was the world to her. If anything was to happen to him, she would lose so much of herself, and I would not allow that to happen. I would be there for her regardless.

Christine still had feelings for the Marine that I met her through. He had met a woman in his time serving in Ethiopia and was getting married. This hurt Christine, and, in turn, it hurt me. It was at that moment I decided to do something against one friend to protect another. I realized that by doing that, I had to stand by my decision and never look back.

I was invited to the Marine's wedding, to be there as he got married to this girl. I wrote my friend, the Marine, and said that for Christine's sake, I could not justify being there. I felt guilty, but I would have felt worse if I had gone. He said he understood, but we haven't spoken much since then. I knew he was mad at me for choosing sides, but Christine was there for me, and she was my best friend. I felt I had no choice but to support her.

We became really close, talking to each other every day, hanging out three to four times a week, doing just about everything with each other. Her father didn't like this; I think he felt I had ulterior motives. I just wanted to be the best friend I could to Christine, and, in turn, that would mean she would be happy, making me happy...

"We got him!" she said to me.

Christine called me on a Sunday morning and told me to turn on the television. Saddam Hussein had been captured by 4th ID in Tikrit. I told Christine, "I knew it! Some guy was trying to tell me where he was, but we didn't listen! Damn it! That could have been me!" She could care less about that; she was more worried about what it meant. "Does that mean you still have to go?" she asked. I told her that it didn't mean anything. I asked her to let me watch the coverage, and I would call her back.

I asked Christine to let me watch the coverage because I needed to take in the situation. I needed time to reflect, to take in the amount of loss absorbed by the people of Iraq, the Marines and soldiers alike. I spent the rest of that morning watching Fox News as they showed images of Saddam going through a health check. I was initially overjoyed. We had captured the tyrant; this justified everything that happened over there. I shed a tear watching soldiers celebrating his capture; it was a proud day for others and for me.

I started thinking more about it and whispered to myself, "Was it really worth it, for just one man?"

Saddam's capture indeed changed nothing. We were still deploying; people were still dying. We spent the weeks leading up to Christmas preparing all of our vehicles and equipment for deployment. With a better understanding of what to expect, we packed items we thought we would need. For me it was Tang and baby wipes. Others brought a year's supply of beef jerky.

One by one our vehicles and equipment were loaded onto ships. We would not accompany them though; we would meet the ships in Kuwait. We would be flying. That's how the Army did things; they would send their equipment out first and then meet it in country. This gave us more time to spend at home and more time to say our good-byes...some for the last time.

Almost 90 percent of the battalion went on Christmas leave. I stayed behind and spent Christmas leave standing duty as Officer of the Day numerous times and spending time with Christine. I got her a Christmas present, a VCR and a Sony PDA so she could use it for work. When she opened her presents, she told me it was too much, but I don't put a price on what someone means to me. I get what I think they would love or need most. She told me that she didn't have my gift yet, that she's still waiting to pick it out, but that it would be something special.

While out celebrating Christmas and seeing all the Christmas decorations, she found some t-shirts with quirky sayings on them. She wanted to buy them for one of my Marines that she fancied. For the first time I gave her a strange look. She was buying him a gift and had yet to get me mine? It started to bother me, and I believe she saw it. The two of them had started to talk more after the Ball. After the Christmas leave block they were going to go out one night. She asked me what I thought about that, and I told her that it was cool, it didn't bother me. I was being honest; it didn't and wouldn't bother me, as long as she did not forget me. When I saw that she was thinking about buying him a gift before getting me one, even if she gave me something as simple as a card, it made me feel as if she was indeed starting to forget me.

I am a man of simple things. I give a little; I expect nothing. If I give a lot, I expect little. I was hurt that she didn't think to get me something for Christmas; I was hurt that she had thought more about what to get this Marine than me. I never did get a gift from her.

What Christine did not know was how much I cared about her. I was not in love with her, but I did love her. After what happened with my family and wife in Yemen, I now loved her more than I loved my wife. We started to argue though; I felt neglected, and it was my fault that I had focused so much of my energy on her. I depended on her to keep me stable. The thought of losing her though, that destabilized whatever was keeping me sane.

Christine had known me to be carefree and happy; this was because of her being around me. She never saw or heard me get upset. The first time was when she compared me to the Marine who was getting married. She defended him even after he had hurt her, and said he was doing more than I was to better himself. That hurt me like a knife in my chest. She apologized, but the damage was done. I told her I would need time; she asked how long and said that she didn't want to lose me.

I felt selfish. I felt as if I was overreacting to this, that I was treating her badly because of hurt feelings. I should just get over it and forgive her. Within an hour I gave her a call and said, "Hey I'm over it!" She was overjoyed, telling me that she loved me and I returned the love back. It was then that I told her that I loved her, but was not in love with her. That I loved her more than my wife, if she understood what that meant. She said that she did.

It came time for Christine and my Marine to spend time together. She asked me to come along. She was nervous, but I just couldn't get myself to do it. I didn't want to go out with the Marines and see her there with them. She sent me text messages pleading for me to come out. I asked if she was okay, she said she was but would feel more comfortable if I were there. I told her that I would not be coming out, she'd be fine.

When it got late that night I sent her a text that said, "Don't do it. I know that I said I didn't care, but I do." I didn't get a response, and I started to worry. I explained through text that I didn't want her to do it, not there, not with all those Marines around. I didn't want her to be used, to be some random girl that one of my Marines hooked up with. She was my best friend.

The next morning she texted me saying nothing happened and that she was coming over to my room. When she got there, I gave her a hug and she sat down. She had a look on her face, a look of guilt. I knew what it meant.

"So how was last night?" I asked her. She told me it was fine, "nothing special." I asked where they had gone and she told me about some bar down near San Diego. I was ironing my uniform for Tuesday. We had Monday off and I wanted to spend time with her on Monday instead of having to worry about getting ready for work that day. I was also watching the AFC Championship game on television. She was very quiet.

"You know how you told me not to? What if I did?" she asked me.

I picked up my cell phone and called my buddy in Massachusetts, a brother of mine who had just got out of the Marine Corps. He was going to be coming down to visit me that week, and we would drive my cousin's car cross country and drop it off in New York City where it would stay while I was deployed. He was a fan of the Patriots and they were playing in the AFC Championship game. "Did you just see that?" I said to him, talking about the interception Peyton Manning had just thrown. I hung up a few moments later and said nothing to Christine.

She looked back at me, staring, hoping to make eye contact. I ignored her; I didn't say a word, just focused on the game and my uniform. Another interception and I call my buddy again. He's going crazy with excitement. "Dude, they're done," I say to him, excited for him. The Patriots were going to go to the Super Bowl, and on our trip east we could stop in Boston and catch the game at a bar there.

I put the phone back down and Christine says, "Khaled?" I say nothing in return, watching the game and looking back down at my uniform, ironing out a crease. She said she was going to leave, that she would see me tomorrow.

"Yup!" I said, cold and uncaring, looking down at my uniform and flipping it over, preparing to iron the other side. She left upset, but I felt far worse. She was my best friend, and I did nothing to stop it. I didn't go out when she asked me to; I didn't object when I should have; and I didn't know the severity of what it would do to how I felt about her. It was my fault, and I didn't catch it in time.

The lights are turned off. I am in complete darkness. Welcome to 2004, the beginning of the worst year of my life.

Chapter 25

A Hundred Days

It was crunch time now. We were just a few weeks away from going back to Iraq. "OIF 2" was its name and there were rumors that it was planned out for more sequels than the *Rocky* saga. I knew this meant I would be spending the rest of my Marine Corps career going to and from Iraq. It was time to prepare and train the Marines for this deployment. The dynamic of what was waiting for us over in Iraq had changed, the enemy was undefined. The word "insurgents" was used, but who the fuck were they?

I was granted a week of leave. My buddy Eric flew in from Massachusetts to help me with the 3,000 mile drive east. Eric was more than a buddy to me, he was my brother. I met him after Thanksgiving of the year 2000 while serving as a Marine Security Guard in London. He was a larger than life character with a laugh and voice equally as large. No one thought I would get along with him, especially since they moved him into the room next to mine after I demanded that no one move into it.

"You're Hafid?" he said to me extending his hand to shake mine the first day I met him. Within a few hours we were hanging out together and he became my first drinking buddy. Before I knew him, I would refrain from drinking, but he was just a blast to be around. He was also loyal, the most loyal person I have ever come to know. He cared about me more than a brother would, and that is why I consider him such. We were so close that even after I left London to serve in Shanghai, we called each other to shoot the shit while we were each on duty. During the September 11 attacks he was in the United States. I did everything I could to track him down over the phone and finally did. When I flew back to London shortly after the attacks, I picked him up from the airport when he returned. I purposely flew to London to see him; I wasn't going to miss his big moment.

When a Marine gets promoted, they are asked who they would like to promote them. When I was a young Marine, I remember thinking to myself, *Wow, that's how you know someone respects you.* I still remember who the Marines were who placed the chevrons on my collar for each one of my promotions. It's an honor you give to those you respect and love; it's more rewarding than any award you could ever receive.

Over my career in the Corps, I have had the honor of pinning the chevrons on many Marines. There was even a time when I was called out by four Marines in one ceremony. As much as I was honored by those Marines, being there for the promotion and being able to pin on the sergeant chevrons on my brother Eric, that was the proudest moment I have had in my military career. When the chevrons were ones I had once used, it made me even prouder.

Eric was now out of the Corps. He missed it so he flew out a week early to stay at my place on base before we embarked on our journey. I would go to work and he'd hangout at the barracks, watching ESPN and catching the highlights of the Patriots over the course of the season. He was a diehard Pats fan and a semi-fan of the Red Sox, but I ignore that. The Red Sox were harmless; they could never beat the Yankees.

At work we held inspections, one of the most painful preparations for any deployment. While in a formation before one of these inspections I heard some of my Marines talking about Christine. They laughed and giggled like schoolgirls, this was the exact reason why I didn't want her to go through with it. I am standing in front of the platoon when I hear the Marine she spent the night with make a smart remark about her. I kick him in the leg in disapproval. He laughs and says, "Sorry, Staff Sergeant."

I had spoken to Christine a day after she had left with me not speaking to her. I finally told her why I had objected and why I didn't want her to be another random barracks' visitor. She was my friend and I was their platoon sergeant; the conflict of interest was obvious. I told her that I also wanted Eric to meet her; I wanted him to see how much she meant to me. I had also started to drink more. While Eric was there, we drank every night. We would go up to LA to visit Christine, and she would know where to go to have a good time. All that week we'd end the day in LA, going to bars and a famous joint called Roscoe's House of Chicken and Waffles. I don't know why they were so famous, the food was okay, but waffles and chicken…sorry, but my stomach did not agree.

All week we had planned to go to Tijuana with Christine and a few others. She wanted to ask the Marine she hooked up with to join us. I was livid, angered more by my intoxicated state. Marines below the rank of corporal were not allowed to go to Mexico, and she was trying to convince him to go. I had told her this ahead of time, and yet she still asked him. I also didn't want him around because I didn't want her to end up doing what she said she'd never do again. The fact that she called him upset me to the point of rage.

Eric was driving and I was controlling the music selection. I put on Blink 182 and picked out a song called "Dammit." I had done this for a reason. The song was loud and fast paced. I raised the volume to sing along with it, "The steps that, I retrace, the sad look, on your face. The timing, and structure, did you hear, that he fucked her?" I say the latter part with force and anger, screaming it at the top of my lungs. She knew what I was doing, everyone knew what I doing…except me. I was overreacting. I was acting insane and overdoing it; I could not stop. As we get closer to the border Christine says she doesn't have her driver's license, which means we can't cross into Mexico. We turn around and stop at a gas station. My anger had worsened and resulted in me cursing out Christine, my hurt feelings relegating me to act this way toward her. We drove back to base; our night was over.

I quiet down, texting Christine, who was right behind me, that I was sorry. She responded with, "I don't want to talk about it." She would be granted that request. We got to my barracks and I got to my room. I prepared the bed for her to sleep in; she was to spend the night. I was going to spend the night on the floor. Five minutes pass, no Christine or Eric. Ten minutes pass, then thirty minutes. Finally Eric comes into the room and says, "Dude, she's not coming."

Eric was outside trying to convince Christine that my outburst was my way of showing pain. She told him she didn't want to be near me, not after that. He told her, "Don't go where I think you're going." He was referring to the barracks where my Marines stayed. As he was telling me this, Eric could see how much it hurt me; he did everything he could to get me over the pain. I called Christine, left her voicemails pleading with her. I got no response all night, until the next morning when she met me outside my room.

We went for a walk around base, something we had planned on doing beforehand. It was during this walk that Christine and I had a heart to heart, trying to clear things up. I explained how it was hard for me to deal with this while heading back to Iraq. I explained how it was hard for me to be dealing with the possibility of losing someone who meant so much to my post war recovery. After our walk and Christine had gone home, Eric says to me, "I don't like her." He has always been honest with me. "I'm only nice to her because you care about her so much bro, but I don't like her because of what she does to you." He wasn't referring to her actually doing things to me; it was how our relationship was affecting me. It wasn't healthy for me.

By spending the night at my Marine's room, Christine forever left doubt in my mind. The last time I had a relationship with a friend who liked another Marine, it didn't end well and luckily for me, Eric was around for that too. The friend and I parted ways because things became secretive, and the Marine could care less either way for her. I remember asking Christine, "Is this relationship worth destroying us?"

It was time to head east, time to drive to Massachusetts to meet Eric's family and to watch the Super Bowl from Boston. With Eric and I both driving we got to Philadelphia in forty-eight hours, New York the next day, and then a few days later we arrived in Massachusetts. On this ride I played a soundtrack one of the Marines made for a picture and video montage of the war. One of the songs was called "The Angry American," and it suited me; it was how I felt. I must have played the song about fifty times.

When Eric was asleep, I would contact Christine by phone. I didn't want him to know. I'd talk to her a little, trying to be nice and mend hurt feelings. I was a shell of myself, lacking confidence, and all I could think about was how fragile I was even after all I had been through. How insignificant this all was in the grand scheme of things, but it consumed my every being.

While in New York we went for drinks with an old friend of mine from childhood. He had just gotten back from Iraq himself. He was there as a contract hired interpreter. He made good money, but I could see he was completely different now. He was also Yemeni, married and had children. He was once religious but there we all were, drinking, smoking, and talking about going back. Whatever we were before the war as kids was long gone; we were no longer innocent. We were young in number, but ancient in experience.

I met Eric's family; they were loving and so kind. They were more parental than my parents and it was so strange to see. Being around them toned down the flame of darkness burning inside me. There was a moment of bliss where I could think clearly, now that I was away from the chaos that I had caused for myself. I called Christine and told her that everything would be alright, that I was just going through a dark time but that it would be okay. She sounded confused by the phone call, probably because I sounded so calm and happy. She asked if I was drunk. I wasn't. I told her that I would call her when I got back to California.

I headed back to New York before going back to California. It was here that I would be leaving my cousin's car. I parked it in a spot where it got two tickets, but I didn't care. My father didn't like my cousin which meant I didn't like my cousin; he could pay for it when he picked it up. I met my childhood friend again before my flight home and had a few beers before he took me to the airport. Things just didn't feel right though. I needed alcohol to suppress pain that I thought I had a handle on. Being drunk made it easier, made me more tolerable of others. I checked into the airport, laughing and completely drunk. I tell the lady checking me in, "I'm going to Iraq next week, aren't you happy for me?" She smiled and thanked me for my service. I look at the ticket and hand it back to her.

"Ma'am, don't you know that I am Arab? Don't you think I should be *randomly* selected to be screened?"

She looks at the ticket and says that I should be fine.

I continue, "No, I would feel safer if you searched me. Everyone would feel safer if you searched me. I am not offended; you have to be sure, you know?"

She takes my ticket and marks it so that I would be searched. I go through the extra layer of screening and am cleared to go. My name is announced over in the airport for all to hear asking me to board. I stumble and get to my gate, telling everyone I see, "Hi, I'm a Marine and headed back to Iraq."

I board and sit in my seat when the flight attendant announces, "Ladies and gentlemen I'd like to let you know that we have a Marine on board and he is deploying to Iraq next week."

There is applause, but I don't pay attention. My head is leaned against the window and I fall asleep.

By going on the one week trip to Philadelphia, New York, and Boston, I had hoped I would cure whatever it was that was bothering me and thought things with Christine would be on the up and up. I wanted to head back to work ready to deploy. By now we had made up all the rosters. We had the names of all Marines who would deploy and the names of the Marines who would be staying behind due to their contracts expiring or orders they would have to execute, sending them elsewhere. Everything was different; we had a new command element on every level. The only constant was the Master Gunz as the senior enlisted man in our platoon and me as the platoon sergeant.

One last inspection!

My Marines get up at 0400, lay out their gear, gear that they would never use but had to bring because the Marine Corps issued it to them. I observe how they set up their gear and inspect it before the battalion commander goes through for the final inspection. I send my Marines to chow, telling them to get their breakfast while the sergeants stay behind. They are my Marines; I dictate how they do things. The acting company gunnery sergeant tells one of my sergeants to do something and he refuses. He tells the Gunny, "Sorry Gunny, but I was told to stay here by my platoon sergeant, and I am following his orders." The Gunny gets pissed at him and looks over at me and says, "Staff Sergeant, he's going to do what I tell him."

"No. Sorry Gunny, he's not..."

After saying that to the Gunny he snaps his fingers and points his index finger at me, as if I was a recruit in Marine Corps Basic Training. Sure, I was junior to him, but as a staff NCO, there is a way you address another staff NCO, especially in front of other Marines. As soon as he points his finger at me I pounce, headed right for him and I get in his face.

"These are my Marines. I don't fuck with your Marines, so you don't fuck with mine. Also, I am a staff NCO, just like you. I demand the same respect you demand, so before you go snapping your finger at me, think about what the repercussions will be!"

He was a cook; his whole mission in the Marine Corps was to serve chow to hungry Marines who do work. He wanted to feel good about himself and impress the new first sergeant. I cannot stand individuals who feel the need to impress others senior to them, especially when you're a senior Marine yourself. I got my way, but he wouldn't shut up about it. When our new first sergeant came to our battalion and then company, there was something familiar about him. When he first called the company to attention, that's when I remembered him. It was October of 1996, Marine Corps boot camp, Parris Island, South Carolina. He was a staff sergeant at the time, and he was the battalion drillmaster. My senior drill instructor received commands from him and before he began to march us, he said under his breath, "Fucking asshole." He didn't like him.

So now, nearly eight years after that, he was standing in front of us, saying things that were borderline gay. Calling us "hard dicks" and other things like that. "How you doing there, hard dick?" he would ask a Marine. It wasn't normal; at least I didn't think so. Say what you will about him though, he was locked on. He made the other staff NCOs aware that they couldn't get away with their normal shit. He was someone I could see eye to eye with.

Well after our little spat, the Gunny went crying to the first sergeant. A few days later I am told that I would be standing an inspection, that my gear would be inspected. I, a staff non-commissioned officer, would be standing an inspection. One of the perks of being a staff NCO was that you didn't have to do shit like that. You served your time, you did your duties, now it was the time to inspect, not be inspected. I had a day to get my things together, but I got it all set up and waited for the first sergeant to inspect me. I waited for hours; he was making a point to keep me waiting. It didn't bother me though, if he thought it would stop me from defending myself or my Marines he had another thing coming. He sent the newly permanently assigned company gunnery sergeant instead, a fellow staff sergeant, to inspect me. The staff sergeant admitted I was being inspected because of what I had done, but he told me that he agreed with what I had done to defend my Marine.

This guy was older than me by about ten years, and he had also been a staff sergeant for about six years longer. He was passed over for promotion and would tell everyone who had ears why he thought he got passed over. What he didn't know was that I remembered him from a year before. He was the vehicle commander of one of the vehicles that took me to question some Iraqis at one position we were holding. The same spot where the Iraqis came to me complaining that their money had been stolen. From that brief moment that I met him in Iraq, I remember thinking one thing, *That guy is an asshole.* I passed with flying colors. The first sergeant didn't know who I was and who he was dealing with. All he knew was that there was a staff sergeant in the company who mouthed off to a gunnery sergeant; he didn't want to have that going on.

Now a day away from deployment, I go to see Christine one last time. This time I had something for her. It was the 21st of February, the next day at around 3:00 a.m., we would be doing what we had done a year earlier…meeting at the armory and getting our weapons. So basically, late that night we would be doing just that. I would meet Christine for a good-bye dinner. It was at this dinner that I spoke of something my mother had told me. I told her what my mom had said about screaming at the television thinking it was me, dead in front of her face. How it tortured her. I cried because I realized I was probably the only person leaving for Iraq that could not tell his family. I would be going there without their thoughts and wishes. Even though they showed me no love when I went to see them, they should still know something. She was the only one that it felt like I could talk to about this, and I lost my composure.

She saw, at that moment, what was going on with me. I had not fully recovered from the first time going to Iraq, and not even nine months later, I was headed back. I told her at that moment that I was scared. Scared that if I died, my family would have said good-bye to me disappointed. Hours from deployment and I was now admitting this—great way to head off to combat.

I hand over a wrapped gift. It was a CD from 3 Doors Down and the album was named "Away from the Sun." I tell her to open it on her birthday and only then, play track number six and only that track.

It was the 21st of February 2004; Christine's birthday was on the 31st of May. I gave her a hug and said good-bye to her, telling her, "Don't forget, on your birthday…" She said she understood and we parted ways.

The opening lyrics to the song on track six?

"A hundred days have made me older, since the last time that I saw your pretty face."

It was the 21st of February, in 100 days it would be Christine's birthday. Yup, I'm a sucker.

But at least I cared.

Chapter 26

Déjà Vu

Yogi Berra once said, "It's like déjà vu all over again." That's what it felt like, getting up early just to get our weapons from the armory and to wait for the buses that would take us to the Air Force base we came back home from just nine months earlier. It was now 4:00 a.m. I checked out both my pistol and rifle and waited by my gear. It was 7:00 a.m. on the East Coast; I try to call a few people to say good-bye to them and to take care of themselves. At the end of each call I would ask the person on the other side, "Please, while we're there, continue to live your life, continue to take things for granted. Act as if nothing matters because your job is not to worry about reality, that's our job."

I saw the value and worth in insignificance. It would be a shield from what really mattered, protecting the ignorant from the cold world outside their view. I envied everyone who complained about a phone bill or a student loan. I envied anyone who worried about things they shouldn't really worry about because they didn't have to worry about the things I, or any other Marine, had to.

I gathered my Marines and loaded them onto the buses. We drove north this time, not south like we had a year before. I looked at the Marines as I counted them individually; some of them were not even old enough to drink legally. Half of them were new to the Corps, joining the Marines after September 11. They were all heroes in my eyes; they'd all joined knowing they would be utilized in combat, protecting their country from terror. Except this time they wouldn't be protecting their country or their people. We were being sent to police the country of Iraq, to "unfuck" the problem the Army had caused by using tactics that separated us from them. We were sent to win the hearts and minds of the Iraqi people, to show them that we are Marines. We would be firm, fair, and courteous; but we possessed the ability to level a city with sheer ferocity. We invested so much in distinguishing ourselves from the Army; the Marine Corps issued us all the new desert pattern of uniform that only the Marines possessed. I looked at myself through a reflection of the bus driver's rear view mirror; I looked too clean, everything was new.

As we drove away, Marines who would be staying behind waved at us, sending us off. How nice of them to show up as early as they did. They must have gone back home afterward to get some sleep. They needed as much rest as they could get. They would be dealing with the wives of the Marines who would deploy. A chain of command for the wives was developed; they would be in contact with the Marines who were left behind. I did not envy them. Nearly half of the Marines who deployed with us last year had gotten divorced. I looked back at the wives crying as we left and I remembered what I had thought a year before. How many of these women would be cheating on their husbands while they were away? How many marriages would be destroyed because of this deployment? How many relationships would end because the wife or girlfriend found a way to justify her actions?

I called more friends on the way to the Air Force base. My battery began to die so I cut short my conversations and saved it for one last call. I saved it so I could talk to Christine before I left. While on the bus I couldn't help but look at the faces of the Marines. For some of them this was their first time over there. For others like me, it would be a return. I felt sorry for those who were first timers; I knew they would never be the same again.

I had called my family a few days before, telling them I was deploying to the Philippines and that calls would be few and far between. I shake my head thinking how crazy it is that I had to keep my deployment a secret. Everyone knew the dangers I would put my family through if anyone in Yemen found out I was going to Iraq. My command knew what this meant for me, but that was not a worry for them; they could use me out there.

We get to the Air Force base and go through a process that was unlike anything I had ever seen before. I don't think we were the first Marines these guys had seen that were going back. They must have had some go through a few days or weeks before because of the way it was set up. It was designed to make us feel good about ourselves, that we were going to Iraq to do the right thing, to do what was in the best interest of our country. The ones telling us this were former service men and women, dressed in civilian attire, wearing baseball caps distinguishing what war they served in. They were experts at putting us through this wringer of sorts. They shuttled us through and made room for more. I felt like cattle all over again. I moo for effect.

I tried to call Christine, no answer. I wouldn't be able to say good-bye to her; I was still a bit upset over all that had taken place. I wished I could have left on better terms, but Christine promised me she would be there when I got back. I didn't have anyone to greet me when I returned last time, and it would be a nice change to have someone to welcome me home. Every returning Marine, sailor, soldier, and airman should be welcomed home by someone. I knew firsthand what it was like to not be.

Boarding the plane was a surreal moment for me. It was as if the last few months back home hadn't really happened. It was as if it was just a dream, and I would wake up back in the misery I had felt months ago. As I got to the top step, I stopped and turned around, looking at the California morning sky. I looked at the roads with cars stuck in traffic. Did any of them care that I was going back? I felt really small. Marines behind me stared at me, wondering what the hell it was that I was doing. I turned around and went inside. There were no seating arrangements made this time around. Staff NCOs and officers took whatever was available in business and first class. I found the first seat in first class, a nice way to be traveling. I wondered to myself, *Did Marines fly first class on their way to take part in World War II?* I put my weapons in a nice compartment to the left of my seat, telling myself to not forget them when I would leave the plane upon arrival.

This time around everyone carried a rifle with them. Our battalion commander made sure we all carried them. I chuckled as I watched others fuddle with their rifles, asking flight attendants to stow them away. This wasn't a coat or a sports jacket. You don't ask the flight attendant to take your gun and hang it up for you.

As we took off, I looked out the window at the life everyone called mundane and unexciting. I hoped I'd get to see it again. I looked down and wondered where Christine was in that mess of cars, trucks, buildings, and homes. I hoped I'd get to see her again.

I slept during the flight. This would be the best accommodation I would get until I returned to the United States; I had better take advantage of it. We stopped in Prague for a refuel. I took this opportunity to spend time with Marines who were taken from my platoon and put in other platoons for this deployment. We sat in a smoking lounge, probably the last in existence, and we filled the room with smoke. The ratio of oxygen to cigarette smoke was probably one to ten. But the cigarettes were needed; I was on edge. After I had a smoke with them, I bought a giant pack of cigarettes that should last me a month.

As we got closer to Kuwait, all I could think about was my prior experience there. I expected to sleep in filth, to freeze in the morning, and eat slop that was sandy in nature. Who would be the first person to piss me off and over what this time? Would someone try to lay their hands on me? If so, how will I react this time around?

We touched down and there is silence, no cheers, no applause. There is a subdued nature going through the plane, even the flight attendants were quiet with a look of worry on their faces. I had seen this look before; I saw it a year ago, painted on the faces of the sailors who bid us farewell. I got off the plane and walked down the steps to a bus. It was cold and dark. We arrived at night. The bus took us to a large receiving tent where a video played for hundreds of troops who had just landed. It didn't feel like it was really happening, but yes, we were indeed there, we were back, and holy shit it fucking sucked again. After a few hours we got back on the buses and headed for our camps, off to somewhere in the vicinity of LSA-5. Great...

The bus ride to our camp was long. The bus driver shut the lights off inside so we could sleep. This ride could have been eight years ago and I wouldn't have been able to tell the difference. In 1996 I was on a bus much like this one and everyone there had their heads leaned forward against the seat in front of them. Back then, when we stopped, a Marine drill instructor got on and welcomed us to recruit training and demanded we, "Get off my bus!" We stumbled and rushed to get off, our lives forever different. This time around, when our bus stopped, the company gunnery sergeant got on, a former Marine drill instructor himself, and tried to do and say the same thing. I rolled my eyes and gathered my things slowly and carefully. Sorry buddy, not this time.

It was now 5:00 a.m. The sun was rising. A few Marines from my platoon were already there, greeting me and a few of the others. We get inside a tent and to my shock it was warm, there were heaters. I looked around and there were cots for us to lie in. What was this place? Oh, and to add to things, there was a mess hall within walking distance, and the food was great.

Okay, so maybe it wouldn't be so bad after all. One of the stipulations I had asked for, if I were to withdraw my separation request and deploy, was that I not be used as an interpreter. I had been promised that by the same man who had promised me an award for my performance last year. I would be able to lead my Marines, and I wouldn't be in harm's way as much. I could do this.

We would be staying in Kuwait for a week this time around. Last year it was an unknown and we had nothing there that would make you want to stay any longer than a day. This time around we had everything we could ask for. We had taken over this camp from the Army. Say what you will about them (and I most certainly will), but they sure do prepare for everything by bringing everything. There was even a Burger King and a Pizza Hut on this camp, "Be all that you can be, in the Aaaaaarrmy!"

Everyone got to Kuwait okay. The equipment had no issues getting there, and the advance party had everything taken care of. All that was left was to get the battalion coordinated by getting each Marine into a vehicle headed north. I had my rosters down precise. There were no mistakes, and there were no question marks. I could tell you the name of each Marine, what blood type they were, if they were married or single, and where they came from. I worked for hours to get this roster on point, and no one was going to change it. The other platoon sergeants in my company? Well, let's just say they weren't up to par. What they lacked in leadership, they made up for in ass kissing. One thing that I did not like about the staff NCO ranks was the lack of intestinal fortitude in some of these men. They were senior Marines, acting like junior Marines. I worked to get where I was because I wanted to be respected for what I had accomplished. Why did these guys want to be where they were?

After a formation in which the company first sergeant told the Marines they would standby and wait for their vehicle assignments, all of the staff NCOs stayed behind so we could figure it out. I had my list with me; I had it right there for all to see. I was prepared, unlike the others. The first sergeant handed the meeting over to the company gunny and walked away. This is where things got weird.

In this meeting were the platoon sergeants for every platoon in Headquarters and Service Company. My platoon had over eighty Marines. A few of the other platoons had the same amount. There were a couple that had less than ten. Yes, less than ten. It was the leadership of these platoon sergeants that was lacking, and we had to suffer for it. Because one of the smaller platoons had a platoon sergeant who was full of shit, the company gunny decided he would move Marines wherever he wanted to, including my own Marines. He started spouting off names and vehicles. Names that did not coincide with the vehicles I had already designated. This made it easy for those who didn't want to do work because he did it for them, but it fucked up my roster, and it would separate my Marines from each other. I wasn't going to have that.

As he rattles off more names I get frustrated and say, "No, we're not doing that. You're not moving my Marines around."

He looks up at me and says, "Shut the fuck up."

My eyes get larger out of shock and I begin to boil over. The other staff NCOs didn't have the balls to say anything for their Marines, and I get told to "shut the fuck up?" Out of the question!

"No, you will not move my Marines around. I don't care who the fuck you think you are. They are my Marines. You're the company gunny, but you do not tell me where my Marines go," I say with other staff NCOs looking on, interested to see where this would go.

"Stop, Hafid. You're being unprofessional," one of the platoon sergeants said. He was one of those who couldn't figure shit out which now caused this debacle.

Without even looking at him I put my hand up to shut him up and say, "You don't need to be speaking right now, so mind your own fucking business." This was the same guy who gave me shit on the ship a year ago; so he doesn't know what professionalism is.

Now the company gunny, a fellow staff sergeant, loses his mind. He sees that I am not afraid of his antics, and that I am not afraid of his words. He makes a scene larger than the head on his shoulders and tells anyone within shouting distance, "I'm going to fuck this motherfucker up. Hold my weapon."

I stand my ground. The other staff NCOs, as ball-less as they could be, back up and one even takes his weapon.

"I'm right here, motherfucker. Why don't you stop talking and do something?" I say to him as he paces in circles. He was all talk, and I knew it. If he were to lay a hand on me, I would have murdered him. I was not in the mood to be fucked with.

"Staff Sergeant, get your fucking weapon! Get your fucking weapon, right fucking now! You're fucking embarrassing yourself!

Get your fucking weapon and get the fuck out of here!" barks the Master Gunz to the company gunny.

My Master Gunz watched as this unfolded. After twenty-five plus years of service, he knew who was at fault. The meeting was over. My Marines were not moved. I looked at the other platoon sergeants and staff NCOs that had done nothing with disgust. They were my peers? These guys couldn't lead a horse to water if they were standing in a swimming pool.

I now had the battalion on notice, I was the staff sergeant that didn't take shit from anyone, and if crossed, I would fight back. The company gunny was told to stay away from me until further notice; he was a pathetic individual who used embarrassment to get his way. It would not work on me; it would never work on me.

Word got around fast; it was just like a year before. Marines were giving me more motivated greetings as a way of thanks for embarrassing a piece of shit who was a bully with staff sergeant chevrons. I went over to the Master Gunz and apologized. I didn't like the fact that a senior Marine of his time and experience had to intervene when there were others there. I asked him if I was wrong, and he says, "Absolutely not. You were doing the job we chose you to do." He was referring to my platoon sergeant duties.

An hour later the first sergeant calls me over to his tent, "That's two, Staff Sergeant," he says to me, referring to the amount of times I had argued with one of his company gunny's. I explained my actions to the first sergeant and told him, "Listen, First Sergeant. I have a job to do, just like your company gunny, but once he crossed the line, what did you expect me to do?"

"Noted, Staff Sergeant, just be mindful," he said as he walked off, dialing a phone number on a satellite phone he had with him.

There wasn't much for us to do while in Kuwait, if we weren't waiting in line for three hours for a pizza or burger, we were in the tents reading or watching movies. I bought a Sports Illustrated magazine with Alex Rodriguez on the cover, donning Yankee pinstripes. A week earlier the Yankees made a trade right from under the Red Sox' noses, so I was beaming as I showed everyone the face of the new Yankee dynasty. I spent my time reading every page of that magazine, reading everything baseball related; I would be missing the entire season.

A day before we got to our staging area, the battalion called in a chaplain I had never seen before. The chaplain is not the regular

Christian type, but of the Muslim persuasion. He talked to each company, and at the end of each formation, he would take a few questions. He spoke about the similarities between Islam and Christianity. Even though I was listening to him with open ears, no one else gave a shit. Islam was a religion of terror to them, not "a religion of peace" as the chaplain had put it. I had been fighting with myself from the moment I joined the Marine Corps about whether or not I was going against my faith by being a Marine. I had been told many times, by Muslims within the Corps, that I was not, but Islam clearly states that Muslims do not kill other Muslims. To do so guarantees hell-fire. I felt as if I were doomed.

No one spoke to the Chaplain but me and one other Marine, a fellow Arab, a Kuwaiti that the battalion had received nine months earlier. I could have used him a few months sooner. The other Marines paid no mind to this chaplain. In their eyes, Allah was a God of different worship. The ignorance was thick. I approached the Chaplain and asked, "Am I doing the right thing, sir? Am I a good Muslim?" He told me that I was, that I was helping Muslims by doing my duties as a Marine. It sounded like a recruiting pitch, but so be it. I asked for his information, so I could contact him when all this was over. I wanted to seek guidance, and I wanted to learn more about our faith and God.

The battalion XO called me into his tent with my platoon commander and a few other platoon commanders from my company. He had heard about my outburst with the company gunny and wanted to deal with the platoon commanders, since we couldn't come to terms. I was the only platoon sergeant there. He asked questions and mentioned serial numbers and vehicle types. I had answers to everything. At the end of the meeting we kept the rosters as they were and he pulled me aside.

"Staff Sergeant, I was impressed by how much you knew. You seem to have it under control. I had heard otherwise," he confessed to me.

"Sir, I am a Marine staff sergeant, if I can't figure out how to assign my Marines to vehicles, and if I can't make sure my roster is accurate, I shouldn't be a staff sergeant in the United States Marine Corps."

He nodded his head and smiled. As he walked away I said, "Sir, what about that award you promised me? It's been a while now."

"Oh yeah, don't worry Staff Sergeant. I'll get it done. Should be easier once we get in country," he said as he patted me on the shoulder. I walked back to my tent and laid down on my cot. My equipment was packed and my Marines were ready to go. I had lost whatever relationship I had (which was none) with the staff NCOs of the company, but I had the backing of those in my platoon.

Marines around me made noise from the packing and the talking they were doing. They were loud and motivated, only Marines could be for this. I felt back in my element, smarter and more experienced from all that had happened a year before. I had been there and done that. There would be nothing I wasn't ready for. I closed my eyes and drowned out the noise around me by putting headphones on, playing the soundtrack of the year before. A familiar song, a song that had symbolized my love for the country and Corps played, and I smiled as I drifted away to sleep. Tomorrow would begin the sequel of the Marine Corps' mission in Iraq. We are Marines, proud and prepared for anything. It was time to shine.

CHAPTER 27

The Road to Whatever Lies Ahead

My platoon commander was filling shoes bigger than his own. He replaced a Marine that we all loved and would die for, so that couldn't be easy. Another thing he had going against him, he was a short fellow. He had little feet too, I am sure. I was sure he'd try to win us over by performance, but to me he talked too much and said things that rubbed me and a few of the others the wrong way. It could be that he came in under bad circumstances, or it could be that he was just not that likable.

Before we staged our vehicles for departure, he talked to the platoon—Marines he barely knew or probably even cared to know. There were more than eighty Marines, and I knew all of their names; he probably knew about ten. I remember standing behind my Marines as he pulled out his journal from his previous deployment. He was with a support unit. He didn't see much action, but he wanted to tell the Marines a story from what he did see.

He encouraged the Marines to take down notes, to write their own journals, to remember their experience as he remembered and was reading from his. As he read from his journal, I could only shake my head in a disapproving manner. What was he trying to accomplish here? He read it as if he was reading the Marines a bedtime story. I could tell what they were thinking—this was a show, this was a display of, "look at me, I care." You don't show you care through words. You show you care by actually giving a shit.

After reading from his journal, the platoon commander walked away; I had the Marines' attention now. I went over the events and how long it should take to get to where we were going. We would be going to Al Qaim, located in the Al Anbar Province. It was near the border with Syria, and to get there we would be driving for three days. I must have had it out for myself because I put myself in a vehicle with the platoon commander, the gunnery sergeant I had an argument with a year before, and our driver was a Marine who was a religious fanatic homophobe hell-bent on "putting a bullet between the eyes" of anyone who was gay. Thank goodness he didn't know I was tolerant of gays.

At the staging area I worked with the homophobe and the gunny to install steel doors on our vehicle. Once again, the Marine Corps had done nothing to fortify our vehicles. Sandbags and steel doors with no windows would be our line of defense against IED's blowing up on the side of the road. While putting the final touches on the door, the company gunny, who had been told to stay away from me, approached with a smile on his face.

"Hey, I heard you have some *reading material* that you'd let me borrow," he said to me. He was referring to porn that I had brought with me. I had a few porn DVDs from the year before and a few others that I had downloaded while I was back in the United States. That coward thought he could come up to me acting as if nothing happened. I guess this was his way of apologizing.

"Bring it back when you're done," I said as I handed the DVDs to him without looking in his direction.

I could feel his shit-eating grin. Much like him, it was fake. As he walked away my platoon commander comes up to me and makes a stupid comment, "I see you two kissed and made up?"

"No sir, he's still a douchebag," I responded, causing him to look at me oddly. I don't think he knew who I was or what he had as a platoon sergeant. You're going to get an honest response from me. If he wanted a "yes man" to smile and nod, then he needed to replace me immediately.

"Can we go now?" I asked as we waited. We were lined up in rows of vehicles called "sticks." We were one of the last sticks to leave and when we finally did, I sat back to enjoy the ride, as if that was even possible. This would be nothing like the drive into Iraq the first time, when it was dark and fires blazed everywhere. This time around it was daylight, and we were driving through as Marines took pictures for their photo albums. "Amateurs," I would say to myself, my platoon commander also taking a photograph of the border entrance. Maybe he'd add it to his journal.

We pushed through and I shook my head. The last nine months had not happened; it was all a dream. This country was just messing with my mind; it let me go for a short while, just so I could get a small taste of what it was like to be home. Now it was calling me back, not done fucking with my head. When we passed through towns this time, kids would line the streets, walking away from the soccer game they were playing. There were no thumbs being raised in the air in approval, just silence and stares. Things had seriously changed, and I could see it already. When we stopped I talked to some of the Iraqis. They asked who we were because our uniforms were different. I explain that we were Marines. "We're not like the US Army," I said.

They nod and I bid them farewell as I get back in my vehicle. The people watch us as we continue going north, counting our personnel, measuring us for what had to be an attack in the near future. They looked confused. We looked different, and we had different vehicles, but who were we? Even though I would tell them we were Marines, they didn't know the difference; we were just Americans to them.

The first day nothing happened; we arrived at our first staging area and rested for the night. I didn't like the looks I was reading from the people; they really didn't want us around, especially now that they were sure Saddam was no longer a threat. Day two saw nothing as well. We got to a place called Al Asad, Arabic for the word lion. We slept on the ground, even though the camp had tents and trailers that soldiers used as living quarters. The next morning the first sergeant decided to have fun with me. "Hey Staff Sergeant, let's get this place cleaned up."

He was referring to the trash Marines had thrown on the ground. I was to ensure the Marines cleaned the desert. I walked from one end to the other, giving Marines orders to clean up. I spent the morning ensuring this took place while others went to the mess hall to have some breakfast. I missed breakfast that morning. It was okay though; I had my MREs in the vehicle, chicken tetrazzini had never let me down.

This would be the last day of the three-day drive up to Al Qaim. There was no word of any casualties. No IED's had gone off; Marines began to relax. When we would pull over to the side of the road for a break, Marines would take pictures with their digital cameras that they would use for this new site called MySpace. Marines would also wander from their vehicles and engage with

Iraqis, offering them money for things Iraqis were selling and paying $10 dollars for Iraqi money with Saddam Hussein on it.

One of my Marines showed off some of the items and money he had purchased to other Marines. Seeing it, I asked him where he got it from. He pointed in the distance to an Iraqi man with items that could be anything. What the fuck was going on here? We were not on a fucking vacation or on a tour of Iraq; this was a fucking combat situation! Not to take a page from the last year, but people were dying.

I looked up and down the column of vehicles that made up our convoy, and I saw more Marines making these purchases. We were setting ourselves up for an ambush, to get punched in the dick, and it would fucking hurt. We were not flanked by tanks or even LAVs. We were a support element of a combat battalion, and the combat element of said battalion? It was nowhere near us.

If your leadership does something, then it must be ok. There were a few Marine staff NCOs just as guilty of buying things from these questionable people, if not more; the junior Marines would follow their lead. I asked my platoon commander to radio the company commander directing the Marines to get back to their vehicles, to stay alert. Before he could even make the command I yelled out, "Where the fuck do you think you're at, Wal-Mart?"

We finally moved forward and not too long after, an IED went off, hitting one of our vehicles ahead. We stopped and assessed the situation. It hit a vehicle, but no one was seriously hurt. There was the first sign it was real. We pushed forward again and then shit began to fall apart. One of the vehicles ahead had an accident; the Marines inside had to be medically evacuated. We were stranded on the road for hours. We fell behind schedule. Half of the battalion had gotten to Al Qaim already, and we were an undisclosed distance away. It's not like there were road signs and exits to get where we had to go.

The delay occurred because we were in an area that made it difficult to get the injured Marines out. We weren't in an open area; it was hilly and dark. An airlift could not be made where the accident took place; to do that would jeopardize those trying to assist. I don't know how they got the Marines out, but eventually we were on the road again. I was exhausted; it was now dark and cold. I couldn't read my magazine or think about what the Yankee lineup would look like for the 2004 season. I could only cross my arms and try to warm myself up as I drifted away to dreamland.

When I wake up we had arrived. I got out of my vehicle and followed someone to a building only because his voice sounded familiar. They led me to a room where there were bunk beds without mattresses, just bed frames. I got on one of them; I didn't even undress or remove my boots. I closed my eyes and tried to sleep, but there was too much going on. When the sun came up I was able to see where I was. We were in an abandoned train station, a huge building that was completely stripped and empty. The room I had tried to sleep in was where they would be installing the battalion first aid station, so that would not be a place I would be resting my head. A morning meeting with the staff NCOs was held by the company first sergeant, getting a count of all the Marines. I was groggy and unaware of things so I was pretty much useless.

The Army had made this train station a base of sorts; it would be our home for at least seven months. There were tents set up where Marines would be staying, and there were bed frames thrown around in complete disarray. Marines were scattered around, lying on the filthy ground, trying to sleep. The Army did not make things easy for our arrival. We had to fend for ourselves, and frankly, we expected it.

It took a few hours for me to gather myself; once I did, I got my Marines together and began planning out where we would stay. We spent the first day setting up those bed frames and laying our sleeping bags on them, cleaning and setting up lighting. We were to stay here for a few months; we needed to make it our home. The soldiers were never to be seen; they hid in an office that would be ours once they left. I took a look inside and the soldiers inside gave me a dirty look. I turned right back around and headed to our sleeping area.

I held a formation, the first my platoon would have in Iraq. I welcomed the Marines to what I called, "home." By now we had set up things in a neat and orderly fashion, I could go out and explore what was around, so I could relay the information to the men. There was an Internet center in the camp; I was completely shocked. I waited in line for my turn and logged into a computer trying to get on AOL Instant Messenger. It was here where I saw Nicole; she had become scarce the past few weeks before deployment. I said hello and told her I had just arrived in Iraq. We chatted for a little bit before she told me that her boyfriend didn't want her speaking to me. She said that she had to listen to him because I'm just some guy on the Internet. I was pissed off but whatever. "Good-bye," it would be.

Christine signed in soon after, and I messaged her. She didn't believe it was me until I told her about the last dinner we had, about the conversation I had about my mother and how I reacted in front of her. She responded with an emphatic, "OMG!" To my dismay, I spent most of my allotted half-hour getting told by Nicole that I could no longer be friends with her; my time had run out. I told Christine to write me, that I missed her and loved her, but I had to go.

I headed back to where my Marines were. They had gotten their areas squared away even further. I told them where the Internet center was and almost immediately they scattered. I took time to gather my things and setup shop. Marines would come and go, greeting me, shooting the shit with me, but ultimately everyone would go and do something while I stayed behind with time to myself.

It was at that moment when I thought I was alone that one of my younger Marines, a quiet and soft-spoken kid named Rudy, came up to me. He was young and full of potential, newly promoted to the rank of corporal. He looked shaken up, saddened by something. He had just come back from the Internet center; I could only imagine what had happened. He said, "Excuse me, Staff Sergeant. Do you have a minute?"

I said, "Sure!"

He sits down and begins to speak. "Staff Sergeant, what would you do if your girlfriend told you that she didn't know if she wanted to be with you anymore? That she didn't think she could do it?"

Without hesitation I responded, "Dude, you're twenty years old. You have your whole life ahead of you. You're doing outstanding in the Marine Corps and when we're done here, you'll go out to the Marine Security Guard program and see the world. Fuck 'em. If you're not good enough for them now, you'll never be, and believe me dude, you're awesome!"

He smiles and says, "Thank you, Staff Sergeant." He walks away confident and feeling better.

I smile and shake my head thinking, *Kids*. I thought I had done well, that I had given him some good advice. Had I known he would die two months later, I would have said something different.

Chapter 28

The Boring End of an Era

The Marines of my platoon were not killers or warriors in the sense that they were on the front lines kicking ass and taking names, they were support Marines. They were mechanics, technicians, engineers, electricians, and any other maintenance related type of occupation. What I loved most about my Marines was that we were all close; no matter what color, race, or religion any of us were, we were all green in each other's eyes.

The Army pulled out of Al Qaim, and we went right to work. The office they were hiding in would be stripped and cleaned of everything they would leave behind. We came up with a game plan as to how we were going to set up this office. It was a lot of work just to clean up, but it was during the cleanup that the personality of my Marines would come out. I could take all the credit and say that the Marines took on my personality, but that would be a lie. They had a personality of their own; the only thing I did was gave them the freedom and confidence to be themselves.

The soldiers left behind a lot of things: clothes, books, even medals. The Army gives away medals for just about anything. There's a ribbon in the Army that is given to a soldier for throwing a grenade. I am not kidding, look it up. There was a medal the soldiers left behind in the office that we found as we were cleaning. It was passed around and each one of us there had a look of confusion, "What the fuck is that?"

With most of the office cleaned up, the Marines took a break. Marines are a proud bunch; they'll complain about some of the little things we do, but ultimately there is not one Marine who would trade their uniform for the uniform of another branch of service. We make fun of other services, and sometimes we play it out in the form of an act worthy of an Oscar. When Marines get an award for valor or service, they are called front and center by the commanding officer, while their citation is read off by a first sergeant or sergeant major. The Marines decide to put on an act, a short one depicting a medal being awarded to an Army soldier. Rudy, obviously feeling better, and another Marine played the Army first sergeant and the commanding officer respectively. One of my sergeants played the role of an Army sergeant being awarded for being a soldier. Another Marine played himself, and he would be the one who would pin on the award.

Rudy stood to the left of the Marine playing the commanding officer. They called the "soldier" front and center. The "soldier" salutes, and does so without a cover. A cover for you civilians out there is a hat. Marines do not salute without a cover. Whenever I am asked why, I say, "Cause we're not the fucking Army." It's a simple answer for a simple question.

As this goes on, I drift to a past memory when not wearing a cover was important…

President Bush is announced on a stage that I am already positioned on. He greets the Secretary of State, the Ambassador to China, the Consul General of Shanghai and salutes me, the Marine sergeant. I did not have a cover on. I was indoors. This was going on in China, so I do a little bow, acknowledging the President. I did not salute the President of the United States in front of a large crowd because it is not within the customs and courtesies that they teach us in the Corps. This probably pissed the President off because after his speech and departure, he shakes my hand and gives me a look of, "You son of a bitch…"

He got me back later on that evening though. While taking photographs with him backstage, he steps on my shoe, scuffing it. My only response to him was, "Dammit sir, you scuffed my shoe." It was the second time I had said something smart to the President. Earlier that day he introduced Colin Powell to me, as if I didn't know him. "Yes sir, I think I know who that is," I said, but I am digressing…

I smile as I watch the Marines having a good time making fun of Army customs. They act out the scene to perfection. A "soldier" is called to pin on the medal of "Soldierly Virtue" as we called it. As he reports, he leans forward and salutes, bringing a smile to the face of the "soldier" being awarded. He pins on the medal, pricking the "soldier" getting a soft spoken, "Oww," from him.

Rudy reads off the citation that he makes up as he goes along, starting and ending every sentence with the word "soldier," laughing as he gets near the end. At the end of the ceremony the "soldier" salutes the commanding officer. Rudy picks up a toy rifle that was found in the office, points it to the ceiling and yells, "BANG!" startling everyone who did not expect it and bringing us to tears. After that artistic display of acting, we get back to work.

The Army must not teach efficiency. They had set up offices within offices and had done so with plywood and two by fours that must have been put together by a blind person. We stripped all of these partitions and walls they had made, stack the wood neatly, and come up with a layout. Another staff sergeant and I had designed the office to be an office, a common area, a bedroom for the staff NCOs in our platoon, and for our platoon commander.

Before we started working on this, our platoon commander called us into a room our Master Gunz had commandeered. If he had been paying attention, he would have known that we had things already planned and had started setting up. I told him that the other staff sergeant and I were to put together the office. He then said, "Good. Make sure you make me a room in there. We'll use that as an office, and I'll stay in there, nothing too special."

This motherfucker wanted us to build him an office and a room for himself and not do any of the legwork? No one spoke up except me, "But sir, what about us?"

He looks at me and says that we'll be able to find room elsewhere. I was livid and he saw the scowl on my face. He then asked, "Staff Sergeant, if you have something to say, say it."

"Yes sir, I do actually. I think it's bullshit that you want us to build you a fucking office and a room for you to sleep in and then ask us to find some other place for us to sleep. We set that place up with plenty of room for all of us, and I just think it's bullshit, sir."

"Well, if you feel that way Staff Sergeant—"

"No sir, we all feel that way," I said to him, interrupting him causing him to jerk his head back in shock.

One of the gunnery sergeants spoke up and said that I had a point. There was nowhere else for us to go and we already had a plan in place.

Little people in charge don't like being questioned. Take Napoleon, for instance. Anyone who questioned him was killed. We were somewhat civil these days and he couldn't justifiably kill one of us, so he had no choice but to keep us happy. "Well fine, just make sure you leave me my own space, away from you guys."

"Don't worry sir; we'll take care of you. Marines look out for other Marines." I put it that way to piss him off; I wanted him to know I thought it was selfish of him to do that. As I left a few others stayed back and he admitted to them that I had a mouth on me. One of the staff sergeants later tells me this and says, "You fucking pissed him off!"

"I don't give a fuck! He could cry me a fucking river. He'll get over it!" From that point on I referred to him as Napoleon, even in front of the Marines.

The platoon commander disappeared for a day, making a trip south to Al Asad. I spent that day with another staff sergeant, building the office with living quarters. We made the platoon commander his very own bedroom; out of spite I made the doorway six feet high. Another Marine walked in, saw it and laughed. I just wanted him to know that he was a small man. I wanted him to know that respect comes with action and performance; he's just a little man to me.

One of the gunny's staying with us looks at the doorway and tells me to fix it. I refuse, saying that it's built structurally sound and that if he wants to change it, he can. I knew that by leaving it the way I built it, it would give the platoon commander ammunition, but he would have to prove that I meant it in a demeaning way. He'd be pissed off, but I really didn't care.

The gunny removes the two by four in the doorway and raises it higher. He knew it wasn't going to lead to good things, "He already doesn't like you, Hafid," he says to me as he nails it in place.

Within a day we had everything set up. The Marines had their living space, and we had ours. The platoon commander had his little squirrel hole in the corner. If I had acorns, I would have left him a pile. We could now function as a platoon, just far, far away from home.

When the other companies that we supported were out on patrols, there was nothing for us to do. For the first few weeks there was nothing, no casualties, no one shot at—nothing at all. Our battalion's mission was to patrol the border with Syria and to communicate with locals in the cities of Husaybah and Akashat. There was another base farther south that had the battalion split into two that patrolled that region, but there was nothing really out there for them.

I spent my days writing emails in Microsoft Word, so I could copy and paste them into an email, thus saving myself time to surf the Internet. While I was writing these emails, I would drink loads of Tang. I remembered how it was in Al Diwaniyah, sitting in a puddle of my own sweat. I didn't want to be dehydrated. The only problem was that I wasn't as active, and it wasn't hot just yet. I had to piss every hour, and it wasn't like I could hold it. I had to put on my gear to go out to piss, but I would have a hard time doing so because I was shaking from having to pee so bad. Marines would get out of my way, as I would rush by them, looking for the nearest portable toilet.

The Marine Corps was now in control. The first thing we did was change the names of all the camps we were occupying. The Army called them FOBs, which was short for Forward Operating Bases, but we're the fucking Marines, they're Camps to us. The Army had special names to go with the FOB. We just named it after the city we were located; it made it simple enough.

One thing the Army allowed was a few locals living on Camp. They set up a chicken market and would sell pizza and chicken to whoever was willing to pay a few dollars. As soon as the Marine Corps was fully in control of the Camp, they were kicked out. A few days later word spread that they were killed by insurgents for helping feed us. I believed it.

It was really boring the first few weeks. I wanted to be around my Marines, but there was nothing to do but sit around and watch movies. It was at that time that I realized I had a terrible selection of movies, and I wouldn't bother to watch them anymore. The Marines were in their living quarters watching movies and then started watching the television series, *24*. "Get me Jack Bauer!" one of the Marines yelled out without warning.

The card game spades was the most popular thing to do. Everyone would take part, and even I did one time, once I got a hang of the rules. I forgot them soon after. Food was served by the Marines who were led by the gunny I had an argument with before deployment, the same gunny who wanted to tell my sergeant what to do. Let's just say that the food was lacking, much like his leadership skills. I raided a box of MREs. I looked at the date displayed on the box and they were a few weeks old. These things were fresh! Chili mac was now my favorite meal.

So, all in all, things were going just fine, as we had expected, once we took over for the Army. There was nothing going on. I felt alone. I was without someone to talk to. The only time I would be able to say anything to anyone was through email, and that was only thirty minutes out of the day. I'd hear from Christine every now and then, but often I would open my inbox and not see a new email from her. Emails from others were nice, but they're different in comparison to a letter. There's just something more personal about a letter that makes you feel more loved.

I picked up a new talent. I took photographs of Marines without them expecting or knowing and I'd make a comic strip of them. There were some fellow staff NCOs that were loathed by the Marines, so I posted comic strips of them and hung it on the walls of their living quarters. There was one comic that had a staff sergeant fixing his collar while looking like he was in pain. The thing on this guy was that he would be a career Staff Sergeant, never to see the rank of Gunnery Sergeant because of his shitty attitude; everything was an excuse; everyone was out to get him. He talked up such a game that if you didn't know him, you'd believe him. The thing was he was a coward and a bully. He would tell stories about how he would blatantly disrespect senior Marines by telling them to go fuck themselves. Other stories were of hookups with the hottest women you could think of. Dude looked like Fred Flintstone. He was full of shit. Whenever someone senior with authority said something to him, he giggled and sucked cock like a champ, pathetic.

He was also not what you expected a Marine to be. Marines are physically fit, capable of doing things that no one would think to be necessary. It's in our nature as Marines. We're bored so often that we come up with stupid things to do. To test our physical skills, we have what is called a PFT or a Physical Fitness Test. This is an event where you are tested on pull-ups, crunches, and a three-mile run. He was one of those guys that would sleep in while I would take the Marines out each morning for a run. He couldn't do one pull-up, and when he would try he'd fall off the bar and grab his shoulder.

Well I didn't like this guy, as I am sure you can tell by my description. He was one of the two shitheads that gave me a hard time on the ship last year. He was the staff sergeant I took a picture of fixing his collar. Well, I had a picture of him talking it up with other Marines (all senior to him, imagine that), laughing and probably talking shit, so for that frame I had this caption, "So I told that Captain to go fuck himself…and he did."

Another frame had him saying, "I mean this girl was gorgeous! Tits so big they were out to here…. Moral of the story, I fucked her."

The final frame was of him fixing his collar looking as if he were in pain, "See it's the shoulder shtud (his way of saying 'stud'). If it were good, I could do twenty pull-ups easy."

These comics had my Marines on the floor dying with laughter. The best was when this staff sergeant comes over to the Marines' living quarters looking for me. He says, "Hey, the battalion commander is in our office. He wants to see you."

I tell him I'll be right there and before he walks out, he sees the comic of him posted on the wall and the Marines look the other way hoping he doesn't say anything to them and doesn't see them laughing. I smile, taking comfort in him knowing that it was I who made the comics, so he couldn't do shit to any of the Marines. Fucking bully.

I get to the office and the battalion commander is right there sitting down at the table waiting for me. He was dirty and looked tired. He knew some Arabic and spoke it to me.

"I need you to go out with Alpha Company in a few days; you'll be attached to them for their patrols."

Without hesitation I say in English, "Aye aye, sir!"

When he leaves Napoleon asks me why he was there to see me. I tell him that I would be gone for a week or so on patrol with Alpha Company. After that week, I would be back to assume my role as Platoon Sergeant.

I would show another staff sergeant what my duties were, and he would act on my behalf while I was away. I didn't mind going out every now and then, as long as I got to go back to my Marines, my men. I emailed Christine and a few others telling them that they wouldn't be hearing from me for a few days, and that I would be back soon. I said good-bye to my Marines and told them that I'd be back. If I had any packages, to leave them on my bed.

As I met the Marines of Alpha Company, Headquarters Platoon, I introduced myself as Staff Sergeant Hafid. Then out of humor with a bit of seriousness I said, "But call me Jo, short for Jose; I am from Puerto Rico. I don't want the locals knowing I am Arabic and have family in Yemen. They don't even know I'm here. Who knows what contacts some of these people have."

As we drive off early that morning I see some of my Marines headed to the mess hall for morning chow. I wave to them and they wave back. "See you next week!" I yell in their direction. Except that I wouldn't. That was my last day as platoon sergeant of Maintenance Platoon of Headquarters and Service Company; my time leading them was over.

Chapter 29

Jack Bauer Approves this Message

I hadn't left Camp since we first got there. So leaving and doing so during daylight gave me more of an idea of what was around us. Al Qaim must have been a busy train station. There was an endless amount of tracks and a yard filled with abandoned trains and passenger cars. Some of them were transformed into living quarters and office spaces. Marines waste nothing.

Light Armored Vehicles come in various types. There is the LAV-25, which has a 25mm cannon. There is the LAV-AT, which is an anti-tank LAV that fires wire guided missiles. The LAV-L is a logistics vehicle that can be used for carrying supplies. The LAV-R is a recovery vehicle, which the maintenance Marines utilize to repair other LAVs. The LAV-AD was an air defense variant that was used the year before but had been phased out. The LAV-C2 is a command and control vehicle used for communication. This was the vehicle I would be riding in.

There is a doorway on top of the LAV-C2 that allowed me to climb in. There is a chair beneath the opening, but Marines do not sit in LAVs; we usually stand to get a better look of our surroundings. I have my weapon on top of the vehicle, my sunglasses on and my Kevlar perched nicely on my dome. The company XO was standing behind me in his own doorway peeping out of the top. He hits me on the back to get my attention.

"Staff Sergeant, we're going to a town called Akashat, a small village where you and the CO will be talking with some of the people there."

I give him a hand gesture to confirm that I understand.

The drive is an interesting one. I hadn't seen what was right outside our camp since getting there, and it was interesting to see people living their lives normally. I mean, how *normal* can it really be when you have an occupying force strolling through town fully capable of leveling a city? Little kids waved, but the adults were subdued, not much coming from them.

I reach over to my daypack; it's called a daypack because you're supposed to use it for a day. I packed my things for the week into this pack. I am just that good. In my daypack are some packets of peanut butter and some cocoa powder. I was going to be sleeping off Camp for a week; I wanted to make sure I would be able to plug myself up so I wouldn't have to take a shit outdoors for a while. I grab a peanut butter packet and kneed it like dough. Within minutes it was ready for me to eat; it's delicious. Until you've tried warm peanut butter from a tube while driving exposed to the elements in cold weather, don't knock it.

In the distance, I see a small town; I look over to the company XO and ask him if that was Akashat. He nods as he puts a dip in his lower lip, and then wipes his finger on his leg. I could never take anyone seriously when they did that in mid conversation. It just looked like a chipmunk storing nuts in its mouth to me. When we arrive things immediately come to a halt. The people stop what they're doing and look at us. I then hear, "Staff Sergeant, you're needed." It could have come from anywhere, all I knew was that I had to get down from the vehicle and meet the company commander.

Dismounting from the top of an LAV is not easy when you haven't done it before, especially from an LAV you're not accustomed to. Add the fact that I had my rifle dangling from my body as I was coming down, and I am sure it looked like I was stumbling and fumbling. I could see from the corner of my eye that the XO was shaking his head. To him I was an amateur, or to put it as a Marine would, a pogue or POG. POG is a military slang term used to describe non-infantry, staff, and other rear-echelon or support units. POG frequently describes those who don't have to undergo the stresses the infantry does, and is generally used as a diminutive for any non-infantry personnel who disagrees or impedes the wants of a grunt.

I go over to the company commander. I met him briefly before leaving Camp. He was a Marine captain, a very friendly man and very well spoken. It looked to me as if he was on his way to a political career the way he addressed and dealt with me. If I had a baby with me, he probably would have taken it and kissed it for the cameramen. With him was his first sergeant, a younger fellow of the African American persuasion, impressive from first look. I would be tagging along with them; I would be interpreting for the captain.

As we leave the vehicles behind with Marines posted outside, children walk past us and toward the vehicles. I watch the captain carefully, observing his walk, his demeanor. Part of why I was so successful the year before was that I was able to read personalities and body language. Without that, I would not have been able to understand most of what was spoken.

This town, if cleaned up, would resemble any town in the United States. There were homes, streets, sidewalks, lampposts, just about anything you could think of if you were to build your own town. We walked the streets, the CO, First Sergeant, a protective detail, and I walking along as if we were tourists. The CO does not bring his rifle, only his pistol to show that he was the leader of the group. I had my rifle and had it ready in case someone was to take a shot at any of us. There were buildings all over the place; we were sitting ducks if they wanted to take shots at us.

The CO gave a look of confidence and kept his smile the entire time. He waved to children, some waved back; he even gave the customary "Salam Alaikum," which drew a smile from me because I always found it funny to hear Americans with no language skills speak another language. The accent is hilarious to me, but no one around knows why I'm laughing.

We go into the police station; we get ushered into an office and speak with the chief of the station there. Our job was to train the new police force, get them ready so when we leave the country, they would be in charge. I don't know what the Army was doing before we got there, but these guys had no training, no funding, nothing. They asked if we would like some tea, and I say yes before they could even finish their question. In the room with us are four police officers, the chief, our CO, the first sergeant, and me. I am to be the middleman, spoken to by the CO and then relaying his words to the Iraqis. As he does this, I can't help but laugh a little by watching as heads turn left and right from me to the CO as we discuss what to say.

The police had not been paid, they had not been trained, and this was all being said by the chief. The CO assures them that we will get them paid, and that we will provide them with what is needed. I am asked by the chief of police, "So what about you, brother? What is your name? Where are you from?" I say in response, "My name is Jose, from Puerto Rico. I was taught Arabic by the Marines when I first joined." This drew a look of "you're full of shit" from them, but they all in unison say, "Ahhhhh."

We walk out of the station and outside waiting is the battalion commander. He and his merry group of men were touring the area of operation and decided to see how things were going with us. He was a busy man, but always found time to go wherever his Marines were. Earlier with my Marines while we were staying on the Camp bored off our minds, he was out with the infantry Marines, a true leader, setting the example.

He asks the company commander, the first sergeant, and me to go for walk with him. We would circumnavigate the entire town; it wasn't that big. Near the end of the walk we spot a crowd of men sitting and drinking tea. We go over to them and greet them. They return a greeting and after seeing that we were harmless, they ask us to join them. I tell them thanks, but no thanks. We had to be on our way. As we walk away I see a boy, probably about seventeen or so. What caught my eye was what he was wearing. I say, "What the fuck? Sir, he's wearing Marine Corps issued sweat bottoms. Where the fuck did he get that from?" This causes everyone to be on their guard, apparently Marines were hit not too far from where we were and some were killed. We question the boy, and he says he bought them in another part of town. There was no way we were leaving without the bottoms, so I tell him take them off right there and hand them over.

This upset me for multiple reasons. The first reason was this boy was wearing Marine Corps issued clothing. He did not earn it. The second reason was that in all probability it once belonged to a Marine that was no longer with us. The last reason was that Marines had been killed; our unit or not, it didn't matter to me because they were Marines, but I was not informed.

"Why wasn't I told about this?" I say to the company commander. He didn't have an answer, but then again, who was I that I had to be told everything?

On our way back to the vehicles the company commander pulls me aside and says, "Hey Staff Sergeant, that was a good job in there and great job catching the PT gear. I didn't even see it. I've already asked the battalion commander, and he said I could have you."

My first thought is, *Who the fuck is this guy and what does he mean by "have you"?*

Am I his fucking boy that has to call him "massa"? I say respectfully, "I appreciate that, sir, but I have Marines that I am responsible for, you can't just take me away from my Marines."

He smiles and tells me that I've very important, complimenting me and giving me praise—the usual bullshit. With someone else this might work, but with me I just didn't buy it. He had just met me; he didn't even know me.

I get back to my vehicle and climb aboard. The XO sees that I was upset and smirks. "He tell you that you're staying with us?" he says. He already knew what the plan was for me. I just didn't want to be used like a piece of equipment, passed around like I was the year before. I'll give it a few days and then I'll convince them otherwise. I just have to do a shitty job and then he won't need me.

Except that's not in my nature. I can't purposely do something half-assed just so I don't have to do it anymore. I had more respect for myself than that. Sure, other Marines got away with doing things half-assed their entire careers, but I was not other Marines. The whole drive to our next position all I could think about was what I was going to do next.

I made the best out of the situation; I met new Marines, including three other Marines who were part of the C2 vehicle team. The driver was a Marine lance corporal, an older fellow, about thirty or so. He had a college degree and was very successful prior to the Corps. He joined the Marine Corps after September 11. He knew history would be made, and he wanted to be a part of that history. Another Marine was the vehicle commander as a lance corporal, a soft spoken Marine but squared away. The XO was a Marine first lieutenant, a cocky and arrogant man, also prior enlisted Marine so he felt he knew how to talk shit. He was a good guy, but he kind of got on my nerves every now and then.

A few days before I would head back with them back to the Camp, I wrote a letter to my Master Gunz. I told him that I did not want to be utilized as an interpreter. I wrote that I had agreed to pull my separation package with the full understanding that I would serve my role as platoon sergeant. I sent the letter with a support detachment that came to give us fuel and MREs. When they returned a day later I asked the Marine I gave the letter to if he had delivered it. His response was, "Master Gunz said he'd take care of it." Of course he would...he's a bad motherfucker.

Word got around about a Marine shooting himself in the arm accidentally. Bullshit, I knew full well that he did it so he could be sent home. It would only be a matter of time before other Marines tried it so they could be sent back. The only problem is, he wasn't hurt seriously enough to be sent home. There were Marines who didn't want to be there? Fine, who really wanted to be here? I mean it would be insane to volunteer to want to come here. So now that the Marine who shot himself was forced to stay, those who didn't want to be there anymore had to come up with other means to be sent home. Before we had left, Marines were coming out as gay, even if they weren't. They would use any excuse to get out of it. It made me feel better about myself for actually staying the course and deploying with everyone. No matter how much I did not want to be there, I couldn't live with myself if I pulled up lame and pretended I was something else.

The week was over; we headed back to Camp. I was relieved that I had made it back to my Marines. I got to my living quarters; everyone looked so clean to me, probably because I was filthy and had not showered for a week. The staff NCOs welcomed me with a "dude, you stink" remark and a "go shower" demand. My platoon commander, thinking he was cool with me, greets me with, "Hey dirty Hajji!" Fucking punk, I should have said something in return, but instead I look for the Master Gunz.

"Hey Master Gunz, did you get my letter?"

"Yeah," he says. "There's nothing I can do."

Here we go again.

I shower up and do some laundry. I clean up hoping that I won't have to be sent back out, but knowing that I probably will. I go and visit some of my Marines, but they look like zombies watching the television they set up with *24* playing without pause. I walk over to the Alpha Company Marines; I had gotten to know a few of them. They were more receptive, more welcoming.

It was here that I found out that the driver to the vehicle I was with was an Orioles fan. "Wow, I never met an Orioles fan before. They still have some of you around?" I said to him in jest. We talk about the 1996 American League Championship Series and argue over which game Jeter hit his controversial homerun. He said it was Game 2. I tell him Game 1, and he makes a bet with me for $100.

After agreeing, I tell him, "Dude, I'm telling you, it was Game 1, bottom of the eighth. Benitez was pitching and Jeter hit it to right field out of the reach of Tarasco." He then says, "Now that you say it like that, I don't know if I should have made the bet." I was right and $100 richer.

I visit the Alpha Company first sergeant, and he looks upset. I ask him what was wrong, and he said one of his sergeants came to him and said he was suicidal, that he didn't want to be there anymore. They took him off of the vehicle he was commanding and sent him away from the other Marines. He knew it was bullshit because the Sergeant was acting it out just a bit much. "He even put a pistol in his mouth to show that he was serious. But that bitch wasn't going to do it." The first sergeant was pretty pissed off about it.

There was a different mentality with these Marines. They were personable but didn't give a shit. They said what was on their mind, but they were simple creatures of habit. I liked it. A few days later Alpha Company got ready to pull out when all hell broke loose. A Marine from another company within the battalion was hit by an RPG. It was a direct hit to his torso. He was dead. The battalion commander, looking for blood, comes back to the Camp and tells everyone to get ready and to load up all the vehicles. We were going to find who did it and kill them. I waited by my gear, waiting for word on when to leave. Time slowed down; a Marine was killed. This was the first attack on our battalion directly. It was on!

I closed my eyes. When I opened them again, a young Marine was standing over me, "Staff Sergeant, we have to go."

I get into the LAV-C2 without complaint this time around. I didn't want to leave my Marines, but I couldn't be a coward either. We drove in darkness. I saw nothing around me; I only felt the cold air hitting my face. I began to remember the feeling of misery when things got bad the year before. When we stopped I balled up in the fetal position in the chair. I closed my eyes, hoping to sleep the remaining six months away.

I opened them some time later. The battalion commander and the company commander were discussing what happened the night before. The Iraqi insurgents had hit, and hit us hard. They were observing us; they saw we were different, that we weren't the Army. Marines are different, but any enemy can be taken down if you have enough intelligence on them. Seventeen Marines throughout Iraq had been killed the night before. Reports on the radio could be heard because I was in the command and control vehicle. I heard casualty reports. I heard the number of who were hurt and who were dead. I closed my eyes, hoping to wake up somewhere else. I open them and see that I am still there in the fetal position, still in Iraq, helpless as ever before.

We had thought that winning the hearts and minds would give us an opportunity to show the Iraqis that we were different. We hoped that the casualties and deaths would go down in numbers now that we were here. Marines are a proud bunch; nothing can take that away, not even death.

I open my eyes and come to terms. My brothers and sisters had been killed the night before. Those claiming to be Marines were trying to get out of the battle any which way possible. I would not be one of those people. I go up to the company commander and say, "Sir, what do you need me to do? I'm all in."

"Just rest up, Staff Sergeant. I'll call you if I need you." He replied.

"Rest up, sir? I just slept for twenty-one hours. I think half of the deployment is gone," I said with a bit of jest and sarcasm. What it boiled down to was that these Marines wanted me to help them, and for me not to help would have been selfish on my part. Sure, who wouldn't want to be watching *24* with the rest of the guys? My hand was dealt the day I walked into the battalion two years before telling everyone that I spoke the language.

"You done bitching, Staff Sergeant?" asks the XO. "Yes sir," I say. "Six more months."

Six more months for those who make it out alive. It could be six seconds, six minutes, or six days for any one of us, though. Fate has an expiration date for all of us, and all I could think of was if mine was sooner than I had imagined.

"We're Oscar-Mike!" the XO says.

And on the move we were, toward the horizon so clear and mysterious. Marines are a curious bunch; let's see what is beyond that horizon…

And let's fucking kill it.

Chapter 30

The Road to Fallujah

I honestly did not know what to expect out of my time in Alpha Company. I was on loan to them through orders of the battalion commander. I should have felt honored to be wanted, but let's be real here. They weren't fighting to keep me because I was a good-looking guy, which I would like to add that I am.

Patrolling with an LAV battalion is not a typical patrol. Normal patrols are on these things called feet. Patrols with Alpha Company and any company with LAVs were done by the LAVs themselves. You could comfortably fit about six Marines into an LAV. By comfortable, I mean being able to breathe. It didn't matter if you had legroom or enough room to stretch. Just get in the vehicle, and if you don't hit your head causing a concussion, you're fine.

I wish the lay of the land was like a map or globe. You know how they have lines where borders are? Well, in the real world that isn't the case. We were given orders to patrol the border with Syria to prevent smugglers from bringing in weapons or explosives, but who in their right mind would bring weapons in when they see twenty LAVs kicking up sand in the desert? They'd just take a different route.

I had now been in Iraq for a little over a month. I hadn't called home or spoken on the phone to anyone. I pulled out my notebook, the one containing names and numbers of everyone I wanted to talk to. I went down the list: Christine would be first, Eric second, my wife third, so on and so forth. Calling Christine was more stressful than anything else. I'd call and she would sound excited only to say, "Hey, can you call back later?" Umm, hello! I am calling from a satellite phone at about $10 a minute from a warzone! I decided to give up calling her.

When I called Eric, we would talk for a while. We'd talk about how it was going out here with "real Marines" as he put it. He always had a laugh that would make you feel better, and he did just that. I would call him at night when everyone else was sleeping, and I could walk away from the vehicles for a bit. I would talk shit about some of the Marines I was with or talk about what happened that day that drove me crazy and he would say, "You know that sound travels better at night?" This was later confirmed by one of the Marines in my vehicle who said, "Yeah we heard what you said about him…" Referring to someone I was talking shit about.

I was forming a good relationship with the Marines of Alpha Company. The officers and staff NCOs were far more professional and laid back in comparison to the uptight individuals from my platoon and company. The senior enlisted man was the first sergeant. He was thirty-three years old, one of the younger staff NCOs, but still the most senior. I believe only two other staff NCOs were younger than him, but they were newly promoted staff sergeants, new to the ranks. The first sergeant and I hit it off; he liked my sense of humor and surprisingly my first sergeant had told him about me.

Whenever we'd stop, form a perimeter and set up watch for the night, I would go and pay him a visit with another staff sergeant. The three of us would sit there and talk shit about any and everything. The three of us were minorities in a headquarters platoon full of Caucasian men. I was Arab, both the staff sergeant and first sergeant were African American. When no one was around, they would let their guard down and we'd just be three men talking up a storm.

I'd be lying to you if I said race didn't play a small role in perception. Race was a small worry in the back of my mind. The company gunny I argued with in Kuwait was obviously a racist, and his two stooges with him were just as hateful. The way they talked to people of color, it was just obvious to me. It wasn't common, but it was certainly around. I remember back when I was a young lance corporal at Camp Lejeune, North Carolina. I was only nineteen years old, but I had gained the respect of the senior personnel for my performance and my attitude. They also liked the fact that I joked a lot about my background. On more than one occasion I was told, "Hey Hafid, you know I hate ragheads and niggers, but you're alright." I didn't know what to say. "Umm, thanks Sergeant," I replied.

I would catch myself thinking about times like that and then look at the situation from the eyes of those same people. We were two niggers and a raghead in their eyes, the eyes of the ignorant and scared, but we were a first sergeant and two staff sergeants, human beings to me. These two guys were awesome. I hadn't had any staff NCO that I considered my friend up until then, but these guys were just that—friends. What made it more rewarding was the professionalism we had when it came down to it. I never once called the first sergeant by anything but his rank. He would call me Joe though; I thought that was pretty cool of him.

During one of these occasions when we were setting up a perimeter, I asked to speak to the first sergeant in private. "Sure Joe," he said, as he got up without hesitation. "What's up?"

I had a hard time speaking. My eyes filled with tears and they rolled down my cheeks.

"What's wrong Joe?" he asked, sounding concerned.

The company commander had given me the satellite phone to call Yemen; it was the first time I had called home. My father answered and he immediately started crying with joy. He asked where I was and I told him I was in the Philippines on an exercise with the local military. He believed it and asked if I wanted to talk to anyone else. I said no, that I just wanted to send my regards to everyone else and that I had to go.

My dad had forgiven me and gotten over how he felt when I visited them in Yemen. Ultimately, I was his son, and I had done things that made him proud. Yes, money was important to my family, but my dad was a little different from the rest. He was tougher than my mother. He ruled with an iron fist, but he was also more loving. He first said "I love you" to me on May 14, 1997, over the phone. It caught me by surprise, but, from that point on, he ended each phone call with me with an "I love you."

Hearing my dad's voice and how happy he was to hear mine was like a punch to the gut. What if something happened to me? He had no idea I was in Iraq; no one did. Guilt washed over me like never before. I was sick; I looked at the phone in my hand after we hung up and stared at it while taking a knee. I took off my helmet and placed it beneath me, providing a seat for me to sit and contemplate what to do next.

"First Sergeant, I don't think I can do this anymore. I'm lying to my family every day I'm here. My wife and son have no idea where I am, and if anything happens, how are they going to feel?"

The first sergeant was sympathetic but assuring. "Don't worry Joe; we won't let anything happen to you."

"I think I might refuse to train," I said. I even shocked myself as I said that, for the first time in my career as a Marine, I thought of quitting.

"Just think it over, Joe," he told me. After our discussion the three of us sat down and talked as if nothing had happened.

I'd had situations in the past when Marines had broken down in front of me, and I had to say the right things to them. It's a pressure packed situation. You don't practice for it; you aren't taught how to handle it, and you can't expect it to happen. Talking to the first sergeant helped. It got me through that day, but it's what happened next that got me really excited.

We got a call from one of the platoons that had set up a checkpoint on one of the roads. They had pulled over three vehicles full of civilians. They were filled with men, young and middle aged. They were questioned but to no avail. I was the Arab speaker there. We left our position and headed over to question these individuals.

The drivers were Arabs, from Iraq driving SUVs with Texas inspection stickers on the windshields. I ask them who they have with them and they tell me the passengers are Indian workers. I tell the CO, and he tells me, "We've gotten reports about some Indians coming into the country."

"So what are we going to do, sir?" I ask him.

"We'll call it in and take them in for questioning. We'll need two Marines per vehicle—"

"Ooh, sir! I want to drive one!" I interrupt him in mid-sentence.

He smiles and sees that it's something that would keep me happy. He agrees, and we all leave for our duties.

I don't know why I wanted to drive a GMC SUV, but I had the itch to do so. Maybe it was because it felt better to drive in and didn't consist of me getting sandblasted by the elements. Maybe it was because I wanted to be an American driving a taxi of sorts in an Arab land. The irony would be epic, but alas, I am also Arab, so no changes there.

When we got back to Camp we dropped the vehicles and the detainees off for questioning. I went back to my living quarters as we were told we had an hour before we would leave again. I saw the Master Gunz sitting down in front of a television, watching a movie. He sees me and says, "So how are things out there, Hafid?"

"Well they're as good as it's gonna get, Master Gunz, but I wanted to tell you something. I think I might tell the battalion XO that I'm refusing to train."

He understood my issues and listened to what I had to say. He recommended that I not do it, but I never said I was going to do it for sure.

"Staff Sergeant, I know you're talking to the Master Gunz here, but I can't stand here and listen to you say you'll refuse to train because you were ordered to do something," Napoleon piped in.

What I wanted to say was, "Oh you were *standing* there? I couldn't see you over that dust ball on the floor." Instead, I just gave him a look, smile and say, "Roger that, sir." He had no business speaking, but he felt the need to do so.

I decided to continue to train. The reasons were plenty, but I cited the conversation with the first sergeant above all. He spoke to me with respect and courtesy, not the way Napoleon had. To him, I was making him look good. There he was, a platoon commander giving up his platoon sergeant for the betterment of the mission. He'd probably get an award for it.

We headed back out, and drove to the police station in Akashat. We were to take the police on a patrol with us in our vehicles and then train them on how to shoot their weapons. As they loaded up, one of the younger Marines was visibly upset and was pulled away by a sergeant.

"I don't want these dirty motherfuckers in our vehicle. I don't fucking trust them," he says to the sergeant. The sergeant does well to calm him down, as I give the Marine a look. I only wonder what he thinks about me. I'd find out eventually. I was going to be with these guys for a while.

After a few hours with the Iraqis, we drop them off and head back out in the middle of the desert for our border patrols. A few times we crossed into Syria by accident, giving the Syrians an opportunity to fire upon us if they so desired. They had done just that the first week the Marine Corps had returned back in March. A Marine was shot in the buttocks, but his unit unleashed hell on the Syrians. I doubt they wanted to take us on again.

The company commander for Alpha Company made a broadcast comment on our way out of camp after we had dropped off the Indians. Over the radio, he said, "Orders might change, standby." A grin washed over the face of some of the Marines, hell even me. We knew what he was referring to. The Iraqis had gotten cocky; they had formed a stronghold in Fallujah, set up IEDs all over the place, and had taken potshots at Marines. The IEDs were artillery rounds, daisy chained to each other and would explode when enough pressure was applied. Marine tanks and vehicles were getting destroyed. Marines were dying left and right in that area of Iraq. The city was considered lost to the insurgency.

This was all over the broadcast waves. It would only be a matter of time before we would launch an offensive on Fallujah, taking the city back from the insurgents. We just didn't know when that time would be.

There really was no mission for us by the border. It seemed like a waste to me, which was the reason why I had bitched in the first place. I wasn't being utilized properly. Why be an interpreter when there was no one to talk to, when I could be a platoon sergeant with Marines to lead? We decided to set up a perimeter and take a break for dinner. The company commander stood outside our vehicle with the radio handset pressed to his ear, listening intently. He handed the radio off to the communications Marine and walked off to, "take a piss."

I don't know why I did this, but I looked over at him in the distance and caught his stance taking a piss. I laughed hysterically and said to one of the Marines, "Dude, check him out."

He was standing with one hand against his hip, as if he were a superhero taking a piss. One of the Marines asked me if I was going to say something to him about it. "Hell yeah I am," I said.

When the CO returned to the vehicle I say, "Hey sir, are you a fan of comics?"

"Not really, Joe. Why?" Yes, he called me Joe as well.

"Cause you were standing there like a superhero taking a piss. Is there any reason you did that? Is it because you were pissing on a bunch of ants and felt like you were Superman putting out a fire?"

This comment drew laughs from everyone around. Probably because they thought it was funny that I would even say something to him something about it. He was a good sport, though. I knew he could take a joke.

"Sir, Highlander actual is calling for you!" yells one of the Marines. Highlander actual was the battalion commander.

Within a few minutes he puts down the handset and tells us all to "mount up."

Without a word we get ready and load up the vehicles with our gear and bodies. When we move out he announces the plan over the radio. I did not have a radio headset, so I did not know what he had said. I looked behind me at the XO; he smiled and raises both hands up in celebration.

"What happened, sir?" I ask.

"We're going to Fallujah!" he says with excitement. "You gonna keep bitching, or you coming with us?" he says as he pats me on the shoulder. He was obviously looking forward to this situation, and so were the other Marines. Where would Fallujah rank in battles throughout Marine Corps history? This was a question I would ponder as we headed back to our Camp to pack up for tomorrow's rendezvous with destiny.

This deployment was just a month old, and I had no idea what the next day would bring. I was just trying to stay alive long enough to see it.

Chapter 31

Gut Punch

Camp Al Qaim was busy; Marines were running around with a purpose. Word had been relayed to the company commanders who then sent word down to their platoon commanders. Back in my living quarters Napoleon was huddled around a table with the staff NCOs of my old platoon. By now I considered them my old platoon because Napoleon didn't care enough to have me around. Why would I want to be associated with him or his platoon? They were discussing who was going to make the trip to Fallujah.

"You guys are going?" I asked.

"Just a few of us. Want to join us, Staff Sergeant?" Napoleon replied.

"No sir, I have better things to do."

I went through my gear and looked for what I would need and what I deemed wasn't necessary. I would pack for a month. I had plenty of underwear, packed away in Ziploc bags. Each Ziploc contained a pair of whitey-tighties, an olive-drab green t-shirt, and some black boot socks. I folded them nicely and as I zipped them up, I left a small opening. This is so I can push excess air out, thus creating a vacuum-sealed pack of undies. I remember commercials for a brand of coffee that was vacuum-sealed; when they broke the seal they smelled the freshness of the coffee grounds. When I break the seal of one of these Ziploc bags, I do the same thing. You begin to appreciate fresh underwear when you're unwashed for over a week.

I have packing my gear down to a science. What would take most Marines hours to pack would take me minutes. Time was critical; I didn't want to waste it unless I was doing my favorite thing…sleeping. Thirty minutes later I was done; I got out of my uniform and headed to the showers.

"Oh look at this," says one of the staff NCOs. "Where do you think you're going?"

"Don't fucking worry about it. If you were out there for a week and you came back needing a shower, I think you'd appreciate it. Now go back to acting like you know what you're doing."

Burn! I took pleasure in standing up for myself, even more when I had a nice one liner to end it. It was the staff sergeant I had made comic strips of; he didn't deserve my sympathy after what he put others through with his lousy attitude. He chuckled, trying to laugh off the embarrassment, but the point was taken.

When I took my first shower, I marveled at how dirt would wash off and go down the drain. For the first twelve years of my life, I bathed, the dirt caked to the sides of the tub. You were basically swimming in your own filth. After discovering what a shower did for time, effort, and opportunity (masturbation for those of you who can't take a hint), I chose showers from then on. By being out on patrols without showers, well it brought about epic drainage filth. It was a sight to see. Imagine a whirlpool galaxy made of dirt. That's what the drain looked like.

I got back to my living quarters; the staff sergeant must have been thinking long and hard about what to say to me when I returned.

"When you going to move your shit out and over to Alpha Company?" he asks, somewhat serious.

"When you going to pull that dick out of your mouth, so I can understand what you're saying?"

I was referring to his infatuation with the Master Gunz. Wherever Master Gunz went, he would tag along. It was pretty pathetic and everyone saw it. I was the only one that would openly call him out on it because, like I said, he didn't deserve my sympathy. He had nothing to say. I didn't think he would.

I set up a chair and put a movie in. I cleaned out my ears with a Q-tip and leaned back to relax. There's something about a Q-tip cleaning your ear that makes you forget everything around you. I'm disturbed by the idiot staff sergeant scolding a young Marine from Alpha Company for knocking on the door and asking for me. See what I mean? He's a fucking bully.

"Staff Sergeant, the CO wants you over at Alpha Company for a meeting in fifteen minutes," the Marine says.

"I'll be right there."

When I get there, maps are laid out, Marines' gear packed nicely and ready to go. I am greeted by the CO and he asks me to have a seat with the rest of the Alpha Company staff. A full offensive was planned with LAV support on the outskirts of the city to kill any insurgents trying to flee and regroup. We knew there would be mass casualties, but we could not allow Fallujah to remain under the control of the insurgents.

"Staff Sergeant, you're going to earn your pay," says the CO with a smile.

"What the fuck was I doing before, sir?" I retort.

We were to leave at midnight; the trace elements of the battalion were to follow later that morning. We're told to get some rest, because we could be out there for a while. I take the opportunity to check my email. I received an interesting email from Eric. He had received a letter from the Marine Corps asking him to come back, that he was needed. It wasn't a requirement. If he went, it would be on his own accord. He asked what I thought about it. He said his family didn't want him to go, but it was his decision. I knew Eric well enough; he was like me. He felt like he wanted to do more. I emailed him back telling him that he should go with his heart. That I would support whatever decision he made, and I'd send him whatever he wanted…to include forbidden alcohol.

As I went into the living quarters of the junior Marines of Alpha Company, I saw a few of them huddled by laptops and portable DVD players. They were watching the gift I had bestowed onto them, downloaded porn. I told a few of them of the news that we'd be leaving later that night, but they had already been briefed. It would be a long ride though, so we would have to stop in Al Asad again for a day. One Marine, an awkward fellow, was watching alone with his laptop and stereo headphones. He came up to me and said, "Staff Sergeant, who is this Heather Brooke lady? I can't stop thinking about her; can you make me a copy please?" Dude was hooked, a little too much, but I didn't blame him; the girl had talent.

I bedded down for the short night and asked one of the Marines from my vehicle to come and get me before we headed out. I got fully dressed and laid down to close my eyes. I couldn't sleep though, not for more than a few minutes.

It's nearly midnight; I've basically been awake the entire time. I grabbed my gear and headed toward the door. I stop to pick up an MRE that was in a pile in the corner. Some people just don't know when to quit. Suddenly I heard someone say, "What the fuck do you think you're doing?"

It's that fucking staff sergeant again. He must have stayed up all night wondering what to say to me.

"Oh wow, that must really suck, because even though you have that dick out of your mouth now, I still can't understand you. I don't speak bitch." I say without delay. Maybe he'd shut up now.

I walk out of the office/living quarters and head to the vehicles already staged and ready to go. The Alpha Company CO is in the battalion headquarters giving his timeline and route. My gear is mounted to the side of the vehicle; the CO comes over to our vehicle and asks, "You ready Joe?"

"Hell yeah, sir. Let's do this!"

We're "Oscar-Mike" once again in darkness. The cool air feels different this time, as I now have something to look forward to. It would be three to six hours to Al Asad. What was I going to do the entire time? I put on my glasses to protect my eyes, but they are also designed to protect them from sunlight. Sunglasses at night is an experience in itself, it's as if you're blindfolded.

I begin to doze off, my head and Kevlar helmet hitting the communication antenna to my right. Hoping the XO behind me doesn't see, I ask, "Hey this thing doesn't cause cancer does it, sir?"

"Fuck if I know, probably does," he says in return.

I start dozing off again. I think to myself that the sunglasses are covering the fact that I am falling asleep, but I get a pat on the right shoulder. It's the XO; he points at me and points down, signaling to me that I need to go sleep. I sit down and lean forward, the hum of the engine and the movement of the vehicle rock me to sleep.

After stopping in Al Asad for the afternoon, the day trip was shortened so we could get to Fallujah before the insurgents could strengthen their position with IEDs. I had in my possession a Cuban cigar. The driver of the LAV-C2 that I was in and I decided that we'd smoke it when the mission was done. I left it in its casing and put it on my flak jacket with the other gear I had tucked away nicely. It is somewhat comical that Cuban cigars are banned from being sold in the United States, but there we were, buying them on a Marine Corps base in the middle of Iraq. I'd never had a Cuban cigar; if I was lucky enough to stay alive, I'd be having one in celebratory fashion. It was something to look forward to; it was the *only* thing to look forward to because if I didn't smoke that cigar, it meant I was dead. Reality set in for a bit, but in no time, we had to move out again.

We got to the outskirts of Fallujah; we were one of the first Marine units in place for the offensive. We were told to maintain a perimeter for the night and await orders. I pulled out my sleeping bag and rolled it out. I could barely see anything, the occasional flare and light from the moon peeking from behind the clouds gave me some idea. I got in my sleeping bag, closed my eyes, and fell asleep.

Morning came to us in the form of an explosion. The Explosives Ordnance Disposal (EOD) team was on site blowing up suspected IEDs. Debris rained down on us, and it was at that time that I realized why we wore our protective gear, especially our Kevlar helmets. A few Marines get up and panic. Others just rolled up their sleeping bags. While my friends and family spent that moment asleep in bed over in both the United States and Yemen, we were waking up with the realization that we were sleeping on live artillery rounds. Had we arrived a few hours later as we had originally scheduled, you would not be reading this right now.

All I could do was laugh. I thought about how it would be a great story to tell one day, and it certainly is. We moved into our position and set up checkpoints. I was sent out to a different platoon within Alpha Company, any who needed an interpreter. The Marines of these platoons were professional, especially their platoon commanders, but as soon as the CO and first sergeant were out of sight and sound…they would say and do the craziest things, especially the platoon commanders. It is Marines like the ones I spent those few days manning checkpoints with that made me love the Corps more. It is Marines like these men that made me realize I had made the right decision in deploying and pulling my separation papers.

Each night we'd head into the desert, out of sight, sound, and mind of the Iraqis in Fallujah. A platoon would be sent out on patrol, and every now and then, I would tag along in the back of one of their vehicles. The nights I didn't tag along were the nights they were attacked. None of the Marines were hurt, but they all had their share of scare. Someone was watching over me.

I asked the CO if he had heard anything about the attack on the city, but he hadn't. We were called back one evening to Camp TQ, which was short for Taqaddum. Marines had a hard time saying Arabic words. Shit, some of them had a hard time saying words with five syllables. Some elements of the battalion were staged over in TQ; we were getting new orders.

"Wait. What the fuck happened in Fallujah?" I asked. There was no answer, no one knew...or was it that no one wanted to say?

We drove north to Camp Fallujah where the rest of the battalion was staged, including Marines from my old platoon. We staged our vehicles in columns and Marines were told to get cleaned up and get some chow in them. I walked over to where my old platoon was situated, and I see Napoleon sitting down with a book in his lap, dead asleep. I felt the need to draw a penis on his face, but refrained.

I see the Marine Staff Sergeant who replaced me and chat with him. He was a great Marine; one of the few in the platoon in the staff NCO ranks that had common sense and didn't piss me off. He was squared away and had a good attitude. I asked him what they had been up to and he says, "Nothing since I last saw you." I had seen him a few days earlier in the middle of what was probably nowhere. We had just enough time to snap a photo with me flipping off the camera.

A Marine sergeant standing with us points to Napoleon and says, "You should have seen him, Staff Sergeant. He pulled out his journal and read to us again. Master Gunz told me he would and said that after he had read to us to make a smart comment. So after he was finished I said, 'Wow! That was great, sir. Thank you so much for reading that.' He told me to shut the fuck up." We all laughed; Napoleon was in his chair, still snoring away.

I was ragged, my hair uncut and my mustache was all bushy. I walked over to where Marines were getting their haircut and asked the Marine to, "Cut it all off. I don't want to get mistaken for a local." We stayed in Camp Fallujah for a few days, still unaware of what was going on, except that we had new orders and things were going to change. In the mess hall, while eating dinner, we watched on CNN as Iraqis celebrated in the streets of Fallujah and CNN filmed the Marines marching out of the city one by one. It looked awful, and frankly it was awful because Marines had died for what? So we could hand the city over to some crooked Iraqi generals? To me it was a campaign ploy. The presidential election was less than seven months away; this was to get votes, not to save lives.

We had a battalion meeting with all of the staff NCOs and officers. The battalion commander would be addressing us. It was odd seeing the Marines from my old platoon and company sitting on one end as I sat with the Marines of Alpha Company at the other. I felt different as well, to be honest, like I was doing a lot more with Alpha than I could with my previous command. We met in a theater; abandoned of course. Every building was abandoned and rundown, hence the *spoils* of war. In the rear of the theater, I overhear a few Marines talking about the NFL draft from the night before. "How the fuck you hear about the draft out here? Who did the Giants get?" I asked in shock.

"Eli Manning. They traded with San Diego who got Philip Rivers."

I knew Eli and wanted him because of his brother; we hadn't had a good quarterback on the Giants since Phil Simms. I wasn't going to count the years with Collins because…it's Kerry Collins! I was excited. I didn't ask who else was drafted; my team got who they and I wanted all along.

"Attention on deck!"

It was back to reality though. The battalion commander had arrived. We stood and he told us to sit down. After explaining why we were pulling out of Fallujah, he went on and told us how he just got out of a meeting with General Mattis. That old bastard was still eating dirt like the rest of us. He explained to General Mattis to no end why he felt we were needed in this region of Iraq more than the border with Syria.

"Well, I got what I wanted and what you all wanted. We're leaving Al Qaim and moving down to Al Asad," he said to the liking of many. "We leave for Al Qaim in the morning, and then back out a few days later."

Al Asad had a great mess hall, and the food was awesome. It was a place that had the logistics part of the conflict figured out. They didn't have the issues we had in Al Qaim, and their living conditions were far better.

The drive to Al Qaim and back south to Al Asad was a blur; we encountered no issues. I was surprised we were able to pack everything up so quickly. Our Mission with Alpha Company was simple, stay off the Camp until you have to come back and patrol, patrol, patrol. It was during this time that I took my first outdoor shit; a six-pound baby turd was delivered after an hour of hard labor.

Like the days of ancient China, I kicked dirt over it and buried it; it must have been a female turd.

I enjoyed my time with Alpha Company more and more. I became friendly with all the Marines of the company. They were just a joy to be around. Though there was one night that I didn't like being told I had to go out on a patrol, and that I would be spending the night out on patrol with a squad of Marines minutes before we would go out, I dealt with it—I'd get over it. We had been out for a little over two weeks, and we would be going back to Al Asad in two days for some rest and recovery before heading back out yet again.

I came back the next day from the foot patrol with the squad of Marines the night before. Nothing was out there once again; I was looking forward to going to Al Asad and getting some mail and some good chow in me in the morning. I walk by the LAV-C2, and everyone was oddly somber, almost avoiding me.

"Hey Staff Sergeant, how you doing?" asked the XO, which he had never done before.

"Umm, fine sir?" I replied and walked over to my buddy, the staff sergeant who hung out with me and the first sergeant. Behind me I heard a whisper, "Did you tell him?"

I loved this guy to death, but he only knew one way to talk, and that was loud and under control. He sees me and says, "Did you hear?"

"No, what happened."

"Rudy died. He's dead," he says to me.

Rudy, the corporal who sat with me and discussed life, had died. Rudy, the twenty-year-old man who sat with me to discuss how his girlfriend was unsure if she wanted to be with him, was dead. Rudy, the man I told had his whole life ahead of him, was now gone.

"You ok?" someone asks.

I walk away in silence, trying to come to terms with what had just happened. This isn't some video game where you get shot, come back to life and fight on. I sit down under a netting of camouflage and stare at nothing. It is getting dark, and it is quiet. The first sergeant comes over to me and asks if I am okay. They all knew he was one of my Marines. I look over to him and say, "I need to be there tomorrow. I need to be at his memorial."

"Don't worry, Joe. We are going back in the morning. We'll be there. Take all the time you need."

"Thank you, First Sergeant," I say softly.

And thank you, Rudy…RIP.

Chapter 32

Never Never-land

"What happened?" I ask the first Marine I see from my old platoon. It was morning; we had just got back to Al Asad. It looked like the Marines in my old platoon were taking it well. They were stunned of course; it just hadn't set in yet. I didn't understand how Rudy could die when there was no need for him to leave the Camp.

Trips north to Al Qaim were made at least twice a week. This was to bring mail, food, ammunition, and any other sort of supplies Marines would need. Each convoy had to have a certain amount of Marines: a driver, someone to assist in driving (or to keep the driver awake), and someone to man a machine gun mounted on the top of each vehicle.

One of the things I was told when I first became a Marine was to never volunteer. Volunteering usually led to you doing some shit detail that would make you miserable. I would volunteer until I realized that there was no benefit to it. Marines who didn't volunteer didn't have to subject themselves to what I had to, yet they were getting paid just the same. The only way I would volunteer is if I was "voluntold." I had a technique I used when I became the one asking for volunteers. I would ask for someone to raise their hand, and when they did, I would say, "Thanks for volunteering." That's what it is to be voluntold.

Rudy was a motivator, soft-spoken, but he was one of my go-to guys. If I wanted something done by a corporal, I would ask him to make sure it would get done. Corporals of the past were now extinct. They were no longer Marines who had the ambition to lead. In my first unit, I was a twenty- year-old corporal, selected to be the platoon sergeant because no one wanted to put their neck out. I did. Corporals of this era lacked the ambition, and I blamed the staff NCO leadership for not instilling it in their men. Rudy was an old school corporal and NCO; he led by example. Leaders never ask their men to do something they wouldn't do. That's why Rudy volunteered to go on that convoy. It is why Rudy volunteered to man the mounted machine gun. It is why Rudy died that twentieth day of May 2004.

I wanted to be mad at someone...mad at them for sending him out there, but who was to blame? He was manning the machine gun on top of the truck as it lost control. It tipped over and he died. No one except the Marines in the vehicle knew what happened. It didn't matter what had really taken place. It wouldn't change the fact that Rudy was gone.

We were told what tent Alpha Company would be staying in. I dropped my gear and headed over to my old platoon to find out more about Rudy's death. I wasn't helping matters. Once again I was thinking I was more important than I really was. I didn't need to know why it had happened, just that it had happened. The Marines I asked all had the same look of disbelief; they were just as shocked as I was. The memorial would be in two days. It would give me time to decompress, take my mind off of things, but my mind was on Rudy and our conversation from two months earlier.

I had told him he was still young and that he had his whole life ahead of him. I basically lied to him, and I hated myself for it. I walked to an area marked "Smoking Area" and stood with a few Marines. The first sergeant was there smoking a cigar. I pulled out the Cuban and started smoking it. It was to be my victory cigar, but there is no victory in war. There will never be victory in war, only loss. Winning and losing takes place between the white lines of a baseball diamond. You can't ever win if you lose a life—one or one thousand, it's a loss regardless.

In honor of Rudy I spent time with my former platoon. I went over to their maintenance shed where they worked on vehicles and threw horseshoes with the Marines. I had never played, so I decided to take part in a game to test my skills, and I found that I was pretty good. The only thing to do was to act like it hadn't happened. We hadn't had his memorial yet, so it hadn't sunk in yet. It was one of those situations where you know something is coming, but you avoid it at all costs.

I had mail waiting for me. It was a box from Christine. I allowed myself to smile as I looked at it covered in hearts and all girlish. It was meant to be a gag gift, a gift to draw attention to me and have others laugh as I opened it. It could not have come at a worse time. I opened it and handed it over to one of the Marines in Alpha Company saying, "Here take this shit. I don't fucking want it." It wasn't her fault, but I was somewhat hoping that she would do something nice for me, like sending me something that I could use. I needed Christine to be a friend at that moment, and all I had to show for her friendship was a pink toothbrush with matching toothpaste.

I emailed Eric, telling him what happened to Rudy. I emailed another Marine who stayed behind at Camp Pendleton. I gave him my honest to God opinion on what was going on. He would later tell me that he sent copies to the Marines who were staying behind with him to keep them informed of what was really taking place. I don't sugarcoat things. I just say what I feel, and it's for someone else to decide what I mean by it.

I stop speaking to any of the Marines about Rudy. I had gotten as much information as I could. There was nothing more to talk about. We just waited for the memorial. The morning of Rudy's memorial arrived, and I awoke feeling eerily similar to the way I felt on March 11, 2002—the six-month anniversary of the attacks on the World Trade Center and Pentagon. I got dressed and headed to the mess hall for breakfast. I ate and headed right to where my former platoon had formed up and were going through a rehearsal for the ceremony.

A little over a month ago I was standing in front of these Marines giving them commands. Now I paced back and forth in the background as I watched their new platoon sergeant. Marines walk to the podium then walk away. In the background someone is standing by audio equipment. There is a Marine Corps and an American flag flapping in the wind. A pair of boots aligned as if Rudy were standing in them at the position of attention. A rifle placed muzzle down between the boots. His dog tags hung from the rifle, and a helmet is placed on top of the butt stock of the rifle, symbolizing Rudy as fallen. Marines from Headquarters and Service Company start taking their positions. I stand behind the platoon I was once a part of; I would be a part of them for this…for Rudy.

The Platoon Sergeant reads the names of Marines who, after their name is read, each yell, "Present!" This is for accountability purposes; he gets to Rudy's name and pauses, he does this three times. He first reads his last name, then his rank and his last name. Finally, he reads his rank and full name. No response. I had never experienced the death of someone close to me. I had known people who had died, and the year before I had watched a baby die in front of me, but I didn't know any of them as well as I knew Rudy. He had so much potential. So much love and joy was in that man, and now his name is called out and there is no response. Rudy is gone and he isn't coming back.

We are at attention and my head is bowed down. I am not looking forward as is customary at the position of attention. "Taps" begins to play and my tears fall to the ground. They do not roll down my cheek. They steadily drip to the ground, as I do not have the energy to raise my head and see what is going on in front of me. It is a nightmare come true.

Three Marines stand by the podium. Each one knew Rudy well. Each one had something positive to say, there was nothing negative to say about Rudy. One by one the Marines tell a story about Rudy. Each tells a tale to make you realize how special Rudy was. I could name so many people far more worthy of the Reaper's scythe, but the Reaper has never been one to choose people worthy of death. He often chooses people unworthy, and that was Rudy. I guess I can say something negative about Rudy—he was mortal.

My sadness becomes anger; Napoleon takes the podium and sheds crocodile tears. He speaks of Rudy as if he knew him, crying and stumbling over his words. What little respect I had left for this man was now gone. Just a few moments before he was fine, joking around with a few people, and now on display, he is emotionally overcome. It would be best for me to avoid him, for as long as I am a Marine in the Marine Corps.

The ceremony concludes and Marines in single file walk by his helmet, boots, and dog tags. I wipe my tears and nose on my sleeve and walk up to Rudy symbolized. I kiss my fingers, touch his helmet, look up and point above with the same hand. Much love Rudy, much love.

Afterwards, Marines huddle together, completely different now that the ceremony has taken place. Reality sets in and each one is devastated. Rarely do you see someone loved as much as this Marine, but how often do you see those so loved taken away first? There are babies, Marines, soldiers, and civilians all dying for what? Some say it's God's plan, but what sort of plan justifies this? I curse God under my breath saying, "What the fuck are you thinking? Do you even give a fuck?"

I take a knee; it didn't matter where I took it, I just needed to do it right then. I take a knee and take off my cover; I stare off into the distance hearing sniffles and hearts breaking. Four and a half months remain and what have we got to show for it? Word has it that we're leaving Al Asad and heading back to Al Qaim. What purpose did we serve down here?

Back in my tent, I grabbed a book and lay down on my cot. I needed some fantasy after this heavy dose of reality, so I reached back into my childhood years and read a book based on the Batman cartoon series. I hadn't read much since joining the Marine Corps, but reading was something that I enjoyed. We were to leave for more missions outside of Al Asad; I took my book with me.

We sat in positions, manning roads and just sitting there out in the open. It was to show presence, but it was a waste of time. I would go with one of the platoons in Alpha Company to a position by some standing water. It was nearly June, so the days of being cold were now over. We sat in the sweltering heat, drinking as much water as we could. You could drink five gallons of water and you'd still only piss once a day. That was after you woke up in the morning.

Flies were everywhere, all around us. They buzzed in your ear; they landed on your lips. In the distance you could see a stream of raw sewage. If you looked long and hard enough, you could watch a fly bath in someone's shit and piss and then fly over and land on your food or in your mouth. All I could do was try to read, but before I could finish a sentence, I would have to shoo at least five flies.

For a few days I sat in this position, fighting flies and reading about Batman. There were people around, but even they knew it wasn't smart to be out there among the flies and filth. We finally headed back to Al Asad. Our mission was over. Batman's mission was over too; he won...again. We had two days to pack our stuff and get ready to head back to Al Qaim. Apparently, while we were away, the insurgency was crossing over into Jordan and back with ease. This border made our border with Mexico look like the Great Wall of China. The gamble to move a majority of the battalion down to Al Asad didn't seem worth it to me, and what did we have to show for it? A dead Marine and an area of operation we left behind without enough resources to ensure it would be secure? Yet we were told that our mission in Al Asad was successful. Bullshit.

"I'm driving," I tell one of the Marines of the vehicle I was moved to. I was now in an LAV-L. General Mattis, who was borrowing LAVs from our battalion, had one of his LAVs hit and needed a replacement. The first sergeant had to give up his vehicle, so he took my spot in the LAV-C2. I was moved, no problem. The LAV-L had more room in the back for me to lie down and sleep anyway.

I get into the driver's compartment and put on the helmet/headset combo. The vehicle commander is a Marine corporal; he wasn't going to tell me no. I get comfortable and start the vehicle. I had driven one of these before, but that was in Kuwait. We're "Oscar-Mike," and I put my foot to the pedal. As we pull away there is a familiar face in the distance, standing by the exit from the Camp. It was our previous battalion sergeant major. He sees me as my head is popped out of the driver's hatch. He raises both hands and points at me. I raise mine and point back at him. He yells something that I can't hear; even if I had I wouldn't have been able to understand him. It was probably my name I am sure.

"Hey sergeant major, they never gave me my award!" I yelled in his direction. He shook his head; he heard me loud and clear. I took my hand and gestured my finger going in and out of a hole formed by my other hand. He nods as he understands full well what I meant. "They fucked me."

I drive, having to concentrate on everything I am doing. This isn't a car; this is a moving hunk of steel that doesn't stop on a dime, and if I hit something, it won't be as forgiving. It feels like I am driving a school bus, and I imagine that I am—anything to keep my mind off the time we had just spent in Al Asad.

The vehicle commander puts one of his earphones under the flap of the headset I am wearing and into my ear. He plays Metallica and I know exactly what song I want to hear playing.

"You got 'Enter Sandman,'" I ask him.

Without a reply he changes the track and the beginning of the song plays. It has to be one of the best songs ever because it prepares you for greatness. What I didn't know was that he and the other Marines in the vehicle had found a way to splice the music throughout the rest of the vehicle. Down the road and driving north back to Al Qaim and whatever mess we had left up there, I sang along with the song. The vehicle commander behind me sang along as well, both of us singing at the top of our lungs. The engine is loud; we're tearing down the road. The Marines in the back were also singing as one.

"Exit light. Enter night. Take my hand...we're off to never never-land."

Chapter 33

Green Eggs and Ham

"What the fuck do you think you're doing here?" I ask a Marine in my living quarters back in Al Qaim. We arrived late, around two in the morning; he was asleep in my bed of all places. The difference this time around though, there was a mattress. He gets up and gathers his things; we were all back and setting down our gear. "No, leave the mattress behind; that can be your thanks to me for letting you use my bed," I say to the dejected Marine.

    I take off my boots and go to sleep. A few Marines who stayed behind greeted us when we came in. We left with Rudy; we came back without him, complete and utter failure in my opinion. In the morning I would be meeting with the Alpha Company staff NCOs and officers for an idea of what was next.

    I get up a few hours after the other Marines do. I was no longer in their platoon, but they weren't going to ask me to leave. I fucking built the place with another guy. There was no way they would get away with that. They probably didn't want to deal with me getting upset; I kind of had a reputation. I rolled out of my bed and see the other staff NCOs are already dressed; I smile at them, knowing they envied my sleeping in, and head outside to brush my teeth.

    At the meeting, we discuss a short mission with another company to help out in Husaybah. With most of the battalion south in Al Asad, insurgents had a field day planting IEDs and anti-tank mines. When I was out brushing my teeth earlier, I saw that there was a graveyard of LAVs that were torn to shreds by IEDs and mines. LAVs look intimidating, but even steel can rip like paper.

    We would be leaving in a few days, which meant I would be able to spend my birthday at camp. I was turning twenty-six years old, and I was still one of the younger Marines in the battalion.

Everyone was taking it easy; Alpha Company was in the back, playing three-on-three half-court basketball. I wanted in on the action, so I say, "I got next!" I pick my staff sergeant buddy from Alpha Company; he's got size and looked like he had coordination. I believe the first sergeant was our third guy, but I am not too sure. The winning team from the previous game got the ball first—first one to eleven wins.

Now, some people exaggerate, but I have no reason to. It's not like I'm going to be drafted by the Knicks by saying I was great. Growing up in Brooklyn wasn't easy, especially when you're a skinny Arab kid in a predominately Italian neighborhood. Going to school where 65 percent of the kids are African American didn't help much either. No one liked you if you were Arab, Indian, or any sort of brown that wasn't Latin. When pickup games would take place, they would never pick me or any other Arab kids, so we had to wait for the time to be right to get on the court. Believe me, if you have to wait for hours to get on the court, you don't ever want to leave it, so you have to be good.

One shot from the key, good. Another along the baseline…also good. Dribble drive, stop and pop…nothing but the bottom of the net. I was lethal. If they doubled up, I fed it inside to my buddy who would then kick it back out to me if he were doubled. We didn't lose one game.

"Damn, Staff Sergeant. I didn't know you could play," a few Marines from the losing side said.

"Why, cause I'm Arab?" I respond. "That's racist!" I'd flashed them a smile showing them I was kidding.

"Man, you're just lucky. It must be your birthday, Joe," said the Alpha Company first sergeant.

"Why, actually it is. Thanks for remembering, First Sergeant."

Our mission in Husaybah was supposed to be a brief one. We were to go out for the morning, find nothing and come back to camp, awaiting new orders. Except it wouldn't happen that way. Things always have a way of getting fucked up.

After patrolling for a few hours and finding nothing, the company commander tells the other platoons to get ready to head back. I get out of my vehicle to take a much needed piss when all of a sudden a sound like I've never heard before explodes somewhere in front of me. It was evil. It sounded as if it was ripping through the air, shredding all around it. I see a small black mushroom cloud and I know exactly what it was. I shake and put away my piece and mount the vehicle. I hear the radio going crazy, one of our vehicles is hit. We're on the move without hesitation.

We get to the area where the IED detonated and see who it was that was hit. It was one of the Marines who had been hit twice before. He was fine, but he was a bit shaken up. "What the fuck, sir? That's three times already! It's like someone's out to fucking get me," says the Marine sergeant to the company commander out of frustration.

We stop traffic and block off the area. We begin a search of the entire visible area to include the homes in the general vicinity. I knew I would be asking lots of questions. I never liked it when someone tried to kill me or one of my Marines.

The answers I got were all very similar to, "We didn't see anything, we were asleep."

Yeah, sure they were lazy, but who sleeps all fucking day, especially when there are tanks and LAVs belonging to another country in the area? I could understand they were afraid of insurgents targeting them, but giving in to these assholes would only make them stronger and more in control, and that's what these people were allowing to happen.

The battalion commander is on the scene. He is with the company commander and me. In the distance we see two Marines calling out to us. They found an IED that hadn't exploded; it had the trigger (a cell phone) still on it and powered, ready to receive a call.

The first thing they tell you to not do when you find an IED is to touch it. Well that's the first thing we do. We walk over to the IED; the battalion commander picks it up and asks the EOD technician, "Can you get me the cell phone off of this?"

"Yes sir, but we'll be dead by the time I do," he responds.

"Umm, sir, what the fuck are you doing?" I ask. "You know that shit is live right?"

"Oh yeah, maybe I shouldn't be handling this."

He places the IED back down, and I give the company commander a dirty look.

He nods and smiles, even he was shocked but it didn't dawn on him until after I had said something. You can't blame these guys though; we had all been blown up and shot at for the past few months. We were tired, without a real mission, and we had just lost a Marine not too long ago.

We get called to a vehicle down the road. Marines from another company have someone in their custody. "This fucker, question him," a gunnery sergeant from that company tells me.

The man wouldn't respond. He was being belligerent by refusing to cooperate. We would be taking him in, but I wanted to have some fun.

"Hey sir, you mind if I do the handcuffing myself?" I ask the CO.

"Sure Joe, go right ahead."

I wanted to show everyone there how handcuffs could be used to take down someone you want to detain. I tell the Iraqi man to stand still; I wanted to show the Marines something. He decides to cooperate at that time. It made no sense to me. I stand behind him and take him down with one cuff on his right wrist. I give a class to the Marines right then and there. I don't know why I felt the need to do it in front of everyone in the middle of the day, but I was feeling froggy I guess.

"If you want to hurt him, move the cuff like this," I say as I hold the cuff with my hand twisting one side of it, digging the cuff into the bone of the man's wrist. He screams, but I feel no remorse. He could have been the one who tried to kill us.

We wait for the EOD team to bring their robot out for the detonation of the IED. The first attempt fails, the robot's battery was dead. A team had to head back to Camp to pick up another battery. This is where Snickers earns their money, because we would not be going anywhere for a while. The first IED went off in the afternoon; it was nearly midnight before we got the robot working, detonated the IED, and headed back to Al Qaim. When we got in, I went right to bed. I'd meet with Alpha Company again in the morning.

The next morning we went out to another part of Husaybah. A few of the Marines put on a happy face and mingled with the children. While I was out walking with the CO and the first sergeant, a few of the Marines pulled out some Maxim Magazines to show some of the boys. They loved it!

"Why are you helping them?" an Iraqi male asks me. "Why are you helping these non-believers?"

This took me back a little; I didn't know how to respond without punching the guy in the face.

"How are they non-believers?" I ask him, "You believe in Jesus and Moses like them right?"

Another day gone and nothing positive to show for it, at least this time around no one was blown up or hurt. We head back to Al Qaim and wait for the CO to return; apparently he has some news for us. We sit around and wait, all of us wondering what it would be. Maybe it would be another trip to Al Asad, maybe Fallujah again? Either way, we knew we weren't going to be staying here. Akashat was our area of operation, but it was as boring as it gets.

The CO walks in with a smile on his face. Rarely is the man not smiling, so it could be anything. He begins his brief. South of Fallujah there is a small Army FOB named FOB Kalsu. It was named after a fallen soldier. The soldiers operating that base to our shock were the same soldiers we replaced back in March. Apparently, as they were boarding a plane in Kuwait to head home after a year deployed, they were told they had to go back to Iraq. Now that is fucked up. How do you give someone the idea of being able to see their family and then snatch it away just because you can? The Marine Corps would never do that to their Marines, no matter who was in charge.

Our mission while down in Kalsu? Well here's the problem.

The 1st Marine Division was located in Camp Fallujah. They have convoys that go up the MSR (Military Supply Route) every day. These supplies can be just about anything: material, ammunition, food, and so forth. This is how we are told. I am paraphrasing, but you can imagine the thoughts each one of us had: "Convoys heading to Fallujah have been hit on a constant basis. Because this has been happening, food supplies have not been able to be delivered to Camp Fallujah. Our mission is to escort these convoys ensuring they get to Camp Fallujah without a problem."

If you read into that you can form your own opinion, but this is what I got out of it…

"The Marines who never leave Camp Fallujah have been complaining because they haven't been able to eat fresh eggs and waffles in the morning. The convoys containing products such as ice cream sandwiches have been hit. So we're going to go down there and make sure these Marines get their ice cream sandwiches."

We would be down there for a month; a Marine Expeditionary Unit (MEU) would be coming out to replace us. Yeah that makes sense, send a company-sized element down to hold down the fort for a MEU inbound. We would leave in the morning.

Now here's a misconception many have. Not every Marine who deploys goes out on patrols and eats dirt like we were. There were many who were staying at the camps, getting fat off the good food and getting paid the same as the ones who were out getting blown the fuck up. We would get a few day's rest and relaxation, but we also got dirty looks from some of the Marines who had to wait in line a little bit longer because we were there taking up their space.

I began to see why there was a divide within the Corps between support Marines and infantry Marines. The grunts felt underappreciated and overlooked, while the support Marines got their fair share of glory and kept their uniforms clean. Sure, I was one of those types once, but when you taste the dirt as you're eating it, you begin to show an appreciation for what one of our commandants once said, "Every Marine is a rifleman." Every Marine needs to be ready; I was now, but what about the others?

We stop by Fallujah on the way to Kalsu and have some breakfast. We figured we could get some good chow in before going to a camp we had never heard of until then. I asked for an omelet and some hash browns; I get something green that looks like it was shaped and then scooped out and something else that looked like foam shavings.

I take a bite out of what they said was food and nearly puke. I start gagging while getting up to throw away my plate.

"Yeah sir, I see why we're going down there now," I say to the CO. "I don't want die, but I would certainly be willing to for some good food."

Chapter 34

Your Way Right Away

I hate sand, I really do. Ever since I had gotten back from Iraq the first time, I had avoided the beach because of my distain for sand. When we got back the last time, some of the Marines I worked with would invite me to go to the beach, but I refused every time. I was not going to go anywhere near sand after that one sandy and fucked up day in March of 2003. You would think I would be perfectly all right with sand because of my ancestry, but I hated it more than anyone else. It would get on your body in places you didn't know existed.

We pull off the road and all of a sudden, out of nowhere, a military base appears before our eyes. We are let into the front gate by the soldiers manning it. Our vehicles are staged, and I get out of mine. My feet hit the ground causing a dust cloud. The sand here at FOB (we would be changing that to Camp real soon I am sure) Kalsu was like baby powder. Any idea of me avoiding it had gone out the window.

There are tents made up where, I assume, we will be staying. They are surrounded by concrete walls that are ten feet high. There are sandbags everywhere. You might as well have them, there is plenty of sand to be put to good use. FOB Kalsu was an area that was just off the main highway, a perfect target for incoming mortars. Apparently mortars were more frequent than rain, because it was drier than a Dane Cook joke.

I head to a wooden building strategically placed in the center of the base. It was made of the cheapest plywood Iraqi money could buy, but put together well enough that it prevented the non-existent rain to penetrate. In the building there were two large rooms and six other rooms in the rear. The company XO stakes out the area and finds a room to his liking. "This one's mine," he says as he points to a room in the far right corner.

The company commander talks to some of the soldiers in charge; they are grizzled, tired, and emotionally unaffected by us being there. They had been in this situation before, on the verge of going home only to be pulled out of a plane on the tarmac, waiting to take off. I sit down at a table waiting to be told what we would be doing next. To my left is a soldier focused on the laptop screen in front of him. He's having a webcam conversation with a family member. He is silent while his fingers are doing the talking for him, probably telling his family that he might be coming home soon, but they shouldn't hold their breath expecting it.

"You have Internet here," I ask him rudely disturbing his conversation.

"Yup," he says without looking up.

I could see that he doesn't want to talk, but I go on anyway, "Looking forward to going home?"

"We'll see," he says.

My buddy the staff sergeant joined in and got about the same response. Our concern was the Internet and being able to communicate with the outside world. We started to plan how we would set up the building by routing Internet into each room and getting it so that we could set up a common area for us to surf the net without having to wait in line for the Internet Center they set up behind the building.

After a few moments, the company commander comes back and gives orders to his platoon commanders. I then ask him what I would be doing; secretly hoping that I wouldn't have to go out on random missions and be able to just lay low for a while. He confirms my wish; that I would be his go-to guy whenever he needed to go off base and see to something. I smile knowing that I would have some Internet time and some time to clean up, or what would be considered clean given the circumstances.

The first sergeant and a few of the Marines from my vehicle would also be staying in the building; they'd each get a room. I decided to stay in a tent that my buddy had set up for us. He was the maintenance chief for Alpha Company, and he was recently selected for promotion to the rank of gunnery sergeant, so he basically got to do whatever he wanted to do. He commandeered a tent for a few of us and we set it up the way we liked it. This included satellite television. Yes, I got to watch the Oprah interview with President Clinton.

My mission at Camp (see I told you we'd change it) Kalsu was simple, but it was better than being a fulltime interpreter. I wanted to help as much as the next guy, but being a Marine staff sergeant and possessing the abilities that helped me get to staff sergeant in five years were not in use. It made me feel useless when it came to being an everyday Marine. I didn't like being utilized as just an interpreter; I was a Marine first and foremost, a leader of Marines above all.

The first sergeant saw this; he knew I was dying to do more than just speak to locals. He must have gone to the company commander with this because he came up to me tasking me with setting up a perimeter for the entire camp. The first sergeant also tasked me with morning duties to ensure that everything was done and done without delay. I was given duty every other night to answer radio calls from out in the field and respond to anything that might have occurred. I was happy to be more than an interpreter and the first sergeant pulled me aside later and spoke to me about it, "You know what, Joe? I gave you a task and you went out and got it done. That's what I like to see, and it's obvious why you've been successful so far in your career."

The first few days and weeks at Kalsu were interesting. For the first time since I had been with Alpha Company, I had a standard routine. I would get up, do my duties, and go on trips with the CO whenever and wherever needed. We even made a trip to Baghdad International Airport. There were rumors of a Burger King in Baghdad, and I wanted to confirm its existence. It was also located in the so-called "Green Zone," and I wanted to see if it was indeed "green." I'd had enough of the sand.

Baghdad International Airport was enormous. There were soldiers everywhere and an endless amount of living trailers where the soldiers stayed. They were the Army. They had the money to buy trailers. The Marine Corps used tents doused with kerosene. It's to keep the rain from causing leaks apparently, because we know how often it rains in the desert. The kerosene experiment didn't last long though. An entire camp once went up in flames; they found other ways to waterproof the tents.

I honestly have no idea why we went to Baghdad International Airport. All I knew was that the thought of a Whopper sandwich made me want one to the point that I believed it to exist without confirmation. I stop by a place where we could withdraw a cash advance from our pay. If there was a Burger King, I wanted to be able to buy enough for the ride back to Kalsu and for dinner that night.

While waiting in line for cash, I spoke to one of the soldiers behind me and asked him if there is an actual Burger King on base. He nods and says it was by the "main exchange." My eyes widen with excitement. They actually had a Burger King; the rumors were true. I guess this is how Juan Ponce de León would have felt if he had actually discovered the Fountain of Youth. I pulled out enough money for eight Whoppers (with cheese of course); I would be dining like a king tonight. No pun intended.

I am finally standing in a line the length of a football field at the Burger King. Everyone is waiting with dreams of a Burger King meal, their stomachs growling with anticipation. Every few moments you'd see a soldier or a Marine walking away with a smile on their face. It is the simple things in life that we take for granted. Give a Marine a cheeseburger, and you give him hope. I hold a place in line for my buddy; he had walked to the main exchange to buy a few items. As he comes out of the building, his facial expression tells it all.

"They sell big screen TV's in there," he says with shock.

That's never a good sign, in my opinion. How long do they plan to make us to stay in Iraq, if they are selling big screen televisions? I place my order and receive a few bags of Burger King goodness. The Burger King was not a building as one would expect but instead a booth. It was no bigger than a booth you would see at a carnival or a fair, but they were churning out burgers like there was no tomorrow. None of us asked where they were getting the burgers from; we just wanted some artery clogging food that actually had some flavor to it.

As I walk away with the same smile I had seen others display when they received their food, I overhear two soldiers talking about stopping by a Starbucks next. Only the United States of America would ever think of bringing a Burger King and a Starbucks to a combat zone. Why not? We're trying to bring democracy to a country torn apart by a dictator and now an insurgency. What says "democracy" better than a Double Whopper with cheese and some fries?

As we head back, I sit down in the back of the LAV. I pull a Whopper out from my bag and unwrap it. The sheer smell of it gave me an erection. I peel off the tomatoes, pickles, and onions because I have never liked anything resembling vegetables touching my food. I hand them over to another Marine who stacks them on top of his burger. My hands are filthy from the dirt surrounding us, by the sand and the greasy vehicle now taking us back to Kalsu, but I have neither the time nor the inclination to wash my hands. If anything, it would add an extra Iraqi flavor to the meal. The Whopper was sloppy and messy, much like the back of the vehicle I was in, but it was delicious!

I get back to Kalsu and back to my tent. Our day is over and I decide to chill out and watch some television. I put the left over Whoppers into the small refrigerator by my cot and grab a seat. I turn on the news to see something that catches me by surprise. It was video of a United States Marine blindfolded and tied to a chair. A sword was placed over his head and a threat was read saying he would be beheaded unless we blah blah blah, the usual terrorist bullshit. He was a Marine corporal of Lebanese decent named Wassef Ali Hassoun. The Marines in my tent watched in disbelief and silence. I, on the other hand, felt quite the contrary.

"Bullshit. He's fucking faking it," I shout. "First of all, Marines don't get fucking taken as POWs. We'd rather be fucking dead. Second, how the fuck does a Marine just disappear in Iraq without his fucking command knowing where the fuck he is? Third, since when do these fucking terrorists hide from the fucking camera's view?"

They didn't know what to say.

I knew what he was thinking. He hated being an interpreter. He knew how to get around; there were some perks to being able to speak the language. If you knew the right people, you could get whatever you wanted. Just in Kalsu I was able to negotiate a television, a satellite dish, two washers, and a few other things such as holsters for our pistols for a modest price. If you establish a relationship with someone in country, you could basically get whatever you wanted.

As much as I could understand the frustration of being an interpreter, I also understand why some Marines become certified Arab speakers as well. They get paid extra for it. Yes, it's about the money. I, on the other hand, flunked the written and oral exam, so I get paid nothing. It doesn't stop the Marine Corps from utilizing my talents as a speaker or someone who was able to read body language. Too bad they couldn't test me on that. I'd be rich! Even with the extra pay, it is a thankless duty. As I have said before, it wasn't until I was given more leadership authority by Alpha Company, originally granted to me by my promotion warrant and with the first sergeant's assistance, that I felt like I was any sort of a leader of Marines during this conflict. I have also given my Marines instructions that if I were to ever be taken by the enemy, to shoot me. They had better unload on those who abduct me. I'd rather be dead.

The video bothered me from two points of view. The first, obviously, was that he was a Marine and Marines are not known for giving up and allowing capture. The other was that he was an Arab like me. If he could do this, what did other Marines think about me? I don't understand why anyone would want to betray another person for their own safety; you still had to live with yourself after the betrayal.

Visibly angered by this, the CO asked me why I looked so upset. I explained why I thought that Marine was full of shit and he nodded his head in agreement. I reassured him that, "I might bitch and complain about being an interpreter, but I'd never do that shit, sir!" I don't think he ever had a doubt in his mind. If I were going to walk, I would have by now.

The next morning we get word over the radio that the United States has handed over "control" of the country back to the Iraqis. This announcement comes two days earlier than expected to surprise the insurgents so they couldn't stage attacks. It's not like we were really giving control over to the Iraqis. It just meant we couldn't shoot unless being shot upon first. A stupid tactic that I don't think anyone really took to be a strategy. If someone is pointing a weapon at me, I'm not going to say to myself, "Wait, he hasn't pulled the trigger…. Wait! He missed me…" Just kill the motherfucker and deal with it later.

Our latest mission was more reactionary than anything else. We provided escort from a place called "Scania" up to Camp Fallujah without attack. It was when we manned the main highway that problems ensued.

A Marine convoy drove by the position Alpha Company's platoons were manning. I guess one of the platoons was too relaxed and their Marines were sitting around, lounging about out in the open. The senior officer actually pulls over to the side of the road and demands to speak to the Marines' platoon commander. Out comes the lieutenant with his sleeve cuffs rolled up once and his uniform hanging off of him like crumbled paper. He was relieved on the spot; our mission would now change.

Word got to General Mattis that this had occurred and our company commander got an earful. The CO convinced General Mattis to allow the lieutenant to continue on, but the company commander had to babysit him. Running the mission from Camp was no longer going to be good enough, for the rest our time in Kalsu, we'd be out on the road and be with the rest of the Marines. Every now and then we'd go back to the Camp to regroup and clean up, but we only stayed for a few hours at most.

It's the Fourth of July and we are finally able to rest. The mess hall was scheduled to be serving what appeared to be a steak dinner! I'm lying on my cot in my shorts and t-shirt. Outside the temperature reads 140 degrees Fahrenheit. It is so hot mosquitoes are bursting into flames. In the distance we hear an explosion. "Oh shit," I say, "I hope that wasn't us."

Within moments the company commander's driver walks into my tent saying, "Staff Sergeant, vehicles from 1st Platoon got hit. We gotta go."

"Did anyone get hurt," I ask.

He tells me it was the lieutenant's vehicle, the same Lieutenant who was relieved a few days earlier. Another vehicle in his platoon was hit too. No one was killed, but they were being medically evacuated. I get dressed, knowing I would be missing out on the steak dinner this Fourth of July day and hoped we would get this sorted out quickly, but I knew I would not be so lucky.

Talk about a bad week…the Marine lieutenant spent a few days wondering if he'd have a career in the Marine Corps after he'd been relieved, and now he was blown up and knocked unconscious, knocked out by an IED that ripped his vehicle to shreds. The other vehicle that was hit was also damaged and shrapnel tore into a Marine sergeant's leg.

One of the most motivating and heroic moments I have ever come to know had just occurred, and it reminded me why Marines are a maniacal bunch. This Marine sergeant, a motivator if you had ever known of one, was a man that talked the talk and walked the walk. He lay on a stretcher bleeding from his leg. As he's being tended to by the Navy corpsman, the helicopter taking him to a military hospital arrives. Knowing that those who tried to kill him were probably still watching, he orders the Marines who are carrying his stretcher to put him down. They do so and he gets up and walks to the helicopter under his own strength, waving off anyone who attempts to help him. He was not going to give the attackers the satisfaction of seeing how badly they had really hurt him.

I begin to question the locals, "I don't know what happened; I was sleeping. It's safe here," would come from their mouths as if it was rehearsed over and over. I was with a squad of Marines who had just seen one of their Marines hurt and their platoon commander knocked unconscious. They were frustrated and wanted payback, but there is only so much payback you can get when your hands are tied by the rules of engagement. Seeing the obvious frustration on the Marines' faces and the realization that this was going nowhere, I made a decision that I was not authorized to make, but was willing to take the heat for it.

Every Iraqi home was allowed one rifle, one AK-47 rifle they could use for protection. This was something they were allowed to have by coalition forces and now that they were a sovereign nation, they possessed that right even more.

"You have a weapon here," I ask a man in the house we had stopped to question.

"Yes, we were told we could have one to fight off the Ali Baba," he replied.

Ali Baba was what they called a thief, go figure. I ask him, "If it is safe here, then why would you need a weapon?

He didn't have an answer.

"Show me the weapon," I demand from him speaking softly but in a firm voice. He walks inside his home and shows me his rifle and magazines without any ammo, completely clean and unused. I take it, hand it to one of the Marines, and walk away saying, "Thank you."

He walks up to me asking me about his weapon. With anger I reply, "I thought you said it was safe here? If it's safe, then you don't need it. Are you saying it's not safe?"

No reply.

I then tell the Marines with me what my plan is. If they all felt it was so safe, I would disarm each and every household. I did not trust or believe them. I knew that someone was hiding something. Someone was hiding someone else. Hell, some of the people we talked to were probably the brains behind the explosives. The Marines had no issue with this; they supported it, and they supported me.

Hours pass, my uniform is drenched with my sweat as if I had gone for a swim. My mouth is dry and my head is pounding. I have disarmed everyone in the vicinity of the explosion and even some further inland. I told the company commander what and why I had done so with a simple response, "Fuck 'em sir."

A week later the 24th Marine Expeditionary Unit arrives with much fanfare. We travel down to Scania, the place I considered home of the ice cream sandwich the Marines up in Fallujah were now enjoying on a daily basis, to help the 24th MEU find Camp Kalsu. They see that it is barely an operational base; I mean we were the only ones there and we were a company-sized element. These guys were huge in numbers!

The MEU had things we didn't have, like money to buy whatever they wanted, manpower, equipment, and the longevity to see the mission through. We had been jumping from mission to mission so often that we would never get to see the results of our efforts. Within a few days the camp went through massive changes. More Marines meant more living areas, and more living areas meant more targets for the Iraqis to drop their mortars on.

The Fourth of July incident had angered me to the point of belligerence. I was introduced to a Marine major who had spent the first Operation Iraqi Freedom in the Pentagon planning and writing reports of what it was we were doing in Iraq. His uniform was clean; his rank insignia was new and fresh out of the box. He had a smile on his face that was so annoying; all I wanted to do was punch him. It's not that he was a bad guy; it's just that I was frustrated over the happenings in this shithole and now we were being shown the door…but not before we went on a humanitarian mission.

Bring out the cameras and reporters; yes, the Marine Corps has an occupational field where you can be a reporter. We were going to win the hearts and minds of these people, and we were going to keep trying to accomplish this by offering them water! Spare me. On this mission, we go house to house once again. I sarcastically ask the Iraqis who had come to know me by now, if they wanted some water. Most of them refused, thinking we poisoned it. I don't argue and walk away, but the major who I had met earlier wanted to stop and talk to every single person. This was annoying the hell out of me. He asked them what their concerns were. They wanted nothing to do with us. When we came across the few who did want water and help, he beamed with pride. On the way back he and I had a conversation that I think was a bit over the top…even for me.

"These people, Staff Sergeant, all they want is water and electricity. I mean they're no different than you or me. They just want the simple things in life," he says to me.

"Sir, where were you last year?"

"I was in the Pentagon watching along with everyone else what was going on over here," he responded.

"Well sir, it's easy to think that all these people want is water and electricity when you're sitting at your desk and we're getting blown up and shot at. They don't only want water and electricity. They want us dead, too. But of course you were in the Pentagon drinking coffee and reading your paper in your comfortable chair while we were out here eating shit."

I say this to him with a stone cold look on my face. I look at the road ahead of me as I speak without once looking over at him. He didn't have to worry about IEDs just yet, but I had been watching out for them since the first one blew up in our convoy months before. The Marines in the vehicle with me and the major stare at me, wondering if the major was going to lash out at me for what I had just said.

"I'm sorry you feel that way, Staff Sergeant," he says to me.

"I am too, sir, but then again, no I'm not."

Chapter 35

Father of Mine

As a reward for a job well done in Kalsu, we were told we would get four days of rest and relaxation in Fallujah. Now tell someone you love that you're going to Fallujah for rest and relaxation, and they'll think you've gone batshit crazy. When we were told this though, we were excited; we would be reaping the results of our work. We'd be able to eat some ice cream sandwiches!

When we get to Camp Fallujah, we're greeted by a master sergeant and shown to a building sectioned off from the rest of the base. We're told this place is a getaway for Marines who earn it. We are put into rooms and shown a recreation center. A few Marines are already staying there, but what was different about them is that they were unarmed.

While there were some who faked mental anguish to get out of being in Iraq, some actually had legitimate demons they were fighting. They were unarmed for fear that they would commit suicide, and from what I saw in the eyes of these Marines, they wouldn't hesitate to end their own lives. Some things are hard to live with when your mind replays them over and over. I could understand that. I could sympathize with them.

It was a nice getaway, a break from reality. Sure we were still in Iraq, but we were able to let our guard down. We were able to get some good food in us, replenish our supplies of Pringles, cigarettes, dip, and for me, some Chef Boyardee Beefaroni. I found a way to heat it up and have a hot pasta meal. I'd wedge a can of Beefaroni between the hull of our LAV and the exhaust muffler. On a road march it would get hot enough that when we stopped, it would be perfect. I cleared the shelf at the exchange on base; I was good for a few days.

The first sergeant and my buddy, the newly promoted gunnery sergeant, had me visit their living space. They produced a bottle of Crown Royal and some Coca-Cola. Somehow the first sergeant got some ice. The Crown and Coke didn't surprise me; it was how he got some ice cubes that really shocked me. We were forbidden from drinking in Iraq. Anyone caught would be dealt with through non-judicial punishment. We were senior Marines, and we had each other's backs. Who gave a shit, if it was just a drink?

We sat there drinking, joking, and laughing about who knows what. It was just good company and then all of a sudden there was a mortar attack. The ammo supply on base was hit and by sheer luck caused a chain reaction that set off the other munitions. For a good hour and a half there was a firework display of ammunition. Marines jumped on top of vehicles to get a good look. I yelled over at them through the window of our room, "Hey, you know some of that stuff can still kill you?"

Accountability is important. We are each told to get out of our rooms to account for everyone. Out of sheer belligerence or stupidity, I walked out with my beverage. Everyone knew what it was, but no one said anything to me. The officers of Alpha Company were doing the same thing, so who were they to judge? Every Marine was accounted for and we were allowed to go back to what we were doing.

Our next mission wasn't really much of a mission; we would be going to assist Delta Company in their area of operation in Western Iraq. It was in a town called Ar Rutbah, and the base we would call home was Camp Korean Village. The word going around was that it had been a construction worker camp before the war where Koreans lived. That made sense to me once it was explained.

It was now July 15. I finish my drink and grab the satellite phone from the first sergeant to call Yemen to speak to my family. It was also my dad's birthday. I didn't think anything of this call when I made it, but it went as such…

> Dad: Hello?
> Me: Hello, Dad. It's me, Khaled.
> Dad: Khaled? How are you son? Where are you?
> Me: I'm good Dad; I'm still in the Philippines. We're doing an exercise. How are you?

Dad: Good, good. You should see your son. He's so big. Here talk to him…
(He hands the phone to my son)
Dad: (in the background talking to my son) It's you father, baba… (My son just breathes heavily into the phone until my father takes the phone back)
Dad: You should see his hair. It's red; he's beautiful. Who do you want to talk to? Your mother?
Me: Sure, where is she?
Dad: Right here. (Calls out to my mom) Get over here. Khaled's on the phone.
Dad: Okay son, take care of yourself, and I love you.
Me: I love you too.

During the conversation with my mom and then my wife I remembered it was my dad's birthday. I tell my wife to wish him a one for me. When she does he says out loud, "Thank you. Thank you son! See my son calls me to wish me a happy birthday. He didn't forget." I ask my wife to make him a cake and to make him feel loved. She said she'd take care of it.

I don't know when my father first came to the United States exactly so what I tell you is based on what he told us, but his story is indeed inspirational.

My father was born into a poor family. They lived in the mountains in a village called Yafa. To his family a car was something that existed only in stories told to them by others who witnessed its existence. Travel was by donkey or foot and there wasn't much money to be thrown around to purchase a donkey. My grandfather is still a mystery to me, and so is my grandmother. They both died before I had ever seen a photograph of either of them. My father was the third child of what I think was seven children. He had two older brothers and the rest, three brothers and two sisters, were younger than him.

My father walked miles on end to bring water to his family. He and his older brothers walked for three days or more to the capital city of then Southern Yemen, Aden, to work for pennies and scraps. My father was a servant for a very fortunate family in Aden. He told me stories of how they treated him and another servant, a woman who took care of their children. They were both fed the leftovers and were given these leftovers as if they were dogs. In fact, he mentioned the dog was treated better than both he and the female servant. My father was only seven years old.

Talk about slaving for pennies and doing what you can. I believe this put a drive in my father's heart. Here was this family who seemed like they didn't have to work for anything, treating him as if he was a being without a soul. My father worked for them for years. He sent money back to his family in Yafa and saved what he could. Somehow, someway, he saved enough money to go to the US Embassy in Southern Yemen to get a visa and a one-way ticket to New York City. He was around eighteen years old. He had done this on his own, by sacrificing himself and probably putting aside his pride. His older brothers joined him. My father knew some others who had escaped the hardships of a Communist Southern Yemen and shared an apartment with them in New York. He lived with seven others in this apartment. He learned some of the language and worked his ass off. He joined the National Maritime Union to become a merchant marine. He started as a deckhand, someone who mopped the floor, scraped paint off the side of the ship, and someone who would tie up a ship in snow, rain, sleet, and wind. His brothers did the same, except my father was not like his brothers at all.

We ask ourselves why we go through some of the things we go through and we wonder why we suffer at times and think it will never end. People tend to give up and give in; my father was not one of those people. His brothers continued to do manual labor and the kind of work that did not put pressure on them. What pressure could one encounter doing manual labor that they could care less if it was done or not? My father wanted to learn. He liked how things operated. He asked questions, and he took in answers and became an expert. He was never satisfied, and it drove him even further. That family he worked for as a child really motivated him. My father wanted to work for more money in the engine room. He wanted the responsibility of the heart of the ship, and he got it.

For years my father worked and advanced. He learned the language with proficiency and embraced the customs of the United States. He had grown to love the country and saved some money. These weren't the pennies he was making as a servant. He was being paid more than teachers, firemen, police officers, and government employees. My father was exceeding the salary and money content that the family he worked for had ever dreamed of. Still, this did not satisfy him. My father had one thing in his mind now. He wanted to show his worth to those who questioned him, and he was going home to Yemen to do so.

He was twenty-five years old now. He and his brothers got together and decided to build a home for their parents and other siblings. The largest home in Yemen was two or three stories and very slim in stature. His brothers and he put their money together and built the largest home in all of Yemen. It was completed in 1969, and people came from far away to see it. It was the same year the United States planted its flag on the moon and became a defining moment in its history. My father planted his flag and legacy right then and there, too. He had indeed arrived.

The village of Yafa is bare. It had few homes and plenty of mountain area. Many families shared homes with each other. My father grew up in a home with about fifteen other families living in it. One family occupied one room. These rooms were comparable to a small studio apartment in New York City. Now here he was with his brothers, owning a home with twelve large rooms, a large front yard, and eight exterior buildings that formed eight other rooms to be used as kitchens, storage, and/or living spaces. Talk about one family to one room, how about one family to twenty rooms?

The house was so large it could be seen from a distance of thirty miles. People would drive by and see this monster of a home and ask, "Whose home is that?" My father's name was not mentioned; instead people used his father's name. They would say, "The sons of Abdul-Hafid." It is always the father of the children who received the royalties and the credit; my father understood and accepted this. His father was looked up to by others in his tribe. He was the father of the men who built this home. I could only imagine how he felt. In another village not far from him, there was a family that my father had heard of. They had a young girl coming of age. My father kept them in his thoughts. Their home, like my father's, overlooked most of Yafa. They saw the home my father had built with his brothers. They noticed it along with everyone else.

By now, my father had gone back to United States. He had become a US citizen; his home was now the United States. His brothers started families in their new home in Yemen. My father waited for the right time. It was a different life in Yemen than that of the United States. He did not seek a girlfriend and look to get married in that way. He wanted to have a marriage the customary way; he wanted to go to that village that he kept in his thoughts. He wanted to ask for a girl he had heard of, one that grew up in the same fashion as he. He asked permission to marry this girl, my mother.

It was April 12, 1971, and my father was twenty-nine years old. My mother was fifteen. That is not a typo; it was common for the man to be older than the woman he was marrying. No one would blink an eye if he was to ask about his new wife and find out her age was almost half his own. My father purchased her gold, customarily given to the new bride, and the marriage was official. There were no wedding bells; there was no walking the bride down the aisle. Weddings were three days long, and on the second night, the bride comes home to her groom. A marriage is consummated via agreement between the groom and the father of the bride. They shake hands; a priest blesses the marriage and questions them both. The father is asked if his daughter agrees to the marriage and if he agrees to the marriage. The groom is asked if he will take care of the bride and provide for her, not much different than what everyone in the United States would consider a normal wedding, except that it doesn't involve the bride much at all. My father now had a family to call his own.

In August of 1972, my oldest sister, Noer, was born. It was my father's first child, a proud moment in his life indeed. He returned to the United States to provide for his small but precious family, but on his mind was a discussion he had earlier with his brothers. Should he do as they did? Should he let his family grow up in Yemen and provide for them from a distance? Should he do what was considered a gamble in bringing his family to the United States? Against his brothers' wishes, he decided to bring his small family to the United States. Everyone mocked him and called him a fool. It was 1975; my mother was pregnant with their second child. My father wanted it to be an American citizen; they left for the United States.

I recall a story my father once told us. We sat there in silence as he told us. South Yemen did not have the same rights as the North, nor did it have the same fairness and human decency. They would take people into political custody for no other reason than to receive a bribe, and if it was not paid, they would be imprisoned or killed. My father spent all of his money to get him and his family the visas and plane tickets needed to get to the United States. If he was to be taken in for a bribe, he knew he would be unable to leave with his family and could possibly be killed. Was it worth the risk? Would you take a bullet to ensure the safety of those you love?

My father, mother, and sister boarded the plane. He was nervous. He knew that as long as he was in Southern Yemen, he was not safe. His daughter and pregnant wife were also not safe. All of a sudden, armed personnel boarded the plane. They went to the captain of the plane and told him to make an announcement. They made an announcement that Mohamed Abdul-Hafid must get off the plane and go with them. He knew for sure he'd be killed; he had nothing to give.

He did not respond, and he did not get off the plane. They thought no one would be dumb enough to ignore their demands, so they figured he could not be on the plane. They left, the doors were shut, and the plane finally took off. My father was still worried; he and his family were still in Southern Yemeni airspace. He knew they could easily have the plane turn around and he could be shot dead right in front of his family for disobeying the armed men. The plane finally crossed into Northern Yemeni airspace. He was safe, and he could breathe easy...for now.

My father could only afford an apartment in Brooklyn in a neighborhood that was questionable to say the least. In October of 1975, my sister Antiseir was born. She was the first American child born to our family. My father now had two daughters who would have a chance to succeed in life that he had earned. The only difference would be that they'd be afforded the opportunity at a much younger age.

My father continued to work for his family. They did not have much. In fact, they barely had anything. He would go away for eight months at a time. Merchant mariners would be out at sea for long periods, and they would be separated from their families for as long as it took. My mother got pregnant again, two months after having my second sister. It was barely enough time a woman needs to recover after having a child and being able to have another one.

My father was away working; he would call home every few weeks or months to check up on my mother. He worried for her; he would be away for the first time during her delivery. He called one day and my oldest sister answered. It was September of 1976, and my sister was four years old and barely able to understand the concept of what was happening. She knew it was my father calling, before he even said hello. She answered and yelled into the phone in Arabic,

"Baba, mama had a boy!" It was the proudest moment of my father's life; he had a son and named him Nasser.

My father knew that if he didn't have a son, he would not have anyone to carry on his legacy and create his legend. In the Yemeni culture, when your daughter gets married, she marries into the family of her husband. She no longer has responsibility to her family, but more to her husband's. It's a bad deal, but it was something that could not be changed. My father knew this and when my older brother was born, he knew that he would have at least one son to carry on his name.

My father still continued to work for his growing family; my mother now had three children to take care of while her husband was away. She spoke no English and was alone. My father came home in the middle of 1977 to spend time with them. He was proud to finally meet his son. My mother was pregnant once again in the fall of 1977. My father hoped for another son. At the end of the year my oldest sister became a citizen of the United States. She was five years old; my father proudly signed her name for her. He got another job and was sent out to sea once again.

My mother went into labor while my father was away. This was common for her by now; she had her uncle take her to the hospital. It was June of 1978; the fourth child came into the world, and the second son. I was born in the early morning and my mother did not know what name my father wanted to give me, so she named me after her younger brother. My first name is traditionally spelled "Khalid," but my mother did not know how to read or write. She had her cousin, who had the same name as me, spell it the same way he did. Khaled was born, and my father could be no happier.

My father worried about the safety of his family in the neighborhood we were living in. My older sister came home from school one day and walked by an apartment in our building that had paramedics, the police, and two murdered bodies of elderly people. They had been robbed and killed just two floors below our apartment. My father had a new goal, to move his family to better and safer surroundings.

My father was away longer than usual. For the next two and a half years he saved everything he could. He partnered with my mother's uncle, her uncle's brother, and two other families they knew from the old villages in Yafa to purchase an apartment building in the neighborhood of Sheepshead Bay, Brooklyn. It was 1981; the asking price for this apartment was $90,000. My father was able to pay his portion, which equaled $18,000. We left our old apartment later that month and moved in.

It was 1982 and my father sat staring out the window. He had his hand to his face and a tear ran down his cheek. I did not understand what was going on. I later found out when I was older that his mother had died. He had not seen her for seven years and her death was a mystery. They found her lying dead next to some bread she was making for my grandfather and uncle. My oldest sister had been named after his mother; he was devastated.

Not more than a week later, my father's friend and partner in the apartment building was murdered in a convenience store late at night. I was friends with his sons, and his wife was pregnant at the time. I remember that morning; it was a somber time to say the least. My father's mother died and now this happened. My mother answered the phone and started crying, and then my sister did the same. She was brushing my sister Antiseir's hair. My reaction was like it was always at that time, confused. A day later, my father's slain friend's wife had their child.

My father recovered and got back on his feet. He took care of their family for a while. He drove their car for them when they needed something, up until his slain friend's brother came to the United States to look after them. My father went back to work to make more money for his family. He was able to continue with his life and to grow his family. My mother was now pregnant with their fifth child.

In March 1983, my brother Nabeel was born, but there was a problem; he was born with yellow fever. I heard the story later on that a doctor had gone up to my father and told him my newborn brother would die. My father broke down and cried. I could only imagine how much heartache one person could take, and he was taking a lot in one year's time. He came home and sat my brother and me down. I remember him telling us something about my baby brother being yellow and he would go to God. My little brother made it through though, and he came home in April of that year. My father now had three sons to carry on his name.

In 1984, a woman and her son came to live with us. Her name was Alya and her son's name was Hussain. Alya was married to my uncle Ahmed; he was one of my father's younger brothers but a troubled brother. I knew nothing of him; he was a merchant mariner, like my father and his older brothers, though he was killed while tying up the ship. The rope to the anchor snapped and cut him in two. My aunt came to the United States to collect the settlement that was due to her. We loved our cousin, and so did my father. My mother and father were due to have their sixth child. One February night in 1985, my mother and father went to the hospital and later that night my father called saying we had another brother. We jumped up and down with excitement; my father was living the American dream. He named my new brother after my cousin, an honor for any living being.

My father now had four sons. His legacy would certainly be intact. He would now start molding his children. He would talk to us and teach us lessons. We were so afraid of him. We loved him, but we feared him. He had this commanding presence over us and most anyone else. I had such fear of him that whenever he would speak, he would make me cry. He would tell us a story, teach us a lesson about life, and then ask us questions about what we had just talked about it. He would ask me, "Khaled, what will you do when you're my age?"

I would have a hard time talking because my voice would start to crack and tears would form in my eyes. This was a sign of weakness to him, and he would slap me. It was innocent in nature, but he frightened me so much, that I couldn't help but cry.

My older brother Nasser was nine. I was turning seven, Nabeel was two, and Hussain was a few months old. My father sat Nasser and me down, told us a story about a kid who was my age, seven years old, and made less than a quarter a week. It was about him. He told us, "You will never watch cartoons or play with toys. They are for babies like your brothers Nabeel and Hussain. When they watch TV, go to your room and read a book."

I started to cry again for not being able to watch cartoons and for fear of my father. He explained again why we could not watch cartoons and compared us to him when he was seven. He then uttered a phrase that defined his belief and intensity to succeed...

"You're men now."

My father was a tough man, but he was a proud man. Years later he would take us all to Yemen and show everyone who doubted him what he had accomplished in life. The people who treated him like dirt when he was a child probably heard of his story and probably wondered if they should have treated him better. I looked at my dad standing above everyone with thousands of people celebrating his return.

My father was a superstar, a man that I wished I could be.

I say good-bye to my wife and remind her to take care of my father for his birthday. I smile thinking to myself that I had done my father proud, and I hoped to become the man he dreamed for me to be. If I could become a tenth of the man my father was, I would be just fine.

"Where'd you go, Joe? You were gone for a bit," asked the first sergeant.

"Oh, I was just wishing my dad a happy birthday. He turned sixty-two today."

I spend the night in darkness, lying in bed, thinking of my dad and his sixty-two years of existence. I replay his life story he had told me about over and over. It would be the last time I would ever speak to my dad.

If I only knew…

CHAPTER 36

The Gamble

A lot happens in a few months in Iraq. Though the wait to get back home makes it seem like years, when you sit back and think about it, the time before is like flipping through a photo album. Each moment leading up to this thought is a moment of reflection. I had already seen a lot, and I had interacted with many. With a little over two months remaining, I could only imagine what would happen next.

It's during the latter parts of a deployment, especially when deployed in a combat zone, that you begin to carefully plan for when you get home. By carefully, I mean you plan with the hope you don't get killed before you can execute your plans. You are so close to the finish line, and while you can almost taste the air of being home, you know not to get too comfortable with the thought, because you'll get sloppy.

Fully rested, we get to Camp Korean Village and stage our vehicles. This place was literally in the middle of nowhere. Our battalion deployed one company to Korean Village and some elements of my old platoon were also there to provide support. In this camp there were homes remade into barracks, others made into command centers. There was an Internet center for us to use and an area sectioned off for training.

After dropping off my gear, I speak with the company commander for Alpha Company. I ask him when I will be returning back to my old platoon. He lets me know that it would be at the end of August, a month before we got back home. We would be in this area of operation for about a month, scheduled to return to Al Qaim in the middle of August.

Our mission was to assist Delta Company, who had been in this area since the beginning. After settling in and taking a walk around camp, I get back to the house we would be calling our own for the month and meet with all the staff NCOs and officers of Alpha Company. We are given details of our mission by the company commander; he gives every platoon commander a task by showing them what area they will be manning and patrolling.

Ar Rutbah was a main city in western Iraq. Travelers from Jordan and Syria go through Ar Rutbah on their way to Baghdad. If you were coming from Jordan or Syria with ill intentions, it would be the way you'd want to travel. By doubling the size of our presence here, our battalion commander felt this could prevent future attacks. While I agreed with the man to some degree, there just wasn't enough we could do to completely prevent it, not with our size at least. We are visitors, occupying land that these people have lived in for centuries; they know the lay of the land better than we could ever imagine.

After the meeting, I ask the company commander what orders he has for us. He tells me that we'd have to wait and see. We would react if a platoon needed assistance. I took this as an opportunity to ask him about MCMAP. MCMAP stands for the Marine Corps Martial Arts Program, implemented in 2001 while I was still in the Marine Security Guard Program. From 2002 and on, the Marine Corps had started to train recruits in martial arts during boot camp, and nearly every Marine in the Fleet Marine Force had qualified for entry level (tan belt) except a few. I was one of those few.

The company commander and first sergeant loved the idea. For one week I would not be going out on missions, but I would be training for my tan belt. A few other Marines were asked if they wanted to participate and by the end of the day we had about ten Marines who wanted to be trained. There had been a rumor the Marine Corps was going to make it a minimum requirement that each Marine be tan belt qualified. If you were not qualified, your promotion could be affected. After deciding not to seek early separation from the Marine Corps, I had ambition to continue with my career as a Marine. I didn't want to miss out on a promotion because I didn't have a silly colored belt.

The tan belt syllabus focuses on the development of the basics of armed and unarmed combat. Students start with the basic warrior stance and break-falls are taught for safety. This is where we practice falling straight to the ground and spreading the impact to a larger area of our bodies. We could not brace, and we could not use our hands.

For an hour we had to learn how to fall down and absorb the impact with our ribs. This was not something I'd call fun.

We then moved to hours and hours of basic punches, uppercuts and hooks, basic upper-body strikes, including the eye gouge, hammer fists, and elbow strikes. Then we worked on the basic lower-body strikes, including kicks, knee strikes and stomps, bayonet techniques, chokes, joint locks, and throw counters to strikes, chokes, and holds. We added some basic unarmed restraints and armed manipulations, knife techniques, and finally weapons of opportunity. Try learning all of that, executing these maneuvers, and then at the end of the day try getting thrown into a gauntlet where you fight four times with four different and far more experienced fighters...what the hell was I thinking?

After my first day of MCMAP training, I got back to the house and the first sergeant began to laugh at me hysterically. I could barely move. My face was covered in powdered sand and my uniform was filthy. I smiled and acknowledged that I had gotten what I had asked for, but by the end of the week I had my tan belt and was proud that it signified I was able to fall down properly. That would come in handy if I ever got into a fight with someone like Mike Tyson.

Now that I had my belt and was appeased by the company commander, it was time to get back out there with the rest of them. The CO, first sergeant and the rest of us would set up a perimeter during the day and patrol at night. The LAV-C2 had to maintain its position for communications with Camp Korean Village, so when we went on patrol I traveled with the mortars section.

These guys were great! They were young Marines who were fun to be around. During the day we'd sit around and talk about going back home and other nonsense like who we would take with us to the Marine Corps Ball in December. We were hoping it would be in Las Vegas this year. One of the Marines offered his girlfriend's sister to me as a date to the Ball. He showed me a picture and my jaw dropped. She was gorgeous!

"Hell yeah, dude! Hook me up," I said to him.

Each day, out in the middle of nowhere, we'd just sit and talk. I really liked these guys. They were in my age group, and it allowed me to be myself. They even let me drop mortars one day...that was awesome! They handed me a mortar round and said, "Here you go, Staff Sergeant." As if I was on my own from there. All you have to do is drop it in the tube and let it fly. It's like throwing water balloons, except these things kill people. It's a different feeling to be dropping mortars on targets than being the target yourself and having mortars dropped on you.

On one of our breaks the company commander shouted in my direction to get my attention. I saw him a few meters in front of me by his vehicle and he pointed to my right. An Iraqi supply truck was headed for our position. We threw on our gear, and I got out there to stop the vehicle. Vehicle Born Improvised Explosive Devices (VBIEDs) were common and Marines had been killed by them before. If this was a VBIED, it would be massive and kill everyone within seeing distance.

I was able to stop the truck and had the driver come out. I asked him where he was going. He pointed to an area over a hill behind me, to a village I couldn't see. We searched his vehicle and found nothing, so we let him go. He had a good attitude and told me to hold on a second as he went back into his vehicle. He pulled out five cans of beer, actual alcoholic beer and began handing it to each of us. I took it and threw it in my cargo pocket before anyone else could decide against keeping them. The company commander didn't want to take it, but I told him he should as a sign of respect. I thanked the man and he drove off.

"Hey sir, if you want, I can get rid of that for you," I tell the CO.

He handed me the beer without saying anything and we headed back to where we were staged. The mortars section saw that I had two cans of beer and were envious. I told them that we'd all drink later that night, as if we were home. One of the scouts with the CO smiles and tells me that he'd come over to drink with us too. He also had a can from the Iraqi we had stopped.

Night came and we would not be patrolling because we'd be heading back to Camp Korean Village in the morning. We all sat by one of the mortar LAVs, sipping beer. We passed the beer around and took swigs. Off to the side, I see one of the Marines with an M-16 round, trying to remove the round from the casing. What we liked to do as a prank was to take a cigarette and dump out some of the tobacco. We'd then take some gunpowder and put it in the cigarette. Then we'd fill it back up with tobacco. I knew what he was doing, so I played along.

The cigarette doesn't explode immediately, but when it gets down to where the gunpowder is, it goes up in flames, startling the unexpected smoker. We start smoking with one of the Marines who picked the unlucky cigarette. I should have been an actor because I played it off really well. A few moments passed as we sat there in anticipation. We know what was going to happen and how funny it was going to be, but it is always funnier than you expected. The Marine's reaction was classic, throwing the cigarette down as he dropped "f-bombs" on us. I laughed hysterically to tears. It was too funny!

As we continued talking, the conversation became serious. One of the Marines talked about where he came from and what he felt about some people. He talked about what he felt about different races and religions including the Iraqis. This was the same Marine who protested us training the Iraqis a few months earlier because he didn't trust them. He didn't hold back from how he felt and even looked over at me to confess something.

"You know what, Staff Sergeant; before I knew you, I didn't like you. I thought you were just a dirty sand nigger, but I know how cool you are now," he said.

I was shocked; I didn't know whether to get upset or to let it go. Here he was opening up to all of us, other Marines nodding their heads in agreement as he spoke. Sure, he complimented me in a way, but ignorance commanded his thoughts. He admitted to hating blacks as well, calling the first sergeant, "Just another nigger."

I was speechless.

The next morning we returned to Korean Village. One of the Marines from the mortars section went with me to the Internet center on base to get his girlfriend to tell her sister that I was taking her to the Ball. She agreed and gave me her sister's contact information. We chatted online for a little bit, but when she found out that I was an Arab, she freaked out. She stopped responding to me and told her sister she didn't want to go with me anymore.

The Marine felt awful. He apologized over and over, but I told him I was used to it by now. I have lived the life of an Arab from day one, reaping the stereotypes that came with it. The girl probably thought I sounded like someone who worked at a 7-11 or drove a taxicab. I didn't want to go with someone who was shallow and bigoted; it was the Marine Corps Ball, it was something special. I wasn't planning on taking Christine either because our relationship was not what it once was.

After a few more missions, Alpha Company was done in Ar Rutbah. In fact Delta Company would also be leaving Ar Rutbah.

Husaybah, left nearly unattended because Alpha Company had been pimped out elsewhere, was now laden with landmines and IEDs. We were planning a major mission in the area, flooding it with LAVs and manpower.

I never agreed with doing something half-assed and then trying to make up for it after you realized that you had screwed up. Either do it right the first time or don't do it at all. In my eyes, we were going into an area that was now a minefield. We were weeks away from our replacements, 3rd Light Armored Reconnaissance Battalion, touching ground and taking our place, and we were just now doing this? The problem was there would never be enough Marines on the ground. War is hell.

I was nervous for this mission, so close yet so far away. On the way back to Al Qaim all I could think about was getting through the few weeks I had remaining with Alpha Company. I was so close to getting home, just six more weeks. For the next two weeks I would be on a path littered with mines, each one set to go off with death on the other side of it. I needed to think of something else. I was getting mentally and physically overwhelmed, but it would be good to see some of the guys in my old platoon; it had been two months since I had seen any of them. When I got to Al Qaim I was greeted by some of my Marines from before. They shook my hand, some hugged me, and others were just happy to see me, with a comment like, "Hey Staff Sergeant, we missed you." When you see someone every day, you don't notice the change they go through, but when you're away you see the changes, and sometimes they are dramatic.

The men were bigger, some of them were fat, and others were muscular. They had enough time to eat and relax. Some chose to use that time to work out and get big, others used that time to eat more.

I get back to my living quarters; my bed was left untouched, even though I had been gone for two months. It was good to see some of the staff NCOs, including Master Gunz. I wasn't too pleased to see the platoon commander though, even though he was a small man, he was everywhere you didn't want him to be, like existence.

While visiting the Marines I once led, we talked about the Marine Corps Ball and how it might be in Vegas. We talked about it more and more, some Marines talking about who they would bring. The Marine who Christine slept with asked me if I was going to take his sister to the Ball. I hadn't even thought of that or considered it an option. His sister and I had started talking over the Internet and phone on her birthday a year ago. He had me prank call her, acting like I was an insurance agent. This had her going and drove her mad. We hit it off from the start. We were cool. I tell him to ask her for me, knowing she'd say yes. I agreed to fly her out and take her to the Ball. She would be my date, so it should be a good time.

I start to think optimistically about going home. I had to because I was so unsure what was going to happen over the next two weeks, my final mission with Alpha Company. I didn't want to think of what could happen on this mission. I just wanted to think of what could happen in Vegas in December. I didn't want to be part of a story where I was a day away from going home only to get killed just before. I didn't want anyone else to go through that, but knowing what we were facing, I figured someone was going to die. Who was it going to be?

CHAPTER 37

Taking a Chance on Life

When you know someone who dies, it changes how you feel about death. Death isn't what you see on television or in a movie, where you have no feeling about the person who has died. Death is real, death is unforgiving, and death is permanent. I saw a baby die a year earlier and though it ate away at my heart, it wasn't the same as when Rudy died. With each death I encountered, I wondered about the family of the person now deceased. I even wondered about this when an insurgent was killed. They had families, too.

After spending a few days in Al Qaim getting ready for the major offensive in Husaybah, I wake up one morning before the mission and have some breakfast. You never wake up knowing what the day will bring; you wake up thinking about what it *might* bring. The mess hall was full, loud, and boisterous. Marines were sitting with the friends they'd made over the years and recent months. I sit back and take it all in, marveling at how fate can bring you to a point in life, but then you have the final decision on what you do next.

I was supposed to leave for Marine Corps boot camp in June of 1996. I had only one class remaining in my senior year of high school. I needed this class to graduate, and while I barely tried, I felt I was on good enough terms with the teacher to rate a passing grade. I was hours away from leaving for Parris Island when I was told I would not be leaving because I had not yet graduated. When my teacher was asked, she refused to commit to passing me. I hadn't earned the right or given enough effort for her to even do that for me.

Even though she was pressured by other teachers, and even though I was offered a credit by another, she wouldn't give in. My guidance counselor did not appreciate me trying to get another teacher to vouch for me and give me a credit, so she let me have it with a verbal tirade. I failed my one class for that term, Psychology; an elective course was all I needed and I failed when it was crunch time.

Had she given me a passing grade I would have left for boot camp that one day in June of 1996, but she hadn't. The delay caused me to have to reapply for the Marine Corps Delayed Entry Program, thus negating the occupational specialty I had earned; I had to get a different one. I was initially given a code for basic electronics when I first joined, but now that I had to redo everything, I was given a code for electronic ordnance. At the time I didn't realize it, but my life was forever altered. That one moment in time led to me sitting here thinking about how I had gotten here, sitting in a mess hall in Al Qaim, Iraq. It led me to meet the people I had met, the people who influenced me to get me where I was.

I went to summer school and finally ended up graduating. I remember the class I failed more than the one I had passed because of its significance to me at that moment. Was it a good thing or bad thing that I failed leading to my time here in Iraq? If I had passed would I be here? Would I even be in the Marine Corps anymore? These were all questions I will never know the answers to, but they will always be questions I would continue to ask.

The wanting to join the Marine Corps over going to college and the choice of staying in rather than getting out of the Corps are all choices we have to make in life. You just don't know what will be the right one until you make it.

A year ago, while we were in Al Diwaniyah, our battalion lost Marines to expiring contracts, and the Marine Corps decided to replenish us with a new supply of Marines. Most of them were new and fresh out of high school; some of them were "career Marines" and were in it for the long haul. There was one Marine who was neither. While in Diwaniyah he called out to me, "Hey Staff Sergeant Hafid, remember me from MSG School?"

I take a good look at this Marine, a sergeant by the name of Cook, to see if I indeed remembered him.

"Oh shit, hell yeah dude. How are you," I say to him excitedly shaking his hand.

I did remember him. The difference between him then and him now was that he had the confidence to approach me and he was now a sergeant. When I had first known him, he was quiet, reserved yet respectful. He was a junior Marine, a lance corporal. I asked him what he was doing with our battalion now, and if he had reenlisted. He confirmed that he had indeed reenlisted.

He had gotten married at his last posting in the Marine Security Guard Program. He had brought his new wife to the United States and wanted to go to school to get his degree. The Marine Corps does not pay like other more heroic jobs like baseball players and actors, so he wasn't able to save enough money to afford bringing her to the United States and going to school. The Marine Corps would pay for his schooling though.

"I reenlisted for school. After I get my degree during this enlistment, I'm getting out," he says laying out his plan for me.

I nodded in approval. This was a good plan. The man had come a long way from being a young lance corporal; he was a sergeant of Marines with a new family—with career and life goals. I loved seeing Marines putting forth an effort to better themselves; anyone who had a plan that would lead to their success was motivating to me.

I saw Sergeant Cook in the mess hall eating with and talking to a group of his Marines. They looked up to him; he was a vehicle commander for an LAV, and the Marines he was with were his crew. Everyone here had a story. Everyone had fate and decisions bring them to this moment, but only a few would be known.

We hit the road in numbers. LAVs and supply trucks carrying food and ammo were attached to us to support the mission. We got off the main road and drove into the desert. The trick was to follow the vehicle directly in front of you by driving in the path they've traveled, their tire tracks. What this does is provide the vehicles in column with a feeling of assurance that they will not hit a landmine. Of course the lead vehicle is the sacrificial lamb.

As we follow along I see one of the other companies break off and each vehicle takes its own path. What the fuck was going on? Why were they doing this? Within moments I hear multiple explosions. LAVs are being shredded to pieces. Marines are getting hurt and are being evacuated to the nearest medical facility. We sat and waited for the Marines to be tended to, and then finally continued on. One of the Marines who was hurt would later die. Word gets to us about him and another Marine who had been seriously hurt.

I didn't understand what was happening. Why were we looking to get blown up? What good was it for us to be out in the middle of the desert when all we were going to do was get each other killed? Prevention through sacrifice, that is all I could make of it. To prevent future attacks, we had to go out there in a show of force, getting blown up in the long run but not allowing the insurgency a moment of opportunity to plant more landmines and IEDs. Tell a Marine that he would be doing this and though he will bitch, he will do his job. Tell a celebrity to do a show for the troops, and they won't do it until their demands are met. Who deserves to get paid more? Oh that's right, the one who gave the rousing performance in the movie you liked so much...

After the moments of chaos, the battalion splits up and gets to work. Alpha Company will send platoons to patrol the streets while the company command element stages in the hills where we can't be seen. We sit and wait; I am handed a book by one of the Marines in our vehicle and told to read it. It is Dan Brown's *The Da Vinci Code* and it came highly recommended.

Hours pass and I find myself lost in the book. Completely taken away from where I was and what I was feeling. In the background I hear Marines talking about who knows what, but it was all muffled to me. I was wondering how Robert Langdon got himself in such a mess and how he was going to get himself out of it. I don't eat. I don't speak to anyone. The only time I move is to move to the shady side of the vehicle. The difference between the sun and shade is drastic.

Night comes and I finally put the book down. I had almost read the entire thing in one day. If I had another hour, I would have been done. It was either a good book, or I was so desperate to be away from reality for just a day. I get ready to sleep under the stars and get into my sleeping bag. As I begin to shut my eyes and dream of porn I had seen in the past, I hear an explosion and gunfire. I knew what it meant.

I get up and get dressed. I put on my boots and my sand covered uniform. I didn't need light to get dressed, by now I had been accustomed to doing everything in the dark, including wiping my own ass. I hear two vehicles start up and drive off. The company commander had just left, and this time he hadn't taken me with him. Hmm, I guess I'll just go back to sleep.

The next morning I was called down to where the explosion had taken place. A few of our Alpha Company Marines were hit and had been taken to get treated. Their time in Iraq was now over. At times it made you think if it was worth getting hit by something, but then you think about the chances of survival against the chances of death. When I get to the area, I see the vehicle that was hit. It was blackened on one side where the explosion had been, but it was largely undamaged. I wait to become useful, so I sit next to a Marine by another LAV. I greet him and take a seat.

What we couldn't figure out is how our Marines could be attacked when there were patrols done by the Iraqi Police. I am now useful to the CO; I walk with him over to the police station. I interview the police chief, who had not been on duty the night before. I was told by the company commander that when our Marines were attacked, the police had fled the station, running from a call instead of answering it.

"How are you supposed to be doing your job when you guys run away from it? You think we're going to be here forever," I ask the police chief.

The CO is getting visibly upset, feeding off of my tone of voice and scowl. The police chief has no answers, when it's his job to have answers.

"They fucking knew, sir. Why else would they be gone just as we get attacked," I ask the CO.

He agrees and tells me that we would be taking him in. I disarm the police chief and he comes with us without a fight. He is in a bad position, but with positions of responsibility you must take on the problems that come with it. He didn't do that, and he was now being arrested by us, taken in for questioning.

The vehicle that picks him up was the same vehicle that had brought me down earlier in the morning. I get in the vehicle expecting to go with them, but I am told to stay behind with the CO to question the other police officers. They drive away with the police chief with his hands zip tied together in a convoy of four vehicles. They drive off and I continue questioning the other police who had fled the night before. Each time I can see the CO get more upset with their responses. They were his Marines who had been hurt so close to going home. A man I had known to smile more times than not looked completely different to me, but I could understand why.

BOOM!

A familiar explosion is heard and a familiar mushroom cloud can be seen. Our vehicles escorting the police chief back to Al Qaim were hit. The vehicle I was supposed to be on was the one directly impacted. The Marines who were in the vehicle were shaken up but not seriously hurt. The vehicle commander for that vehicle was knocked unconscious; he was taken to Al Qaim for treatment.

Had I not been told to stay there for questioning, that would have been me. If I had been there, would I have been so lucky to only suffer a concussion? I had been in Iraq for a total of eight months, but I had never seen so many attacks targeting us. The people who were out to get us were going to get as many of us as they could. It didn't matter if we killed three hundred of them. If they got one of us, it was considered worth the loss of three hundred of their own. I didn't understand the rationale behind it, but eventually they would all be killed right?

After a long day we get back to our position hidden in the hills. I sit down, dirty and salty from the sweat, and pick up where I left off in the book. As I am finishing the last few words I hear the company commander say a familiar name, "Cook."

"Did you say Cook, sir? Do you mean Sergeant Cook," I ask him with concern.

He nods his head and tells me what had happened. Sergeant Cook's vehicle was hit with a double-stacked landmine causing the vehicle to tip and roll over. Sergeant Cook and another Marine were standing in the turret when this happened; when the vehicle was hit it rolled over and pinned Sergeant Cook from the waist down.

With tons of steel on top of him Sergeant Cook knew he was going to die. As the company commander is telling me this, I realize that he was still alive. The only thing keeping him alive was the weight of the vehicle, that once removed, would be the cause of his inevitable death.

I overhear the CO telling his XO that they were trying to call Sergeant Cook's wife, so he could talk to her for the last time. I do not know if he ever did speak to her.

A girl meets a boy, falls in love with this boy, and marries him. This boy came to her by chance, a Marine Security Guard who was assigned to her home country randomly. She goes to the United States with him, supporting his decision to stay in the Marine Corps to get further educated for the betterment of his new family. This boy leaves for Iraq and comes back home to her safely. Just as this boy gets comfortable being home with this girl, he leaves again. The boy tries to call the girl one last time to tell her he loves her but that he would die soon after saying "good-bye."

Moments pass as I sit there in silence replaying the meeting I had with Sergeant Cook the year before. He was sure that he was doing the right thing when he reenlisted. I was also sure of it. The decision to stay in so the Marine Corps could pay for his school was not the reason he was killed, but it put him on the path to his eventual demise.

Over the radio I hear his name and the words "killed in action" follow. I put my head down in silence. I had no tears to spare; I had no feeling other than to say, "This fucking sucks."

Our mission in Husaybah would conclude days later. When I got to Al Qaim I attended the memorial for the Marines who had fallen during the mission. I don't remember how many had died, but one is too many, and it was certainly more than that.

My time with Alpha Company was over. In all actuality the war was over for me. I'd now be granted my wish to go back to my old platoon. Alpha Company was going back to Ar Rutbah for the rest of the deployment in Iraq. The show of force, of machinery and manpower was like throwing a gasoline can into a raging fire…then turning around and walking away.

These Marines did not have to die, but that was irrelevant. Just because something does not have to happen, it does not mean that it will not happen. They were still dead.

Chapter 38

The Calm Before the Storm

I'm bored. Each day I wake up is one day closer to getting home and doing things I have always wanted to do. I get up to brush my teeth and spend the day visiting the Marines in my platoon. Though I am back with my original platoon, I am jobless. The new platoon sergeant is more than adequate and the Marines give him their respect; he's earned it.

We're a few days from 3rd Light Armored Reconnaissance Battalion making it to Al Qaim. They were already in Kuwait and you could almost smell the freedom their arrival would signify. Without anything to do time comes to a halt. You can only watch a movie enough times before it becomes unwatchable. I spend most of my day walking around the camp, going to the Internet center more times in a day than I have in all the time I had spent there before.

With Alpha Company now in Ar Rutbah for the remainder of the deployment, there wasn't much I could do. All I could do was wait for the word for us to go home, and that was only a few weeks away.

I wanted to travel light; I didn't want to carry all the gear I had brought to Iraq. There was a Post Office in camp that we could use to send items home. I packed my cold weather gear and shipped it back. I wouldn't need it; we were leaving soon.

I mostly kept to myself. Though I was around other Marines, I didn't speak to them much. I spent more time silent than I did speaking. I was just exhausted. I would go over to the Marines' living space and would watch movies that I had seen more than twenty times. Within the first ten minutes of each movie, I would fall asleep. When I would wake up, there would be no one around. They had all gone to have some chow.

I walk over to my living space; the other staff NCOs are lying in their beds either listening to music or reading letters. I grab the propane burner, a frying pan, sliced bread, canned cheese, and bottled butter spread. I take two slices of bread and shake up the canned cheese. I spread the cheese evenly on the bread and put the slices together. The frying pan is now hot enough, so I lower the temperature. I squeeze some butter spread onto the bread and place it on the frying pan, the sizzling echoes in the room. The silent, and at the time, focused staff NCOs hear this and smell the aroma, breaking their concentration; they get out of their beds and make their way to where I am, conveniently starting a conversation with me.

I halfheartedly offer them a grilled cheese sandwich, hoping they'd decline, but they jump on the opportunity. I make them each a sandwich and finally get to my own. I don't burn the sandwiches; I cook them well. I cannot stand a grilled cheese sandwich that is black on each side from overcooking and attention loss. I finally get done with theirs and bite into my very own sandwich. The crisp sound of the bread fills the room; the taste is uncanny. Though made in an unconventional way, it works just the same. It's delicious and bad for the arteries, just the way it was meant to be.

It was like the movie *Groundhog Day*, every day. I wake up, brush my teeth, find something to do in the time between Internet center visits, make some grilled cheese sandwiches, and go to sleep. The only time I deviated from that schedule was when I had to take a shit or go over to the mess hall and ask the cooks for some butter and bread. My constant Internet usage was attributed to the continuing relationship building of my future Marine Corps Ball date. We'll call her Kelly.

Kelly was excited and we'd always talk about the Ball. She would say, "I have the best date for the Marine Corps Ball." I would respond with, "Duh!" It was a platonic relationship, she was the sister of one of my Marines, and though he had hooked up with Christine, I still loved the guy. Kelly was his younger sister, and she had just recently had her heart broken by a longtime boyfriend. Relationships can really suck. I was glad I had one that was basically a "here you go, you're both married" relationship. I spent my online time with Kelly to get her psyched for the Ball, because thinking about her broken heart would do nothing for her.

I really looked forward to the Ball; it would be a great way to celebrate the Corps and to celebrate the lives of those we had lost. It would be a time we could come together as a platoon once again and lift our glasses up high for Marines like Rudy and Sergeant Cook. We would hold our glasses up high for all the other Marines that we might never have met, but felt their influence on our lives. To have Kelly, a good friend, there with me would be the cherry on top.

As I chomp down on a grilled cheese sandwich I hear a familiar rumble and roar. LAVs were inbound, but there were more than a company-sized contingent. It was a battalion-sized element; 3rd LAR Battalion had arrived with their tan colored LAVs. They were based out of 29 Palms, California. It is where the largest Marine Corps base is located, large not because of the amount of Marines on base, but because of the impact area. A lot of training is held at 29 Palms and nothing else really. It is about as exciting a place to be as Al Qaim, but it was still the United States.

The Marines looked cleaned and determined. They looked like they were brand new, fresh out of the box. We looked like we were worn out and ready to be sold at a garage sale. It was a sight for sore eyes to see these Marines. They were our replacements. We were going home!

It was mid-September now, and we would have a week of turnover with 3rd LAR Battalion. If you were to imagine a parallel universe and if you wondered what your counterpart from the other universe was like, I am sure this would be something much like it. The staff NCO counterparts of our platoon were comical to say the least. They had a platoon commander and a Master Gunz like we did, but they were nothing alike. I, on the other hand, had no counterpart; I had no job, so it was the perfect time for my Master Gunz to play a trick on one of the staff sergeants from the other battalion.

"Hey Hafid, I told him you were an Iraqi and that they let you sleep in the same area as us. I then told him they gave you staff sergeant chevrons, so if he looks at you weird, play along."

That Master Gunz, he loved to have some fun; I played along because it would be a hoot to see how he would react to me walking around with a weapon around American Marines. The staff sergeant's face was classic, especially when he heard me speak. He could never figure out how it was that I had an American accent. He must have thought I was educated in the United States. When I would have an intelligent conversation with him around, he would stare in silence and nod his head. I didn't like him though because when he was told that I was given staff sergeant chevrons to wear, he said, "Fuck that. He doesn't rate that shit. I'm gonna snatch it off his collar."

I wish he would have tried.

The Marine Corps was going through a massive turnover throughout Iraq. They called it "RIP" for Relief in Place. We doubled our size in country. If there was a time to launch a major offensive, it was now. One of the plans to save the Marine Corps some money was to leave all of our equipment back with our replacements; this meant that if we weren't in LAVs, we'd have to get down to Kuwait by other means. It also meant that I didn't have to spend any time in the same vehicle as the platoon commander. The platoon sergeant got us together to give us the order in which we would be leaving. It was really happening. We were leaving Al Qaim but not without a last good-bye, or was it a hello?

The new units in country were hit and hit hard. Marines were killed within the first few days, including senior Marines in command positions. When senior leadership is killed, it's an eye opener. These Marines had served for so long and had seen so much, for them to fall as casualties meant the Iraqis were getting better at killing their targets, or they were just lucky.

Seeing vehicles towed back to Al Qaim bloody and destroyed served as a wakeup call. Though we are no longer in charge, we are still in harm's way. As I pack I find myself recalling a conversation I had with a Marine gunnery sergeant during a wait for my turn on the Internet. He told me to be careful and not expect the transition home to go smoothly just because it was initially planned that way. "Shit happens, plans change," he told me. I ignored it for the most part, thinking nothing of it.

I packed my gear, lightweight because I was smart enough to have sent it all back through the mail. I get on the back of a seven ton truck with other Marines from my platoon and ride down to an area where we were to be picked up by helicopters and flown to Al Asad. I had never been in a helicopter before. I was afraid of flying already, but at least airplanes had wings.

I have to admit, flying in a helicopter is far less stressful than flying in a commercial airplane. That's if you take away the possibility of being hit by a rocket from the ground. The takeoff is slow and smooth and the landing is something you barely notice. The sound of the engines churning and the blades cutting through the air are deafening, but they were music to my ears.

Good-bye Al Qaim, and go fuck yourself for me.

When we get to Al Asad the company commander and the first sergeant of Alpha Company are waiting for me. It was good to see them; they had arrived earlier with their Marines. They drove in with their LAVs; the LAVs were going back to the States for upgrades. They asked me to join them for dinner that evening. I accepted their generous offer. These were classy gentlemen, these Alpha Company Marines.

We get into our tent and drop off our gear. I choose a bed to my liking and drop my gear there. I see the platoon commander chose his bed, one that was without another bed on top. We had bunk beds, but because he was who he was, he had his separated so he could have his own spot. He didn't want anyone sleeping above him. He left his gear on his bed, and I thought I'd do something nice for him. Since he was so short and since we had extra bunk bed equipment lying around, I decided to grab a ladder from one of the beds and place it on the side of his. This way, if he needed help getting into his bed because he was such a small man, he'd have a ladder.

"Fuck you, Hafid," he said when he saw the ladder. He couldn't top that one.

"You're welcome, sir," I said in return. The other Marines laugh hysterically but not too much in front of his face. We didn't want Napoleon to hop around all mad, though that would also be funny. He was still our platoon commander and could be a dick if he wanted to be.

I meet with the first sergeant and company commander for Alpha Company. We go to dinner and talk about a rumor that had been going around. Rumor was that the battle for Fallujah was going to kick off soon, and that we would be called back into action, possibly staying until December.

"That's not happening, right sir?" I ask the company commander.

He looks over at the first sergeant and then back at me.

"Well, that's why we wanted to talk to you, Joe."

It was real. This wasn't like Jennifer Lopez dying; this was the real deal. We were so close to being home, so close to being home in time for October baseball and the Marine Corps Ball. I lose my appetite as the first sergeant and company commander speak glowingly about me and how they look forward to working with me again, that they missed me in Ar Rutbah. It wasn't helping though. I was sick to my stomach.

I get back to the tent looking dejected. The other Marines had heard about the rumor and now confirmation of said rumor. Some had complained, but I complained most of all because while they would just be sitting in their tents eating and getting fat, I would actually be in Fallujah, and all because I spoke this cursed language! It was something I regret. I should have set a better example.

"Just do your fucking job," the platoon sergeant tells me sounding annoyed.

"Show me where it says this is my fucking job, and I'll gladly fucking do it! It's easy for you to say that from where you are because at least you are doing your job," I respond with anger. We weren't angry with each other, we both respected each other. It was just the heat of the moment.

I wake up the next morning and realize the worst that could happen would be what I should expect to happen. I am sitting alone in the mess hall when both the first sergeant and the Alpha Company commander sit next to me. They have smiles on their faces and give me shit, a little ribbing in the morning.

"So when should I move my stuff over to Alpha Company, sir?" I ask the CO.

"Don't worry about it, Joe. The battalion XO just told me we're not going now," he says with a look of assurance.

I smile and can taste my food for the first time in twenty-four hours. I walk back to my tent hearing Marines speaking of the rumor that we wouldn't be going anymore. I confirm, citing sources close to me. The Master Gunz later walks in and confirms it as well. A promise was made to us that we would be going home in October, and the Marine Corps senior leadership was not going to let us down. I grabbed a satellite phone to call my sister; now that I was sure I would be going home, I called her back in the United States to make a confession.

"Umm, you know where I am?" I ask her as she picks up. "I'm in Iraq. I've been here for seven months now. We're going back to Kuwait next week."

My sister was shocked, a little angry but she understood why I hadn't told anyone where I was. I tell her I would call her from Kuwait, but that everything else was fine. I had to go to a formation.

I say good-bye and hand the phone back off to someone else. I head to the formation where I am pulled aside by the company first sergeant.

"Oh he'll love to hear that," says the Master Gunz to the first sergeant. I didn't hear what they were referring to.

"What's going on Master Gunz?" I ask wondering why I was called aside with a few other Marines. He didn't respond.

The company is called to attention. We are ordered front and center. Headquarters and Service Company had a new company commander; I halt the small detail of Marines I was with, face them toward the CO, and order them to salute, "Present...arms!"

The company commander stands in front of me with the first sergeant to his left. A citation is read out loud for all to hear. It was an award for my duties during this deployment. I was being awarded the Navy and Marine Corps Achievement Medal by the Marines of Alpha Company. I was honored, filled with joy, but somewhat saddened that they were not there to present it to me. As the citation was read, my chest swelled with pride. My mind drifted away to my father. I couldn't wait to show him this award, and I got it during combat, too. His timid son has done more than he could ever imagine. He just doesn't know what I've done yet.

After the formation the Master Gunz gives me a hard time for the award, thinking it will make me feel better for being snubbed the previous deployment.

"Oh believe me, Master Gunz. This is an honor, but it doesn't change the fact that I was forgotten last year. This is a different award for a different action," I say in response. I say it with all due respect and he understands.

I walk right over to where Alpha Company was staying and thank the company commander, first sergeant, and other Marines from that organization.

"Oh come on, Joe," says the first sergeant, "You didn't think we would leave you hanging did you?"

I didn't because while I was promised something in the past, these Marines had promised me nothing and had delivered everything. I will always remember my time with Alpha Company and the honor it was to serve with them.

I walk back to my tent later that evening, still clutching the award I was given. It meant the world to me. It meant I had done something and had made a difference somehow. That's all I had ever wanted to do, to make a difference.

As I am about to walk into my tent I see one of my Marines, an older corporal, a Marine junior to me in grade but senior to me in life. He speaks softly to the Master Gunz as tears roll down his face in force. Had I been the platoon sergeant I would have known what was going on, but I wasn't any longer. I ask what had happened to the Marine, and to my sadness the platoon sergeant says, "His father died. We just got the Red Cross message."

"Man, that's too bad. Right before he goes home, too," I say.

He would leave the next morning, but before he does, I go outside to see him and ask him if he needed me to do anything for him. Before our deployment in 2003, his stepson was murdered, and I had collected money from the Marines to help him. There is nothing I could say or do right now. How does one deal with the loss of a father? I look at him and he maintains his military baring, his respect, and he addresses me by my rank and speaks to me in a military manner, like a Marine.

"Dude, relax. I'm a human being, just like you," I say to him feeling uncomfortable about my standing in the Corps in front of a man my senior in age.

Morning comes, and he departs; he would be home in two days. We, on the other hand, would be leaving Al Asad in two days. We would be on a C-130 headed to Kuwait, a place that seemed like heaven in relation to where we were at that moment.

Our new company commander holds a formation and asks that all the staff NCOs and officers depart. He is a man with a raspy voice, probably from all the yelling he had done prior to his arrival. He was motivated and cursed more than anyone I had ever heard curse. He was a warrior, another one of those Marines you leave in a glass box and break in time of war, but he came to us a few months late. I liked this guy, and he was always respectful of those around him. While he was speaking with the Marines a rocket attack takes place nearby. He pauses and jokes about how we had dodged a bullet by not going to Fallujah and how we had just then dodged a few rockets. The Marines come back from the formation with smiles. This was a good man, and you could see it in the faces of the Marines.

On our final day in Al Asad all I could do was daydream about what I was going to do when I got back home. I would be bringing my award back with me and pictures of what happened to show my dad. He'd give me a hard time for not telling them about it, but in the long run he'd understand that I was doing it for his benefit. I didn't want him to be stressed out thinking about me. It feels like I am nine years old all over again, the night before the first day of school and I could barely sleep. In the morning I'd be up and on a C-130 headed to Kuwait and Camp Arifjan. I didn't care what was there; all I knew was that it wasn't Iraq.

It didn't seem real though, boarding the C-130; it didn't seem real when we took off from that runway. None of it seemed real until the moment the men manning the machineguns on each side of the aircraft took off their protective gear; it meant we were now in Kuwaiti airspace and out of danger. Oh, there's this one little thing called landing the plane, something I have always hated while flying.

We made it of course…if not, you wouldn't be reading this right now, now would you?

CHAPTER 39

The Angry American

Camp Arifjan, Kuwait was like nothing I had ever seen. There were barracks, there was a fitness center, there was a main exchange that could put some back in the United States to shame. There was a Subway, a Pizza Hut, a Burger King, a donut and coffee shop, a barbershop, a mess hall (should have been called a mess structure because it was huge), recreation centers, phone centers, and an Internet center that had no time limit as long as you paid for the service.

We would be staying in a massive maintenance bay. It was redesigned to house Marines or soldiers by the thousands—all heading back home. I was one of the first Marines to get to Arifjan, so the rest of the platoon had not yet arrived. The platoon sergeant would be the last to show up because he was making sure everyone left Al Asad without issue. A good leader does that. A good leader is the last to do anything because he gives his subordinates the opportunity to get done before him. The platoon commander was the first to arrive; he picked out a spot for us by an exit.

The Master Gunz, who arrived with me, asks me to get a count of who we had on the ground already. I write down a list of Marines who had already arrived with or before me. I go off memory and write down the other group of Marines to follow. I remembered all of the names of my Marines, where they were from and how long they had been with our platoon. It's something good leaders do.

One by one the Marines filter in and grab a bed to call their own. The platoon sergeant arrives, and I give him the list of names I had written. We were all accounted for. Camp Arifjan is a bit different than any other base we had been to. We cannot carry our weapons with us, and we have to salute officers. Though we are deployed and technically in a combat zone, we are required to render the appropriate greetings. We don't salute officers in combat or in the field because they are the ones snipers will pick off first. If you want to get someone shot, salute them and hope a sniper is perched on some rooftop nearby.

Our schedule was light; we would clean our equipment and gear, get it inspected and then be on our way. There wasn't anything more for us to do in regards to training, though our platoon commander wanted us to go on a run around the camp one morning. I thought this was a great idea coming from a three-foot tall man. The Marines were worn down and tired from months of ups and downs and had not had the opportunity to run regularly, but he wanted to prove a point. Marines fell out of the formation; the platoon looked pretty bad. I yell at Marines to motivate them and to implore them to keep up. I was in pain and exhausted myself, but I wasn't going to let the little prick have the satisfaction of embarrassing me. Some people get off on embarrassing others.

It was a good feeling to walk around base without the added weight of a weapon, but every now and then you would reach for it with fear, wondering if you had lost it. You don't want to be the guy that loses his weapon. Every now and then you'd have to salute an officer, getting back to that again was interesting to say the least. I could have sworn some of the junior officers were standing around the exchange just so they could be saluted by the Marines exiting.

I frequented the Internet center. I now had the time to contact my friends. I used this time to chat directly with them and sometimes respond to an email from Eric. I was now leaving, but he had arrived a few months ago. We did not cross paths in Iraq. He would be in on the future attack on Fallujah; I couldn't help but feel guilty for being there in front of a computer emailing him about going home. This was my brother. I was now worried for him.

Being involved in a war is a constant roller coaster ride. One moment you're elated because you just talked to a loved one, and the next moment you're on your knees crying, asking God why he killed a friend of yours. There is no in between really; it's either ecstasy or misery. I now understood why so many people avoided dealing with the situation head on. I had a friend from my younger years, by younger I mean when I was seven years old. Her name was Heather, and though we weren't friends when we were kids, we became friends later in life, when I wouldn't stop bugging her with constant messages through instant messenger. Now that I was able to contact her without a time limit, we spoke freely through messenger and she was so happy to be hearing from me.

Heather was one of the last remaining memories of my childhood. I had the life I had in school and the life that I had at home. They were separate, and they were completely different. The life I had in school was awkward and confusing, so every time I spoke to her I felt like an awkward and confused kid again, but she always made me feel better because she sincerely cared about me. It's funny how things work out. For years I hadn't spoken to her because we didn't know each other well enough, and now I sit here in front of a webcam smiling and waving at her from a combat zone. I loved her dearly.

I believe that once your friendship is tested, for instance, when someone you love is put in a position where you don't know what will become of them; you begin to realize how important they are to you in life. I cannot imagine how Heather or anyone else felt when a newscast reported the deaths of Marines, but I could see through the webcam that she was relieved to see me sitting there with a smile on my face. She even took a picture of the screen to remember the moment.

When you grow up, you think the friends you have as a kid will be the same friends you will have when you're older. This is rarely the case, but Heather did have a friend that once knew me, but we didn't get along when we were younger. Heather knew this friend cared about the troops in Iraq, and because she knew me, she felt she should talk to me. I was keen to the idea and Heather linked me to her friend, Carolyn.

I messaged Carolyn and the back and forth was amazing. I smiled for hours while sitting there, forgetting what time it was and even what day it was. Other Marines and soldiers would come and go, and I would still be there. I was motionless from the neck down, sitting there smiling at the screen with the love and admiration showered down on me from these two. At that moment, I knew Carolyn would be a permanent fixture in my life. You just get this feeling when you know something to be true.

It was October the 4th, and I was four days from leaving Kuwait and heading back home. The Marines would all sit in a large area in the center of the base located in front of a stage. They would sit in the stands and bleachers surrounding this area eating all the various food they couldn't have for the last seven months. A few of the Marines went into the exchange and bought non-alcoholic beers. They'd sit around and have a few beers with each other. They would motion over to me and offer me a beer. I had to say yes. It reminded me of the time we all drank the night before our first deployment together. I thought back and remembered Rudy being a part of it and raised my drink to the heavens before sipping it.

"You gonna sing tomorrow, Staff Sergeant?" asks one of the Marines.

There were flyers around the base encouraging anyone and everyone to sign up for the talent show. The Marines knew I had the desire to be on stage in front of everyone, if it drew a laugh. I thought about it and said, "Yeah. I will." I knew exactly what song to sing for them too, and it wasn't going to be a Ricky Martin song.

The next day I wake up and head over to the Internet center. I sit down at a computer and to the right of me is a familiar face.

"Hey, Christine is online," says the Marine.

I chat with Christine for a few moments. I ask her if she would be coming to see me in a few days like she had promised months ago. She said she wasn't sure because she might be busy that day. This angered me because a promise is a promise. It's not like I was asking her to come see me after we spent the weekend together. I was coming back from Iraq. She tells me that she is busy and has to go, but she remained online. What she didn't know was the Marine who hooked up with her was sitting right next to me. When I told him that she had to go, he says, "Well she's still here talking to me."

I didn't get it with Christine; I didn't understand why she would treat me with such carelessness, when it was obvious I cared about her greatly. When I tell her that I knew she was talking to the guy, she gets incensed and ends our conversation and her screen name appears as "offline." The Marine continues telling me that she was bad mouthing me. Christine told him I reminded her of a character in Shakespeare's "Othello" named Iago. If he was still talking to her and I saw her as "offline," that meant only one thing. She had blocked me.

That's okay, I thought. She'll come around eventually, like she did the first time when she thought I was crazy. She can't be that bad of a person right?

I had been defending Christine and her actions even though I knew them to be irrational and hurtful. I was very forgiving the first time she made me out to be a crazy person, and was sure I would this time around. When you care for someone, you do things to show your care and support. When her father was ill, I went with her to see him. When she revealed what she did to her younger sister and began crying, I hugged her and told her to forgive herself for it. Friends are there when the chips are down. That's what separates the friends from the scumbags.

The sky grew dark and most of the Marines from our battalion filled up the stands to watch the talent show. A few soldiers and Airmen trickled in, but it was obviously going to be a Marine event, a 1st Light Armored Reconnaissance Battalion led event. One by one Marines performed on stage to thunderous applause. Some of the humor could only be understood by Marines.

After a guitar duo with two Marines mimicking the mentally challenged, I was called on stage to thunderous applause. Marines from both Alpha and H&S Companies cheered for me, wondering what I would be singing. I chose the song because of the situation we were in, who I was surrounded by, and because I remembered where I had been at the start of the year. I had been in a car headed east with Eric, dealing with the Christine fiasco. I played a song over and over because it symbolized what my life was about.

I was born and raised in the great United States of America, and I was fucking proud of everything that said I was American. I was proud of the uniform I was wearing, proud of the ID that I carried with me, and I was proud to have been raised by my father who was surprisingly patriotic when we were growing up. He took us to the Fourth of July celebration marking the 100th year of the Statue of Liberty. He bought us flags and we flew them outside our window every day that year. But I was angry too. Just three years before our nation had been attacked and forever changed. I put in for reenlistment without knowing what was to come and now my brother Eric was defending our nation. He was angry also. It all came together and without a doubt I was going to sing, "Courtesy of the Red, White, and Blue (The Angry American)" by Toby Keith. I got on that stage and asked the Marines to sing along with me if they knew the words...

American girls and American guys
We'll always stand up and salute
We'll always recognize

When we see Ole Glory flying
There's a lot of men dead
So we can sleep in peace at night
When we lay down our head

I decide to change it up a bit to play to the crowd...

My daddy served in the Marine Corps (thunderous applause by the Marines in attendance)
Where he lost his right eye
But he flew a flag out in our yard (Our fire escape)
Till the day that he died
He wanted my mother, my brother, my sister, and me
To grow up and live happy
In the land of the free. (Yes he did)

Now this nation that I love
Has fallen under attack (September the 11th 2001)
A mighty sucker punch came flying in
From somewhere in the back
Soon as we could see clearly
Through our big black eye
Man, we lit up your world
Like the Fourth of July

Hey Uncle Sam
Put your name at the top of his list
And the Statue of Liberty
Started shaking her fist
And the eagle will fly
And there's gonna be hell
When you hear Mother Freedom
Start ringing her bell
And it'll feel like the whole wide world is raining down on you
Ah brought to you courtesy of the red, white, and blue

Oh justice will be served
And the battle will rage
This big dog will fight
When you rattle his cage

And you'll be sorry that you messed with
The U.S. of A.
'Cause we'll put a boot in your ass
It's the American way

Hey Uncle Sam
Put your name at the top of his list
And the Statue of Liberty
Started shaking her fist
And the eagle will fly
And there's gonna be hell
When you hear Mother Freedom
Start ringing her bell
And it'll feel like the whole wide world is raining down on you
Brought to you courtesy of the red, white, and blue

Uh oh (Marines sing along)
Of the red, white and blue
Oh, oh, oh
Of my red, white, and blue

    I stand there, arms to my sides, with a smile on my face and tears in my eyes, looking above at the blackened sky, my voice hoarse from singing at the top of my lungs. I had a microphone in my hand, but I wanted to be heard with all my might. I wanted God to hear me thank him for the opportunities he gave me through my dad. I stand there before these Marines standing and clapping for the performance. I leave the stage and receive hugs and handshakes from Marines all around. A few of the senior staff NCOs had a few sarcastic words to say, but I didn't give a fuck, they were haters. I was going home to my country, to my family, and I had Marines with me that loved and respected me. Every word in that song meant something to me, especially the part about my father. I wished he was here to see it because I felt like he would have loved to see his son in front of God and everyone, fearless and proud.

    I wake up the next morning and call my sister, so she could stop worrying. I was okay, and after the night before, I was better than ever. I have always been about the little things in life. Something as small as a talent show song allowed me to recognize what I felt, allowed me to put in front of everyone what I was thinking. I did something that made me feel amazing.

"Hey Khaled, how are you? Are you okay," says my sister shaken up and crying.

"Yeah I'm fine. Don't worry about me. I'm sorry I didn't call you sooner," I say in response, thinking she was relieved to be hearing my voice.

"Khaled, listen. I have bad news. Like really bad news," she begins. "Our father died last night…"

My voice cracks. I am out in the open, and I want to stay strong, "What?" I ask in disbelief.

My sister goes on to tell me how our father died; he died not knowing where I was, or what I was doing. He died without me knowing, while I stood in front of Marines and soldiers singing at the top of my lungs. He got up that morning, covered his face, and walked out of the house alone. On the night before his death he asked to see my son, the son that bears his name. He held onto my son, knowing what was to become of him the next day. He left the house without telling anyone where he was going, and he died. He didn't want to die in front of my mother, sisters, or anyone else he loved. He didn't want them to see him brought down by sheer mortality.

I hang up the phone and walk over to my Master Gunz. I tell him, "Master Gunz, my dad died." Saying the words you know it to be true, but you hope that your mind has a sick sense of humor.

I don't cry. I don't say anything other than that and walk outside alone. I walk to the Internet center thinking that while I was singing the words to that song, the verse where it talks about him dying, he was actually dead. Was that the reason why it felt so different and powerful?

I had seen enough death this year, first in Iraq and now this. My mind focuses on only one thing now.

"I hope the Yankees win today," I say to myself. Only they could provide me with comfort and escape…

CHAPTER 40

The Departure

When I walked outside I felt guilty. Not because of my dad's death, but because I felt like I had caused a problem for my Master Gunz, that maybe I had put him in an awkward position. I had Marines tell me that someone close to them had died before, but this time I was the one telling my leadership someone close to me had died. It's never a good feeling to give or to receive bad news, and for that moment, I felt awful that I had put that on the Master Gunz.

After I told the Master Gunz, I saw him walk over to the platoon commander. I just wanted to get away. I didn't want to tell anyone else, and I wouldn't for now. I didn't want to take away from the Marines going home. They'd be with loved ones soon, waiting to get off the bus in Camp Pendleton. Before I got the news about my dad, I had heard Marines who served with us a year before telling the newer Marines what it was like when they came home for the first time. It wasn't about me; it was about the Marines as a collective bunch. I was just one kid who lost his dad.

I walk to the Internet center and sit down at a computer and log in to see who was online. I tell Heather and Carolyn about my dad, but it just didn't feel right. What was telling everyone doing other than drawing attention to me? What was it doing other than reaffirming the fact that he was indeed dead, and that he wasn't coming back? "I'm sorry" was the common response, but it only angered me for some reason.

"Why are you sorry? Did you kill him?" I'd ask knowing that wasn't the case. They were just showing concern.

Kelly was also online. When I broke the news to her she, too, apologized. I saw her brother in the Internet center with me; he was a few rows away. I nodded my head at him when I walked in; he didn't know what I had just found out, but within moments of telling Kelly I could feel his eyes shifting to look right at me and he sent me an instant message even though we were in the same room.

"Yankees suck," it said. The Yankees had lost the first game of the ALDS to the Twins. They weren't at their best today, neither was I, but he knew that a little ribbing would distract me.

"Yeah, but how's that 1997 series feel," I asked in response. He was an Indians fan and 1997 is a painful reminder of how close they had been, only to lose. After a few more comments of childlike banter I felt comfortable in telling him something I was sure he knew, "My dad died."

He confirmed Kelly had indeed told him. He, like everyone else to that point, apologized for something he hadn't done. I didn't know what else to do though; I wanted to come to the Internet center to get away from the idea of my dad not being there for me anymore. We wouldn't talk about things like life and success. We wouldn't talk about why I never got to disagree with him once in my lifetime, out of fear and respect for him. I avoid articles or sports web pages after a Yankees loss, so I had no distraction, just death.

Kelly and her brother were in contact with Christine. I thought she would surely talk to me after finding out my father had died…but she didn't. I sat there at the computer knowing they were each talking to her, and not once did she bother to drop me an email or an instant message, sending her condolences. This girl was indeed something other than a friend; she was unworthy to even be deemed an acquaintance. She might as well have died along with my father, at least he gave a shit about me.

I walk aimlessly around the camp trying to avoid crossing paths with anyone I knew because word travels fast in the Corps. Whether it's true or false, word will get to someone within seconds. I walk to the mess hall to attend a company-sized meeting regarding our return home. As I walk in I'm approached by the platoon commander and Master Gunz. They ask me if I am okay. The H&S Company first sergeant then approaches and out of annoyance I say, "Listen, I don't want to fucking talk about it!" They leave me alone and head to their seats. I felt like I was a child, like I couldn't function without someone doing something for me. That's how I was being treated. The platoon commander, to my dismay, kicks a Marine out of his seat, so I could sit by him. It angered me more than anything because now Marines will know something is wrong with me. It also made that Marine feel like he wasn't a part of the platoon. I remember nothing else from that meeting.

On my way out of the mess hall, Alpha Company's first sergeant sees me and says, "Hey Joe, why do you look like someone just died?"

"That's because my dad did, First Sergeant," I tell him.

His face goes from joking to serious. He asks me what happened. I couldn't say anything other than, "I don't know." He understood not to push too much and asked me to join him and the Alpha Company commander at dinner the next day at the departure camp. I agreed because I knew they really cared about me. They cared about me as a person first and foremost. I shake his hand, thanking him as he offers to help in any way. I know he means it; it isn't an empty promise, like the ones I'm sure I will hear from Napoleon.

I walk back to the bay where we were staying; Other Marines don't say much to me. Those who knew were examining my facial expressions; others just noticed that I had a blank look on my face, still unsure of what it was that had happened to me. The platoon sergeant asks for all the staff NCOs and sergeants to meet him by the exit. I show up because I am still a staff NCO, just because my father died doesn't mean I can disregard my obligations to the Corps and my Marines. I am told that I don't have to be there, but I tell the platoon sergeant not to worry about it. Another Marine tells me he heard what happened and that he is sorry. I laugh and tell him what I have been telling everyone else.

"Did you kill him?"

When someone's immediate family member dies, they are sent home immediately. I was leaving with everyone else in two days, so it wouldn't make sense for me to push the issue. The platoon sergeant tells us the battalion will be flying out on two separate flights. The Marines who were out getting blown up on a daily basis like the Marines of Alpha, Delta, and Weapons Company were going to get on the first flight. The rest of us were going to be on the second one, except for our fearless platoon commander. If I had been in his position and one of my Marines had someone close to them die, I don't think I would have kept that flight. I would have offered it to that Marine. But that's what separates me and a few others from Marines like him. I just shake my head as the platoon sergeant explains why Napoleon is on the first flight, because he is "mission essential" and has to ensure everything is in order when the rest of us got in. Isn't that why we sent an advance party home a month early?

I was tired, tired of this place, the circumstances, of everyone and everything. Just get me home so I can figure out what the fuck it was I was going to do. I try to sleep that final night in Arifjan, but I find myself staring at the empty bunk above me, staring at the stitching, the spots, and stains on the mattress. I turn and try to close my eyes, but the hours tick down to sunrise.

I get up to shower, shave, and brush my teeth. I want to be done with the personal hygiene as soon as possible so I could catch the score of the Yankee game. I pleaded with God for him to let them win; he'd already done enough to me. The tension was too much. I leave the Internet center as we are trailing by one run in extra innings. Why would God take my father away and torture me by putting my Yankees down 2-0 to the Twins? After a quick donut breakfast, I go back to the Internet center to find that the Yankees had come back to win. God is great!

We still had to have our gear and weapons inspected. The weapon inspections are done by the staff NCOs, so, one by one, I go down the line of Marines. I was never a drill instructor, but I always wanted to be one. I stop and face a Marine; he greets me and executes a seven-part rifle movement known as "Inspection Arms." On the last movement, I snatch the weapon with force and intensity, as a drill instructor would. I inspect and hand the weapon back to the Marine and continue on to the next. I have yet to shed a tear for my father; I have yet to speak about him to anyone other than a few condolences given to me. I was delaying my mourning by filling my time with work.

After the weapons inspection some Air Force personnel come by to inspect our gear for excess sand. There was no way we were going to get all of it out. I remember joking about the gear, drawing the ire of Master Gunz. He didn't want me to joke about the gear while we were going through the inspection. Anything taken seriously by the inspectors could delay our departure. I didn't care though, who the fuck was waiting for me back home?

After the inspection we threw our gear on the back of a truck that was headed right for the airport. We would not load the bags onto the plane; this would prevent anyone from tampering with the equipment, thus bringing something illegal back to the United States. We would load onto buses and head for a camp near the airport in a few hours, so I took the spare time and went to get a haircut. I had to look presentable; I didn't want to give anyone an idea of what it was that was going on in my head.

Going from Arifjan to the next camp was eerie for me. It was odd to be on a bus and drive down roads knowing you wouldn't get blown up, but I still felt the need to look at everything on the side of the road. I didn't trust the drivers, locally hired people, whose purpose was to take us from one camp to the next. What if they were compromised? What if they had ulterior motives? Why wouldn't they want to see us dead? We were a symbol of American imperialism and what everyone else considered "infidels." They'd be heroes…as you can see my mind was racing out of control.

At the next camp, I get off the bus and head into a tent without speaking to anyone. We were separated by flight groups. Marines leaving first would be in different tents. Marines leaving second would be in the tent with me and others nearby. I drop what's left of the gear I was taking with me and pull out a book. I had read all of *The Da Vinci Code*, so I decided to give *Angels and Demons* a try. As I begin the first few pages, I look up to see a face inches away from mine.

"Staff Sergeant, if you need anything, you come to me. There is nothing I won't do to help, if you need it."

It was the H&S company commander, and he possessed a look that I did not have. He looked like he was emotionally drained, speaking softly, saddened by the loss of my father. I thanked him and got up to leave. I didn't want to be reminded of it right now. I just wanted to try to enjoy the idea of going home, but still, who the fuck was waiting for me back there?

Outside my tent were both the Alpha company commander and first sergeant. They were ready to take me to dinner. I had nearly forgotten. Thankfully, they didn't bring up my father's death. The company commander brought up the Yankee's game, and I say, "A-Rod, sir, the guy is clutch," referring to A-Rod nearly carrying the team in that game. Maybe my dad would be on the side of A-Rod and the Yankees, wouldn't that be a story?

It would be our final day to rest. Tomorrow we'd be going from tent to tent to receive classes. They figured if we were given classes in dealing with Post Traumatic Stress Disorder in a condensed setting, it would be enough. It would cover their asses when one of us went on a shooting spree. I knew I wasn't able to sleep the night before and that tomorrow would be another day without rest. I tried to go to sleep but couldn't. There was no curfew at this camp, so I spent eleven hours in the Internet center talking to Kelly, Heather, and Carolyn.

The next morning I walk out of my tent and see the battalion sergeant major standing outside, smoking a cigarette. He looked pissed off.

"What flight are you on, Hafid?" he asks me. I tell him I am on the second flight and he storms off, throwing his cigarette to the ground. I am sure he knew about my father's death. His reaction was because I was leaving second. I was with the Marines of Alpha Company during the deployment and my father had died, yet I was still going on the second flight while Napoleon would be on the first. It doesn't take much for someone to see the irrational judgment that led to that.

It was too late though; I was going on the second flight, no matter what anyone would say. The only person who could really push the issue was the one man that could have given up his seat, but that was never an option in his eyes. A few hours pass and the first plane departs. I think about all those Marines. How every one of them deserved to be happy and to feel proud for what they had done, all except one tiny human being who wore the uniform of a teddy bear. He disgusted me now more than ever.

It had now been two days since the news of my father's death. I go through the mandatory "decompression" classes, as if I wasn't there. I go through the motions, slowly but surely making my way closer to the plane that would take me home to…God knows what. The looks on the faces of the Marines resemble joy and excitement. Me, I stare at nothing though my eyes continue to wander.

I finally board the plane and head to my seat. One of the Marines asks me to look over at him and he snaps a picture. I don't smile; I just look at him as I let him take it. I sit down in my seat and listen as the plane begins its trek to the runway. I close my eyes and listen to the sounds around me. The pilot gets on the intercom and begins thanking us for doing the work that many couldn't do and would never do. He finishes to a round of applause by the Marines and all I could think of is how the Marines were silly for applauding themselves.

The pilot instructs the flight attendants to take their seats and the engines rev louder as the plane picks up speed. My eyes remain closed as the nose of the plane lifts off the ground with the rear following. Unlike the year before, I am not clutching the armrests. I could care less what happens on this takeoff. The Marines roar in excitement as we clear the runway and gain altitude. I share no excitement with them. I left the United States with a friend in Christine, a Marine in Rudy, and a father in my dad. I am leaving Iraq with none of them. Maybe if I closed my eyes long enough I'd wake up and see that it was all a dream, but with how things were going, this was just the start. I needed a drink.

CHAPTER 41

Ignorance Is Bliss

As slowly as time passed in Iraq, the blur that is the aftermath began with a common denominator, my friends Jose, Jack, Miller, and some German guy named Jäger. The Marine Corps did all it could to get us ready to return to a world that had gone on without us. The Marine Corps talked to us for hours, days, and had weeks to prepare us, but it means nothing until you set foot on the ground of the land you call home—the home you defended in the name of so many people. But who really gives a shit? I just didn't see it.

I do the same routine I had done the year before. I turn my weapon in and head somewhere other than where I was. Families were cheering our return, but none of them were mine. The looks on the faces of the Marines were priceless. They deserved this homecoming, but I couldn't help but think to myself, "Will I ever get one?"

Napoleon is long gone. His leadership was stellar as usual. He put himself above his Marines and probably used a ladder to do so. I meet some of the Marines who were left behind for various reasons, most of them hurt or injured. I ask one of them for my car keys and he gives them to me. I head to one of my Marine's home, and he offers me a drink. The cap is twisted off before it reaches my hand, and in one motion, I lift it to the ceiling and look up at it. No words needed to be said, just, "Oh yeah, I heard…"

Waiting for me were a few items I had left with Christine—a Yankee jersey I had asked her to wear for me when the Yankees played the Dodgers on my birthday. She was also asked to hold onto my wedding ring. Before heading to Iraq, Eric went out of his way to retrieve them from her. He knew it was a relationship headed for failure. He knew me too well. Brothers have that gift. Christine never went to the game for me. Am I surprised? Absolutely not.

I head to a hotel room on base. With all of the advance parties in place, they still had nothing for us when we got back. No one who was married and a staff sergeant or above was given a room in the barracks. There were beds, yes, but we were not allowed to use them. Had I not had my buddy get me a room, I would have been sleeping in my car. In the hotel that night, I watch as the Yankees are losing 5-1 to the Twins in Game 4 of their series. Out of stress and anger, I leave my room and drive off base. I don't know where I am going to go and don't know where I went.

I call my friend Heather, and I can hear the compassion in her voice. It was the first call I made when I got back. She asked what I had planned, and I told her I would be driving around since the Yankees were probably going to be headed to a stressful Game 5, exactly what I needed. I remember the drive vividly, going over a bridge and making a right turn before I left the front gate; but from there I don't remember much, my mind went blank. When I return I see the Yankees had made a comeback and had won their game and series with the Twins. They'd now face the Boston Red Sox, and I knew what that meant…stress but an eventual series win. We never lose to the Red Sox, and with my father looking down on me, he wouldn't allow me to go through anymore pain.

The next morning I get up and put on a sweatshirt I had purchased from some home shopping network the year before. The sweatshirt showed my affiliation and allegiance to the New York Giants. Why was I wearing it? I was headed to a game in San Diego between the Chargers and Jacksonville Jaguars. I would never wear another team's apparel; I didn't care if the Giants were playing in Dallas that day and I was all the way in San Diego. I was G-Men all the way. My buddy picked me up; I hadn't seen him since he left a month early from Iraq with the advance party. He had a few other guys with him. We were all staff NCOs in the Marine Corps, but I was just twenty-six. They were in their late thirties or early forties.

I felt like the kid brother, and frankly I was. I was a child all over again. Pain settled in, and I felt lost. My buddy did all he could to steer the conversation away from what had happened to me and gave me a beer. I had never gone to an NFL game before, so it was interesting to say the least. The tailgating was fun, the food was amazing, and the drinks were plenty. I was heckled by other fans as they walked by me saying, "Thanks for the draft picks, Eli sucks!"

"Hey how'd you guys do against the Niners in Super Bowl Twenty-nine?" I would ask them. I'd get no response. Most of these fans were fickle in nature, they knew nothing of their team's history. The Chargers had won two games so far this year, half of what they won the year before and all of a sudden they're better than my Giants? Kiss the rings, people. We have two of them, and with Eli Manning I am sure we'll get some more.

I take in the atmosphere around me. I was there but also completely gone. My buddy handed me beer after beer, and I lost count for a moment. If I ever lose count drinking, then I have had too much. I turn to him and say, "Twelve beers, dude! I've never drunk so much, but this is delicious!" My buddy just smiled and nodded his head. He could see I was dying inside. My vision is blurred. I am barely able to walk, but we head to the stadium. More hecklers comment about my Giants shirt, but even though intoxicated, I spout off facts that they would never know, "You guys have Brees. He's a decent quarterback. You don't need to be dicks about it and draft Manning. What's up with that?" In the stadium I look for my seat. The security guard in our area was a volunteer Marine who I had a great conversation with. He was new to the Corps, and he volunteered his weekend to provide free labor to an NFL franchise. I went to buy more drinks and even bought some for my section.

"Hey, sir," I say to an older gentleman and his wife. "What are you drinking?"

He tells me he wants a Heineken, and I head off, making multiple purchases for people I don't know. I get back to my seat and see on the scoreboard that the Giants were laying a beat down on the Cowboys. The national anthem is set to begin, and I yell for everyone to take their hats off and stand. I stand at attention and face the flag as the anthem plays. Tears stream down my cheeks. The anthem always does that to me, but I still look forward to it.

Something happened on the field, but it didn't matter. I was no longer paying attention. I sat at my seat and drifted away, looking at the thousands of fans in attendance. I looked at the players on the field and the cheerleaders on the sidelines. Everyone had something going on in their lives. Everyone in the stadium was enjoying something, while thousands of miles away my brothers and sisters were dying. My brother Eric was now in harm's way, and I detested everyone around me.

The Chargers showed their *support* of the troops by showing a few Marines or sailors in attendance and in uniform on the big screen. The crowd cheered but would soon get back to what was going on in the game. The Marines and sailors were soon forgotten, but not by me. I looked at the sky, it was blue and beautiful, everything reeked of goodness, but the world is not good. The world is far from good.

I open my eyes and hear someone behind me saying, "Is he okay?" The man I had purchased a drink for earlier was asking my buddy about me. I don't know when I drifted off to sleep, but it was now halftime, and I wasn't feeling too well. I get up and head for the exit; I needed a bathroom and needed it badly. Someone must have caught me on camera and noticed the familiar look of sick that covered my face. I had to walk up stairs to get to the exit and then down another flight to get to the bathroom. What was a one-minute walk for me any other sober day, was now a treacherous and trying march.

I fall to my knees and to the crowd's pleasure begin to throw up. I was way past my limit but I was still able to think and feel; I had tried to drown it with more alcohol. With each heave I hear a cheer from the thousands of fans; my buddy grabs me and carries me to the bathroom. The Marine who was volunteering as a security guard is concerned and asks if I needed help. I get everything out of my system and we head to the car. I was apologizing over and over to my buddy and his friends. They laugh and tell me I was on the big screen in the stadium and the crowd could see everything. They were even cheering for me. At least I provided them with entertainment.

I wake up hours later on a couch alone and unaware. The first thing I do is grab the remote control and turn on the television to see what happened in the second half of the game I left. Apparently the Chargers had won, but I was more concerned if they had shown me on local television. Luckily I was not, and I begin to wonder where the hell I was.

My buddy walks in through the front door. I am in his house and he asks if I am okay. With him is a friend of his, and he introduces us. Getting and understanding the hint, I tell him I would be heading back to my room at the hotel. He gives me the keys to his car, and I take off. I get to my room and call Kelly. I tell her what happened earlier and she laughs hysterically. Kelly was due to arrive with her parents that weekend to see her brother. It would be nice to finally meet her. I mean she was to be my Marine Corps Ball date; you kind of have to meet them beforehand, don't you?

For the next few days I didn't have much of anything to do. I'd go to work and my first sergeant would ask me when I was going to Yemen to visit my family. I told him I didn't know because I honestly didn't know, and frankly I didn't want to go. But I knew I had to. I focused my energy elsewhere, like Games 1 and 2 of the American League Championship Series where the Yankees put the Red Sox in a familiar place, in a series they were going to lose.

After each game I called Kelly and talked to her. She became the one friend I could call at anytime of the day and we would talk for hours. I talked to her more than I talked to her brother, and he worked for me! We flirted with each other, and I would say bizarre things. It was part of the humor that made her laugh most when talking to me. I asked her if she wanted to go to the World Series because when the Yankees won I was going to get tickets. She excitedly said yes. In another day or so she'd be in California.

As for my family, I called them once since I'd been back, and it was depressing. Everyone sounded dark and helpless. My mother could barely speak, and I started to see that she wanted me to feel sorry for her. She said things about her possibly dying next and it annoyed me. I even told her it annoyed me because I didn't like how she was begging for sympathy, "Hey, he was my father you know? How do you think I feel?" I would ask her. Luckily the phone cut off as she continued to mope, and I didn't call back.

At work there was nothing to be done. Everyone was scheduling their trips for the leave block. No one would bother me regarding how I felt or what I was thinking about. I was masking the pain; covering it with the 2-0 ALCS lead the Yankees had over the Red Sox. The Yankees were going to get me through once again; they were my outlet and my love. I get called into Napoleon's office, expecting him to say something that would piss me off, but instead he asks me how I am doing. I told him I was fine, I just needed to do my job as a leader of Marines. He says to me, "If you need to talk to anyone, they have people for that." I didn't get what he was saying.

It was my first Friday back in the States and Kelly would be arriving later today. I stayed at work for as long as I could to pass the time away. My phone rang and a familiar voice said, "Where are you?" It was Kelly; she had arrived and was with her parents in her brother's barracks room. I told her I would be right there; she demanded that I hurry up.

I leave the office and head to my car. I was a little nervous to meet Kelly, you never know what it would be like to meet someone you've only seen through pictures and heard through a phone. I get into my car and drive out of the parking lot. The drive to the barracks was literally fifteen seconds. It took longer to start up and put the car into gear than it took to drive it. I could have walked, but I needed a delay.

I walked up the flight of stairs and got to the room. I saw her parents and introduced myself to them. I turned to her and said, "Umm, do I shake your hand or hug you?" She initiated the hug, but by the look she gave me, I knew there was something else there. I talked with her, her brother, and their parents for a few moments. A few of the Marines living in the barracks were also there, they see a girl and they flock to the room she's in; it never fails.

"Let's go to the Cheesecake Factory," I said to everyone. "Just give me a few minutes to change."

I go to my room and change into my Yankee jersey. I had to wear my team colors proud. I was hoping a Red Sox fan would try to say something, but they weren't around. It was funny how they seemed to shrink when they were being dominated...again. I picked up a few of the guys and we drove to the Cheesecake Factory near San Diego. I found myself weaving in and out of traffic, traveling at top speeds. Kelly called her brother who is with me and told him their dad is pissed at my driving. He laughed and you could hear her laughing as well through the phone.

We sat down at a table for about twenty of us. It was a great setting; I sat in the corner and whispered over to the waitress, "When the bill comes, give it to me okay? Just remember, the one with the Yankee jersey." She nodded and walked away. I told no one what my intentions were; I looked at the television, showing the NLCS game between Houston and St. Louis. I was hoping Houston would win so we could face two of our former Yankee teammates.

I asked for three bottles of champagne and the waitress brought them to us. The champagne was poured and I stood to give a toast. I thanked the parents who came to the dinner and thanked their children for whom they represented. I then toasted to those fallen and we all had a drink. I drank the glass in one gulp and sat back down. Kelly tried to talk to me as the night went on, but she was more nervous than I had been before I went to see her.

I didn't eat much. I just sat there looking around at everyone, listening to the conversations and basking in the happiness that surrounded me. After dinner we'd go bowling, one of the things I loved to do. The waitress came over to me with the bill and I handed over my credit card where no one else could see. When she came back, I signed the slip. Kelly's dad got up and scolded me for paying. I told him to just let me be me. Kelly looked at me, and I could tell she was studying my thoughts and actions. Even I didn't know what was going on in my mind. It was mush, but I was covering it up pretty well.

The waitress thanked me, and I tell her I would not be giving her a tip on my card, but I reached into my pocket and gave her the tip in cash. I tell her, "Listen, don't freak out about what I'm giving you, but I pay for services rendered, and this should tell you how you've done."

On my way out of the restaurant she brings her manager over to me and says, "This is the nice guy I was telling you about. He wanted to tell you something."

The manager thanked me for my patronage, but I tell him he should be thanking his waitress and staff for giving me and my friends a great night. They didn't know us, each of us could have been having a bad day, yet they still maintained their professionalism and were kind and caring. You can't teach that. You can't train that. You can't fake sincerity. The waitress hugged me, it was a first for me, but when you tip someone $200 I guess it comes with the territory.

I thought of the amount I gave her as I started up my car, "You just made my week," she had told me as she hugged me. I thought about my father looking down at me. I know how he and my mom were with money, would he disapprove or would he understand what I was doing?

Kelly's parents left for the night, but the rest of us go to a bowling alley. I was introduced to a beverage I had never heard of before—Jägermeister and Red Bull, a "Jäger Bomb." At first I didn't drink it because I had to drive back.

"It's for Rudy," one of the Marines says. "You have to drink it."

He was right, I did have to drink it, and as we made our toast to Rudy I toasted my dad in my head. I had three Jäger Bombs and headed to the car. We dropped Kelly off at the hotel her parents were staying in. We would hangout again the next night, but this time with a smaller crowd.

The next night was the last night she'd be able to go out with all of us because it was Saturday. We were off the next day and she was leaving on Sunday night. I met everyone later in the night because I was watching the Yankees demolish the Red Sox and put them on the brink of elimination.

"We won 19-8. One more win and you get to go to the World Series," I told Kelly. I then said, "How lucky are you? You get to go to the Marine Corps Ball with me and now the World Series. You're lucky for a blonde."

I had also finally made plans to visit Yemen. I would be flying my older sister, her daughter, and my younger brother with me. I'd be paying for their flights, and it would not be cheap. I'd be leaving for New York on Monday, by then I'd have tickets for Games 1 and 2 of the World Series. After that, I'd fly to Yemen to see my father's grave. At least the Yankees were making me happy, and at least I had Kelly in my life now. She had been more amazing in person than I ever expected.

Sunday was departure day for Kelly and her family. Her brother would be going home with them for his post deployment leave; she called me throughout the day to update me on what they were doing—they had gone to the zoo. I found it cute, she was checking up on me, but I knew what it really meant. She had a crush on me, and she was pining over me through the phone. I was a gentleman about it, but would throw her a quick jab, "Aw, how cute. You love me more now!"

She told me to shut up but would not deny it.

"Shit," I interrupted her in mid-sentence.

"What happened," she asked.

"The Red Sox just tied the game in the 9th. It's okay though, we still got this," I said to her.

It's funny how things work out. When things look benign in nature, the next thing you know there's a slight change in the universe and the dominoes begin to fall. I say it's funny, but what came next was certainly not.

Chapter 42

Blown Save

As I sat down at work waiting for the evening to arrive, I logged onto a computer in another office to see that the Yankees were leading in the seventh inning by two runs. I was at ease and hopeful the Yankees would pull it out so my flight to New York would be a joyous one. I see the box score change innings to the eighth. I was more at ease and left work for the day. I headed to one of my Marine's home and waited for a few hours with him before he'd take me to the airport.

Kelly had gotten home in the early hours that morning and had been texting me all day. On the way to the house I received another text from her, this one telling me the Red Sox had tied the game in the eighth inning against none other than Mariano Rivera. My heart sank, all Yankee fans prepared for the worst, but demanded excellence. The precedent the Yankees were about to set would be legendary.

On May 23, 1995, I changed the channel on our television to eleven. The channel used to be known as WPIX, but Warner Bros. had a hair up their asses and decided to have a network of their own called "The WB." It was around 10:00 p.m., and my mom was not home. She was in the apartment upstairs with her friends, which meant I had control of the television. Our best pitcher, Jimmy Key, was injured. The Yankees called up a twenty-six-year-old pitcher from Panama named Mariano Rivera.

I looked on as the Yankees did nothing against Chuck Finley and the California Angels in the first inning, but I was more intrigued about who this Rivera "kid" (as the announcers called him) was. He was not your typical prospect I had heard of that year; he was far older and didn't have the upside that a highly touted prospect would have. He wore number forty-two, like the great Jackie Robinson once did. He took the mound looking as skinny and as frail as I did, but I was still eager to see him pitch.

At that time in my life, I was relatively new to baseball; sports started off as a love interest for the New York Knicks with the New York Giants and Rangers coming in at second and third on my list. The 1993 Yankees swept in and took over my heart and the top of the list. There was just something about that team. As little as I watched baseball back then I was still able to watch how pitches moved and could determine if a pitcher was going to have a good game or not. "If the ball looks small, the batter won't have a chance, but if it looks big, they're going to kill it," I'd tell my younger brothers who listened to everything I said back then. It wasn't scouting, but it honestly looked smaller to me when a pitcher was pitching well. When he was getting rocked, it looked like a beach ball.

Mariano stood there on the pitching rubber and started his windup. It was smooth and would rock you to sleep, if you were already tired from a long day. His first pitch was a fastball and it looked as if the ball was a dot. It was at ninety-five mile per hour fastball, and the first batter, Tony Phillips, had no chance. "This guy is going to be a star," I told my brothers. I was hoping I was right, but when I made that proclamation I knew I made a statement I had to stick by, thinking to myself, "I hope he is; then I can brag about being right."

That day, Phillips went down on a strikeout and the next batter, Jim Edmonds, followed with the same result. I was ecstatic, instantly thinking I would be right, but a few bad pitches a couple of innings later and Rivera was out of the game and forgotten. Chuck Finley was the star of that game, striking out fifteen Yankees and putting on a pitching clinic. If Mariano was going to be a star, he should watch tapes of how Finley pitched.

Mariano Rivera struggled that year, but I still had faith in him. The Yankees offered him to Toronto for David Cone, but Toronto saw nothing in him and declined. They offered him elsewhere for starting pitching, but no one wanted him. They didn't see any upside in him. I went as far as calling the local radio station, WFAN, for the first time in my life asking the hosts if there was a way we could get David Cone without trading Mariano and an outfielder we had, named Gerald Williams. They laughed when I asked that question; they didn't think the Blue Jays would want either player.

Flash forward to the first American League Division Series. Mariano had been moved to the bullpen as a reliever. The Yankees had acquired Cone from the Blue Jays for some pitchers they thought would be better than Mariano in the long run. The Yankees faced Seattle in the series and no one could get Griffey Junior out. He had the Yankees' number. I think the manager, Buck Showalter, brought in Rivera to face Griffey in extra innings in Game 2 because he had no other answers. Griffey flied out to the outfield and the Yankees had a chance. They came back to win that game, but I remembered John Sterling's reaction to Rivera's outing, "Mariano Rivera just became a man."

I had seen perhaps the greatest of athletes in my life in all sports. In the NHL they had guys like Gretzky, Messier, and Lemieux. In the NFL they had Lawrence Taylor, Joe Montana, and Dan Marino. In the NBA, they had Jordan, Magic, and Bird, but Mariano Rivera became my favorite athlete past or present. He'd become such a star, one that teams like the Blue Jays wished they traded for, one that teams like the Red Sox wished never existed. He made me feel at ease when the game was on the line, but this was a different year. This was 2004.

I now sat in front of the television; Joe Torre brought in pitcher after pitcher, just as he had done for the past two games. There were no more off days in the series; I knew it was now or never. After the Yankees failed to score for the fifth consecutive inning, I asked the wife of my Marine to change the channel; my heart couldn't take it anymore. If we won, I'd be relieved, but if we lost, I didn't want to see it.

It was time for me to head to the airport, my phone rang and it was a friend of mine who I had met in China years before. "Please tell me we won," I asked her.

We did not win. I sulked and nearly cried, showing more emotion than I did when hearing that my father died. I knew what was going to happen now, "We're gonna lose. You know that, right? There's no one in the bullpen that's able to lift their arm, let alone pitch," I said with my voice cracking. I was asked to keep the faith, but what had that brought me so far? Nothing.

I slept on the flight to New York and when I arrived I saw the back pages of all the papers reliving the failure from the night before. I felt exhausted and sick to my stomach. I called Kelly to see how she was doing and to see if she could cheer me up. She was frantic and as stressed as I was because she had made a bet with a Red Sox fan at her school about what she would do for him if the Red Sox came back to win. If I were that fan, I would make that bet any day. She was like me, overconfident.

When I got to my apartment in Brooklyn, I find that my youngest brother had left it in shambles. When I say it was in shambles, I mean just that. I looked at the mess and knew it would take me days to clean it up. I went and purchased garbage bags and a vacuum cleaner to begin cleaning. I don't know where the original vacuum cleaner went, but I assumed a rat or cockroach ate it. Twenty bags later I was able to finally see the carpet.

My sister called to say that she and my brother were on the way. They were coming via Amtrak from Detroit. It would take a day or so to get here, but I go on and on about how disgusting the apartment was. She didn't believe how bad it was, but when I told her about the towers of pizza boxes I had to throw out she started to understand I wasn't exaggerating. I was afraid I'd find a dead rat or something under the pile of trash; that would have been it for me.

In the middle of the cleaning I go over to the desktop computer in the bedroom to see what the score was in Game 6. I was still a bit hopeful. It was 4-0, Red Sox. I got up and went back to cleaning the apartment. In the ninth inning, the Yankees threatened to tie, down 4-2 with the tying run at the plate. I looked at the ESPN live box score update and hoped to see a ball appear in the strike zone that was blue and said, "run(s) scored," but like everything for me so far this year, they came up short. I knew what we were headed for; the next day I didn't even watch the start of the game. It's not that I was a bad fan, but when you see your team show nothing, they've already lost.

I was in the city with friends I had met in China a few years back. After spending time with them I would visit a friend I had met in London, also a few years ago. The friend from London was a Red Sox fan and asked me to go to a pro-Red Sox bar in New York and watch the rest of the game with her. She asked me this the day before, and I had agreed. I looked at my watch while with the first group of friends and saw that the game had started.

My phone rang minutes later, and Kelly told me it was 2-0 already. I told her to calm down, let the game play out. Moments later she called nearly crying, "Damon, just hit a grand slam! It's 6-0 Red

Sox!" I didn't say anything over the phone. My friends saw the pain in my face, another death was imminent, this time it would be the Yankees and the Curse of the Bambino; I could barely speak. It was 8-1 by the time I left the first group of friends to meet my friend at the pro-Sox bar. I bought a couple bottles of Smirnoff Ice and took them with me as I got into a taxi. The driver had the game on, and I could hear the silence of the stadium.

I opened the first drink and downed it. The second one followed, and I was done with it as the cab arrived at the bar. Inside I met my friend who was already celebrating with another friend of hers. They were both excited to see the end of an era, an era of futility and they had just ushered in a new era for the Yankees by doing something that had never been done before.

The final innings end one by painful one. Finally, a ground ball hit to second and as the throw is made to first base I ball up inside, crushed, and defeated once again. Just a few days before, I was enjoying another Yankee victory over their bitter rivals, and now I was sitting in a bar in New York drinking heavily, surrounded by Red Sox fans cheering and singing a familiar song.

"Start spreading the news…" they all shouted, mocking the Yankees closing tune in victory.

I didn't go home that night, instead I slept on the floor of my friend's apartment. I was completely drunk, trying to ease the pain from another loss near and dear to my heart. When I woke up I had to find my dad's car I left parked somewhere in the city. The city was somber, quiet, and no one spoke of the night before. We all knew what the other was feeling.

My brother, sister, and her daughter got in that afternoon. I didn't say much to them. We still had an apartment to clean up. I picked up the tickets for Yemen and showed them to my sister. That night we all sat down after finally getting the apartment cleaned up and looked through family photos. When I got to my father's pictures my sister collapsed and cried on my shoulder. I didn't know what to do. I didn't hug her or anything; it felt very awkward and unnatural. To me she was reacting in a strange way. I still didn't let out anything, holding in the pain of my father's death and hoping to mask it with a Yankee victory. The Yankees didn't come through for me; I had been counting on them to.

We left the night of Game 1 of the World Series. It was a Saturday, and all I could hope for now was another year of World

Series futility for the Red Sox. I didn't want the curse to be completely over. They couldn't win in my lifetime; it would be the cherry on top of the shit that was my year. Twenty runs were scored, and before we took off the Red Sox had won the first game.

My sister's brother-in-law picked us up when we arrived in Yemen. He drove us to the village where my mom stayed, where my dad was born and later died. There was no fanfare upon our arrival, just sadness and darkness surrounding everyone. My mother was up in her room, covered in black and looking sickly. I hugged and kissed her on the forehead; she began to cry, shaking as she held me. My brother does the same and after fifteen minutes of tears and emotion from all of them, we sat down with her. It's Ramadan and everyone was fasting, so no one offered tea or any food. We sat there asking each other how we were all doing. I saw my son, now fourteen months old but not yet able to walk. He looked at me in bewilderment.

I asked him to come over to me, but he refused and stayed with his grandmother, holding onto her. My wife sat across from me; not much was said, just hellos and other greetings. We stayed for a few moments, I still had my son and wife to spend time with so I left and headed to the room I would be staying in for two weeks. My sister and brother stayed to keep my mother company. She looked like a mess and I didn't blame her.

I talked with my wife and held my son. The son my father loved so much because he was mine. I asked my wife how my father had died and what happened. She talked about how the word got to everyone in the village before it got to my mother. She told me that my father had been sick, but no one thought it was serious. He was sick for about a week, but the day of his death he got up and got dressed. He covered his head and face, leaving only his eyes visible. On his way out of the house he didn't stop to greet anyone, something he'd done every day.

My uncle saw him before he left. He said his eyes were bloodshot and he was non-responsive. My dad went to a meeting with other villagers concerning drinking water being distributed among everyone evenly. As he was talking, he collapsed, fell to a knee, and onto one of the men sitting there. They laughed and told him to stop fooling around, but soon found out that he wasn't.

They rushed him to his car and tried to bring him to the hospital, but it was too late. He was dead and word of his death began to spread. The house we were building next to the house he had built many years before was full of workers that day; all of a sudden my mother saw them from the roof of his house stop working and leave the building. My mother sensed something was wrong with my dad and asked my cousin if he knew what had happened to him. He already knew the news; he was the one to tell her that he died.

They brought my dad's body home for them to see one last time before they buried him. Islamic law requires a person who has died be buried within twenty-four hours. My father was washed, covered, and buried hours after his death. The stone they used on his grave came from the floor my oldest brother claimed in the new house we were building. They deferred to the eldest son, though I knew my older brother did not love him as much as I did.

My wife continued on, obviously shaken and mentioning how pale my father looked when they brought his body to them. He didn't look real to her; it was not something I wanted to picture in my head. I still couldn't believe he was dead, but it was certain that he was because this was the first time I had ever been in Yemen without him being there.

I would only be in Yemen for two weeks, but in that time I went to see my father's grave with my son and nephew a few times. We said a prayer and walked back home each time we visited. I spent a few hours a day with my mother, talking to her and helping her get through it. She started to speak about our cousins who worked in Saudi Arabia and what they had done for their mother.

My family likes to point out the deficiencies of others in the family to make them look better to everyone else. I found it to be petty. My aunt was bragging to my mom that her sons sent her 1,000 Saudi Riyals. This proved their love to her she said, and then without skipping a beat asked if I or my other brothers had sent anything. My mother brought this up, not even a month after my dad died. She then went on to say that our cousins told her that her sons (my brothers and I) are in America, yet are not successful. They say to her that they are in Saudi Arabia and have money and riches, that they are better than us. She goes on and on, obviously making a dig at me, which she had always been known to do. The concrete on my father's grave was still wet and she was bringing up money.

"If you're going to listen to those scumbags, then claim them as your sons. I told you before that if you listen to what everyone tells you about your children, and if you believe it, then you've chosen them over us. Don't worry, we'll all be better than those idiots. We are our father's children," I said to her in defiance. I left the room frustrated and spent more time with my son. He didn't speak, so he wouldn't bring up anything as stupid as that.

Time with my wife was worse now than before in that she really showed me no compassion. Everyone else made it about them, forgetting those who were really mourning. My wife mourned the loss of my dad and could barely look at me, solidifying my loss of love for her.

Days went on; the trip to Yemen was nothing more than a guilt trip and exploitation. All the vultures who were waiting for my father's demise were now flying overhead, waiting for the four sons to be in charge and to be completely lost. The burden of leadership would fall on my eldest brother. He was not bright by a long shot and had never been a leader of anything. This would be a trying time for him, but did he show up? No, he was more concerned with making more money at work than to stop everything and visit my dad's grave. Much like a baker, after he'd make his dough, he would come at a later date. He was my mother's son.

My father's voice was gone now; the things he taught us would now be tested. My other sister told me that before he died he had told her, "If I was to die, I would be happy because my children are good." I was now certain he knew he was going to die, and had he not known who he had in his children, he would have fought harder to live.

I woke up in the middle of the night before I left to head back to New York. I had a dream that the Red Sox swept the World Series and indeed put an end to their curse. This dream woke me up. I looked at my phone and saw three text messages from friends of mine in the United States who were Red Sox fans. It was confirmed, the Red Sox had won the World Series, and I was lucky enough to live through it.

When I got back to New York I called Kelly to give her an update on how things were going. While joking around about hooking up at the Ball, she made a sarcastic remark about my father, forgetting that he had died. This shook me a little, but I knew it was a simple and honest mistake. I told her that I had to go and she began to apologize and cried hysterically. I told her to relax; she could make it up to me at the Ball. I said that to her without a laugh, she giggled.

My sister left with her family who had come to pick her up. I gave the Yankees jersey that I asked Christine to wear to my oldest nephew. I didn't want it anymore. It was cursed, and it was with a cursed person. As they were leaving, my sister's husband told me that if I needed anything, I should ask, but when anyone says that, I know what it means. It translated to, "Hey, I don't want to sound like a dick and say don't call me, but I will say call me just to cover my ass. But please, try not to call me or ask for anything because I have a life of my own."

It was just my brother and me for a few days before I would leave and head back to California, back to the Corps. I went to watch a Knicks game before I left; I took a friend I once had a huge crush on in high school. She was the first person who didn't treat me like a beaten child. She let me be me. It was a good end to my short time in New York, but I was still hurting inside, more than before. I put too much emphasis into the Yankees saving me, but not even the great Mariano Rivera could save the games or me. At least I had the Marine Corps Ball to look forward to. That would make everything all the much better.

Chapter 43

A Broken Heart

Throughout life's travels you will meet many people. Some of them will have an impact, others will be forgotten. Some will be close friends of yours, but with time and separation you will lose touch and eventually they will be a distant memory. While I was a Marine Security Guard in London I made some good friends, Eric being the greatest friend I could have ever asked for. We met up and went out at night to bars and lounges. It seemed like we weren't even there for work, just to have a good time.

In the Marine house, where we lived, we had a picture board. On this board there were pictures of all of us doing various things. Some of us were in costumes for a Halloween party; others were taken of us playing softball or barbequing; name it, and we were doing it. When I first got there I was the new guy and none of the pictures looked like anyone I had known. Toward the end of my tour there, all of those pictures were gone, replaced by the ones we had taken.

When I left England for China, a group of friends came to see me off. Some cried, some held it in, but all in all, it was a sad occasion. It was sad because you knew you might never see each other again. This was a common occurrence for me, for all of us. All we could do was exchange email addresses and hope for the best. We all looked at the photos, and each of us would point to one of them saying, "Remember when we took this one?" Of course we did, but we knew that like the rest, our pictures would be taken down and we'd be ghosts, memories of what once was…and then forgotten.

The first time I ever maintained contact with friends from another place and eventually saw them again was Thanksgiving of 2002. My friend Erin from London invited me to her parents' home in New Jersey, and I got to meet her family. I remember telling her, "You know you have a friend for life when you see them in more than one place." I believed this, because I felt that if you were a friend, you were not a friend through convenience, you were a friend through time and opportunity.

After I had gotten back from Yemen, Erin and a few of our other friends planned on meeting in San Francisco. It would be a reunion of some of us who were posted in London. We would be coming in from all parts of the world, some from New Zealand and the United Kingdom. Some came from all parts of the United States: Ohio, Wisconsin, and, of course, New Jersey.

I was given an extended weekend by my command, surprisingly Napoleon had no issues with this and encouraged it. We left late one evening and arrived in San Francisco early in the morning. I found San Francisco to be a wonderful city; it was a mix of the best of San Diego and New York. I checked in early then walked around and called Kelly. Luckily with the three-hour difference in time, she would already be awake.

I didn't like to sit alone because it got me thinking. There wasn't much to think about really, just a dead father and the biggest collapse in professional sports. I tried to think about my son, but doing that brought on thoughts of my dad because of how close they were and how my son had his name. I walked around for a few hours, talking to Kelly for a few minutes or so as I walked. I stopped by a Burger King that had a sourdough sandwich I had to try. I guess sourdough was the thing in San Francisco, though I will admit, it was rather tasty.

I got back to the room, by now the first wave of friends had come, and we all met and sat and talked. We would wait for the next morning before the rest would arrive. It was good to see them all, but it was also strange because we hadn't seen each other since our time in London; and so much had happened since. Sometimes you just have to tell yourself that it's really happening. We went to bed late the first night, but I found myself waking up early. So I would go back out and walk the city yet again. I just wanted to take in the sight and sounds of it and to get some more sourdough egg sandwiches.

It was a short trip, a small getaway for people I had known years before. We were all older, somewhat wiser, and far more experienced in life. The one thing I didn't enjoy was the, "Are you okay?" questions I kept getting from them. The more you get asked that question, the more you aren't okay. The night before we left, we all met up in one of the rooms. We would be going out one last time then leave the next morning. I told everyone I would be right back and headed to my room.

I walked in, sat on my bed, and stared at the window. In my mind I was thinking, *What the hell are you doing staring at the window?* It didn't register though. I couldn't move. My roommate, another Marine, came in and asked if I was okay. I told him I'd be fine, and I'd be there in a few minutes. I lay down perpendicular to the bed with my lower body hanging over the edge. I stared at the ceiling and closed my eyes. When I opened them, it was morning, and it was time to go. My short trip with friends was indeed short, and it was now over.

The ride back was long and uneventful, but then all of a sudden I felt a sharp pain in my chest. It was persistent and ran down my left arm. I was scared, but I didn't want to alarm the other Marine so I just told him that I felt a twinge in my chest and that when I got back I was going to the hospital. He asked if I was okay, and I told him that I would be fine. We got back to the base and he got into his car and took off. I called Kelly's brother and he said he would take me to the hospital.

It was a Sunday night and now very late. I was admitted into the hospital on base to be checked by a doctor. My blood pressure was high, and I laughingly asked the nurse if it meant that I was dying. She said no, that it was expected for anyone who was in a lot of pain. I was in a lot of pain, but I didn't want to tell anyone that I was in mourning.

The doctor met me, and I told him how I was feeling. He checked my pulse and listened to my heart. He made the familiar, "hmm," that doctors make when something peculiar is happening, so I ask him what was going on, "Am I having a heart attack, sir?"

It wasn't a heart attack, but he said my heart sounded like it had a murmur, but that I should be okay. He wanted to do more testing. He advised me not to do any physical exercises and to take it easy. Taking it easy would have been an option that I wish I had, but what could I do to stop all the negative thoughts from racing through my head?

I got to work later that Monday morning with copies of my medical reports. Napoleon called me into his office; I had called the platoon sergeant the night before to tell him I was going to the hospital, so he obviously had told him. Napoleon asked me how I was feeling and asked me if I had talked to anyone yet. I asked him what he meant and he said that this could all be stress related; that I had a lot of things going on and that it could be a result of that.

I told him I was fine and left his office. The Master Gunz' office was next to his and when he saw me walk out he asked how I was doing. He sounded very concerned and I could tell because he had his sunglasses off. The thing with Master Gunz was that he wore his sunglasses everywhere, including indoors. For him to take them off and to look me in the eye showed me that he was concerned. Maybe I should have been, too.

I never told my family. I didn't want my mother or anyone else to think the worst. I also didn't want to seem like an attention seeker saying, "Hey look at me! I'm dying!" I called my mom to see how she was doing and what she said to me was unreal. She asked when I would be sending money so we could finish the house. I told her I just spent a ton of it flying my brother, my sister and her daughter out to come see her. It's not like they paid me a lot. When I got money, I would send it. I told her not to worry, my diet of ramen noodles would help.

She called me a liar and said that all I ever did was lie. I made promises about money but never delivered. I explained, once again, that I was a U.S. Marine, not a Merchant Marine like my brothers or my father. I didn't come anywhere close to what they made, nor would I. I was getting angry with her, telling her I didn't know why I ever called her because it was always the same. The phone cut off and I wouldn't call back. I didn't plan on calling her back anytime soon.

My chest hurt again. My left arm tingled, and it felt more and more like I was having a heart attack. I laid down on my bed and waited for it to pass…it finally did.

At six o'clock each night, I was required to call Kelly. I say required because she demanded I call, otherwise she'd, "kick your ass," as she so eloquently put it. The reason why it was six o'clock for me was because at nine o'clock her time, her cell phone minutes were free. She was short on money, complaining about her phone bill and not having the money to pay it. I asked her how much it was and she told me. I asked her if she needed a loan to pay it, and she reluctantly said yes. I drove to the nearest Western Union and wired her some money. She got it and called me outside the free minute time and said I was crazy.

"I didn't ask you to send that much," she said. I had sent her a few dollars more because I knew she needed it. Did it mean I had to really be careful with my money? Yes, but I didn't care. She made me smile, and I was helping out someone I cared about. "That's okay; I'll make it up to you at the Ball." She paid her phone bill and bought a pair of boots…figures.

The Ball was a week away, and I was excited. The Marine Corps Ball was surely going to end this nightmare of a year I was having, and it would be in Las Vegas. It would also be on a Thursday night for some reason. Typically it fell on a Friday or a Saturday, but because the powers that be could not find a venue or day that would be adequate, we had a Thursday night Ball. Each day that passed I became more excited. Kelly would leave an away message on her AOL Instant Messenger that said she had, "The greatest Ball date EVER!"

A few days before the Ball the Marines from Alpha Company invited me to a pre-Ball drinking party for all the staff NCOs and officers of Alpha Company. These Marines were certainly classy. This required me to leave a night early to bring supplies, so I told Kelly I would have to leave a day early for the Ball. She was flying into San Diego the night before the Ball and would drive with her brother and his friend, another one of my Marines, to Las Vegas the morning of the Ball. She balked at the idea, but I told her not to worry, she'd be with her brother and a few of my Marines, she was in good hands.

On December 1, 2004, our battalion had a motivational physical training session that had different stations. Marines would wrestle, fight, run, swim, and anything else they could think of. The company with the most points would win the event. After the event we'd be released for the long weekend, to celebrate the birth of our Corps, for the 229th year. I was not taking part in these events because of my medical condition, but I cheered on the Marines.

While I was watching the wrestling tournament, Kelly called me. She said she was nervous and was mad that I was leaving tonight. I told her I had to, the Marines from Alpha Company were brothers to me; they asked me to come to their event and I couldn't say no. She would be with her brother and some of my Marines, she would be fine. After the call she texted me and said, "I'm going to the Marine Corps Ball with the greatest Ball date EVER!" I smiled and put the phone back in my pocket.

The physical training event was over, and we were told to go to the parade deck for a battalion formation. We all knew this meant we would be released for the weekend. It was quick and when the word, "Dismissed," was commanded, a loud roar overtook the parade deck. Marines scattered, most of them running to their cars or their rooms. The faster they moved the more time they would have in Vegas.

I drove up with a few other Marines; they had kindly added me to their carpool. Vegas was only few hours away. I don't know why we never made more trips there. When we got there we all checked into our rooms and then hit the slots. I brought a bunch of alcohol my buddy had given me to bring for the party tomorrow. He would be flying in the next day; the least I could do was bring the alcohol to Vegas for him.

My phone rang and it was Kelly telling me she had been picked up earlier by her brother and one of my Marines named Kevin. They would be staying at Kevin's place for the night. Kevin was one of the latest groups of Marines that had his wife leave him and file for divorce, except that Kevin had known about it for a while. He was sent home early with the group of Marines who were with General Mattis. Kevin was on the LAV team that provided maintenance for these vehicles.

While on the phone with Kelly I tell her I couldn't wait to bring her into the Ballroom and to see her again. She joked about going with Kevin instead, but I didn't find it funny. She heard no laughter and then said she was joking. I told her to go catch up with her brother and to have a good night; I'd be seeing her tomorrow before the Ball started. She told me to have a good night as well, and we hung up. No more than a minute later, a text from her reads, "How would you really feel if I went with Kevin instead?" I wrote back, "Well, all I know is that I flew you here to go to the Ball with me. It would be rude, don't you think?"

I thought nothing of it, just a little ribbing from Kelly before our night tomorrow. I gambled $10 and won $30, so I called it quits. I never gambled too much, and never went below breaking even. I headed to my room and went to sleep; the next night would be epic.

Ah yes, the day of the Ball. I took out my uniform and put on all the ribbons and medals I'd earned. A year before I looked the part of a young Marine Staff NCO, but now I had six medals across my chest and another three rows of ribbons complimenting them. I was what one would call, "stacked." I took out an ironing board and put sharp creases in my trousers. I took Windex and Pledge and cleaned and shined my shoes. I took a cloth and shined all my medals and anything else that needed a shine. This was the night where Marines came together and celebrated each other, my favorite time of year.

Kelly and I texted during the day; they had left earlier that morning and would be arriving in the late afternoon. It was now late afternoon and I hadn't heard from her yet. I sent her another text and didn't hear back. I got dressed and headed to the pre-Ball party with the Marines of Alpha Company. My buddy had come by my room earlier to get the box of liquor from me. He was putting them to good use behind the bar. He handed me a drink with an apple in it.

"What the hell is this," I asked.

"Try it, you'll like it," he said. He was right.

When you go to battle with Marines, you see them for what they are. When you are at a Marine Corps Ball, it's the one time people can look at you and see what you've done. All of us were combat warriors, distinguished by our Combat Action Ribbons; I walked over to the Alpha company commander and pointed to the star on my Navy and Marine Corps Achievement Medal. I said to him, "See, sir, someone gives a shit." I was referring to the award they put me in for and for the one I was not given the year before. It meant the world to me to have it, especially from whom it came from.

The drinks were flowing, the camaraderie was there, and Marines were showing love for each other the only way they could…by talking shit. I stood there smiling and taking it all in. The night was amazing and the Ball had yet to begin. That reminded me, I needed to check my phone. I looked and saw no text from Kelly. I sent her a message saying that it was almost time for the Ball. When was I going to see her and walk her in? She finally responded and said she would call me when it was time. I could wait for her in the Ballroom.

I left the pre-Ball party and headed to the Ballroom. Outside the room Marines were all greeting each other, hugging each other and telling each other how much they loved the other. It was Vegas, the drinking started early. The ceremony was getting close to starting; Marines were walking in with their dates, but still no call from Kelly. I decided to wait inside where I could mingle with the Marines and their guests.

I called Kelly's phone and there was no answer. I put it away and visited with my platoon and my Marines and stood around talking to each other. I then saw a few of them look over to the right and one yelled, "Hey dude!" He was shouting at Kelly's brother who was bringing in his date. With them was Kelly, arm and arm with Kevin, one of my own Marines and the girl who was supposed to be my Ball date. I just looked at her in disgust and shook my head. I greeted her brother and his date; I passed by her without a word.

I grabbed another drink and downed it, another to follow and finished that off too. I sat over with the Marines in Alpha Company, because one of my own Marines had just fucked me and no one said anything of it. I didn't want to sit with them. My chest hurt, yet again, but I didn't care. I drank myself into a stupor, trying to forget what had happened to me earlier that year and what had just happened. My Ball was ruined; I went back to my room and took off my uniform. I changed into a shirt, jeans, jacket, and a New York Knicks cap.

Later that night a few of my Marines called me over for some drinks after the Ball. Kelly's brother was there with his date, but Kelly was not to be found. On my way out I saw Kelly, she was in her room and Kevin was also there. I said good-bye to the Marines and walked by her without a word.

"Khaled," she said, trying to get my attention, "Come on."

Her brother came out, fully inebriated and demanded we sort out the issues we had. I sat down with Kelly on the stairs. She explained that she hadn't meant to walk in with him; but that she wanted to walk in with me. I didn't really believe it, but I gave her the benefit of the doubt. I didn't know anyone who could be so heartless as to do that, so it couldn't be true. She told me that when we got back to California we'd do everything we said we'd do, including having breakfast together. I gave her a hug and said goodnight.

The next morning I headed back to California. On the way there Kelly and I texted each other, but it wasn't as frequent as it used to be. Some messages went unanswered. I wanted to go to San Diego with her that day, but the hands on the clock kept moving; the sun in the sky kept setting. The day was half over and Kelly hadn't reached out to me. They finally got back that evening; she had spent the day with Kevin and her brother.

"When are we going to hangout," I asked.

"Tonight, I promise. Come to Kevin's. Everyone is going to be there," she said.

"No, I mean just you and me, like we had planned for months," I replied.

"Tomorrow, okay? For breakfast, I promise," she said, sounding more sincere.

I went over to Kevin's house and saw everyone else there. The gut punch of having my Ball ruined was still fresh, but I was still respectful and courteous to them both. I even pulled Kevin aside and talked to him like I had a few months earlier in Iraq. Back then when I was in the mess hall in Fallujah he told me he was heading home early with General Mattis. He told me that his wife was catching shit from the other wives because of their husbands having to stay while he got to go home. I was offended by this and told him, "They can go fuck themselves, if they have a problem they can write me. If anyone gives you shit, you tell them to come see me." He thanked me and said good-bye.

This time I told him that if he needed anything, that I knew what it was like to lose someone. I could help him. I was still being good to this man, a man who had no loyalty to me as his former platoon sergeant and fellow Marine. He thanked me and went back to the party. Kelly avoided me like the plague. Her sincerity was full of shit. I overheard her brother's date talking to some of the other Marines, "Yeah, she likes him, but doesn't know what to do."

Kelly and Kevin went into his bedroom together and shut the door behind them; I left for the night as everyone else was passed out on the couches or floor. I didn't want to be there so I headed for my car. When I closed the door and walked down the stairs I heard the door lock behind me. He locked the door as soon as he could once I was out, obviously not wanting me there. I had been drinking, so I slept in my car. When I woke up in the morning I was freezing and drove to a vacant parking lot.

I was supposed to have breakfast with Kelly that morning, except she wasn't responding. When she finally answered I asked her, "Why are you doing this to me?" She didn't know what I meant; she thought I was overreacting. She told me that Kevin's wife left him and he needed a friend. "What about me?" I asked her. "Don't I need a friend?"

She gave the phone to her friend, her brother's date, and she said to me that I was really acting weird about this, that I was making Kelly feel uncomfortable. She then said, "After this, I don't think the two of you should talk anymore." This meant that a trip to Ohio to see her and her family wouldn't happen now. I had planned to go there for Christmas. I didn't know where any of this was coming from. I headed back to base and showered in the barracks.

I got a call from the current platoon sergeant. He asked if I wanted to have some coffee at Starbucks. I picked him up in my car and took him there. As I was about to park some guy backed into me. He was in his BMW. He got out and blamed me. I was waiting there for him to back out and he backed into me. My chest began to hurt more; I took down his information *and* his parking spot. It couldn't get any worse now could it?

The Marines invited me to go bowling. I invited the platoon sergeant as well and he agreed to go. He wouldn't be drinking, so that allowed me to drink. I tried my best to be a good sport, but this was too much. I'd had all I could take. Kelly's brother brought out Jäger Bombs for us to drink. I downed about five of them in succession; all the while my chest was killing me.

Kelly must have said three words to me that night; and as the clock struck midnight it was now the 5th of December. Kelly was talking to her dad; then her brother took the phone from her and was talking about me to him. He handed the phone over to me and I talked to him. He was very consoling for some reason. When I looked at my watch I realized that it was two months to the day that my father had died, and I had not yet grieved for him.

"You know I never cried about my dad," I told him as my eyes welled up with tears. "He was always there to teach me. Now who's going to be there for me?"

I put him in an awkward position. I handed phone off to anyone and I knelt by the bushes outside the bowling alley and finally mourned the death of my father. I cried for what felt like days. It didn't and wouldn't stop. I was exhausted and beaten, a man less of what I was a few years before. Everyone filed out of the bowling alley, as it was time to close up. As I sit on a bench outside, I began to feel weak. The pain in my chest was more than it was before, and I stopped breathing.

I collapsed, gasping for air and clutching my arm. I was in a great deal of pain as everyone surrounded me. One of my Marines cried and said, "Please don't fucking die, Staff Sergeant!" An ambulance came and took me away; I was in and out of consciousness but still knew what was going on around me.

In the hospital I was put into the emergency room and put on an IV. I woke up to a doctor examining me, listening to my heart. He asked me if I had any conditions, and I mentioned the heart murmur. He looked away as he listened to my heart. "Doctor, what's wrong with me," I wanted to know badly, but even he didn't know.

I was released and walked outside. Waiting for me was the Marine who begged me not to die and the platoon sergeant. Everyone else had gone back to Kevin's; I was of no concern to them. I asked to head back to Kevin's so I could say good-bye to Kelly. When I said good-bye to her I knew what was wrong with me.

My heart wasn't failing; it wasn't going to give out on me like it did for my father. My heart was diagnosed with a murmur, but why wasn't it found years before? As I said good-bye to her and heard her say to me that she didn't think we should talk again or for me to go to Ohio for Christmas, I knew what it was that was ailing me. With Rudy dying, Christine out of my life, my father dying, and the Yankees losing in the worst way possible to the worst opponent, it had all bruised my soul. But what Kelly had done to me on the one day I needed her…

It broke my heart.

Chapter 44

Happy New Year

They say to forgive but never forget; well I would love to know who "they" are so I could tell them to set foot in my shoes. With that being said, it's hard to forget the good and easy to discard the bad. Whenever someone special does something wrong, you have this feeling of hope they will revert back to the ways that caused you to love them in the first place. I have always called it "The Hope Factor," and I was certainly hoping Kelly would eventually see the light.

I was now at the lowest of lows, rock bottom if you would. I didn't care about anything and could give a shit if it all ended. Each morning I would wake up, I would first hope that it was all a nightmare and then look to see if I had any texts from Kelly. I was now blaming myself for what Kelly had done, even telling her brother that I had screwed up. I just wanted to have Kelly to talk to again; sure I lost out on a lot of money by flying her in and paying for her ticket, but I just wanted to have my friend back. You can't put a price on how much you care about someone. But wouldn't it be easier if you could?

I was kicked out of the base hotel, but a few of the Marines who weren't witness to the Kelly fiasco invited me to stay in their room. I was basically homeless, balancing the life of a Marine and a providing father with the amount of money I was making. It was not easy, and it was certainly no fun. Kevin would come from his apartment to spend time with the Marines who were his buddies now. He'd see me and talk to me normally; evading the wrath he should have received. His phone would ring and he'd walk off talking to a person on the other side, everyone knew it was Kelly.

To be replaced by someone because of your deficiencies is one thing, but to be replaced by someone for something you hadn't done was another. I wrestled with how I could have screwed up and caused Kelly to do that to me, never once thinking she might just be a coldhearted bitch. Usually, the answers to our questions and problems are the simplest of answers and solutions.

I was reduced to someone I was not, lacking confidence in my being. I reverted to texting Christine, telling her that she was the best Ball date I had ever had. This was an interesting statement, because I once had a Ball date in London years before, she was a friend of a friend, and Kelly never really spent the Ball with me so she didn't count. Though my Ball date in London was sweet, I was timid and quiet. If I was telling Christine she was the best Ball date out of them all, there was obviously a problem. Christine did respond to say, "Thank you."

Kevin gave his phone to Kelly's brother and he told her who he was with and what he was up to. He disappeared into his room and closed the door behind him. A few minutes later my phone rang and I saw Kelly's name on the screen. I answered the phone and she began with a, "What's up?" It was monotone, forced even. I was so happy to hear from her that I overlooked it, but it was indeed good to hear her voice again. We talked for a few more minutes and said goodnight. We talked about getting back to the basics; she said it had gotten weird for her, but of course it had. I asked her about visiting for Christmas and she told me that she didn't think it was a good idea, that her parents weren't too keen to having me over anymore. I understood.

I walked back outside with a smile on my face that had been missing for a few days. I had a smile on because I felt that we would be able to rebuild what we once had. I talked to all of those around me and asked for a cigarette. A few of the guys would be leaving for the Christmas leave block in a week; I still hadn't made any plans as to what I would do. I was going to go to Ohio and visit Kelly's family for Christmas, but now that idea was shot. I hadn't even put in for leave.

As the week went on I'd hear from Kelly one day and another day I wouldn't. She'd be "busy" as she put it, but she was never busy until she met Kevin. I took it. I allowed her to walk over me hoping that one day she'd look down at her shoes and see that I was there. Maybe when she did, she'd see my eyes and all the hurt she had caused. At the end of the day, all I wanted from her was an apology because deep down inside I knew I didn't deserve what happened to me.

The Platoon Sergeant went on leave, so the job went back to me for a few days. Everyone would be leaving to spend time with their families back home, wherever home may be for them. It was good to see each Marine getting time to go home for Christmas. Every day that passed another Marine would depart, including Kelly's brother. The exodus would be on a Friday night, so I asked the remaining Marines if they wanted to have a final get together in 2004. They all agreed…except Kevin.

"I don't know Staff Sergeant, I have a lot of packing to do and a flight to catch tomorrow," Kevin said.

"Dude, what if I gave you the rest of the day off to pack, would you come then," I asked.

"Yeah, that would be cool," he said.

I told him to take off and to keep his phone handy, so I could call and tell him where we were. He agreed and left for the day. I got back to work, preparing phone rosters for the impending departures. We had to be ready for anything. We were still at war, so at any time we could get a phone call and be called back. At the end of the day we all went to our evening formation and got dismissed for the weekend. Half of the Marines left in the formation were leaving the next day; it was all a formality anyway.

It was time to leave and we all met at the barracks. I'd be driving a few of us in my car and a few others would follow along in another car. I called Kevin's phone but got no answer, so I left him a text. I called again a few minutes later but still no response. I asked one of the Marines in the car with me to call his phone thinking maybe he was avoiding me.

"He's not going to answer," the Marine said.

"Just try," I asked him again.

Kevin answered this time around, telling the Marine that he wouldn't be going out with us. This upset me because I let him leave work early with the idea that he'd be joining us. I took him at his word for some reason, but once again I was proven to be the idiot. The other Marine defended him, "Come on now, he's got a lot going on. He has to pack because he's leaving tomorrow to see Kelly and her family."

After he made that comment he stopped talking, realizing he had let the cat out of the bag. I said nothing, but my temperature skyrocketed. I felt no pain in my chest this time around, instead I felt anger. We stopped by the house of one of my other Marines to pick him up and have a few drinks. While there I sent a text to Kelly's brother. I told him that I had been a reasonable man about how things had gone down, but I could only take so much. I forked up the money to fly Kelly to go to Ball and spend time with someone else, so I'd be damned if I was going to pay for having someone fuck me over like that.

He replied, sounding shocked, which annoyed me even further. What I didn't understand was that he had the opportunity to step up and tell both Kelly and Kevin that what they were doing was wrong. They could have waited until after the Ball, but he hadn't. He didn't see the harm in it, and his shock to my demands was confirmation of his ignorance. He asked me how much she owed, and I told him $800.

The night went on and we moved down to Pacific Beach. There was a strip of bars some of the Marines would frequent. I had a different approach to the night, liberating myself from the blame and reverting to anger actually helped. I didn't feel sorry for myself; I just realized I was played for a fool by just about everyone I knew in my platoon. Were some of them out that night with me? Yes, but I didn't care. I was going to do my duties as their leader and get them home safely.

As the night came to a close, we headed back to my car, none of the Marines were able to get anywhere with any of the women they tried to hook up with. In fact, one of the ladies another Marine was trying to speak with ended up putting her number into my phone. This was while wearing my wedding ring and telling her I was married. As I got in my car my phone rang. It was Kelly.

I ignored the call, hitting silent after each time she called. All of a sudden I was a priority for her. Where was the insistence to call after the Ball? Finally, the Marine who broke the news about Kevin answered my phone and tried to calm her down. She was crying over the phone, begging him to tell me to reconsider. I would have felt sorry for her, but I then realized she had shown no compassion for me, that for too fucking long I had been showing her and everyone else more love than I had given myself.

"I'll talk to him. I'll convince him…" the Marine said to her, as if I was a pushover.

As soon as the phone conversation was over I let him hear the whole ordeal from my point of view. He couldn't say anything so he said nothing. I dropped everyone off and got to my room. I logged onto the Internet and purchased a roundtrip ticket. If I was going to survive any of this, I needed to get back to the basics, back to before all of this ever became an idea. I needed to go to the only place I ever considered home, New York.

The day of my flight out to New York, I sat outside the barracks and spoke to the one Marine other than the platoon sergeant who had waited outside the hospital and begged for me not to die. He had been living with Kevin for a few weeks now and was starting to witness the truth that was Kevin. Kevin began to wonder if he had gotten in too deep with Kelly. She was calling him "too much" as he put it. She was expecting so much from him. He never wanted any of that, he just wanted to hook up and now it was getting too serious.

I laughed because she deserved to be treated as such, to be considered less than someone to care about, because that's how she treated me. I also thought it was funny that she traded me, someone who sincerely cared about her and treasured her phone calls for someone who now considered her a burden after he'd gotten what he wanted. Now while he might sound like a complete dick, which, yes he was, Kelly didn't have to go and fall for it. Women talk about finding a good man but always seem to find the douchebags, that's because they wouldn't know what a good man was if he punched her in the face…which is what a douchebag would do.

I had come to really appreciate the Marine telling me all of this. He was the only Marine I looked forward to seeing again, when I returned in a few weeks. When I returned, I would work on one thing, getting away from the battalion and putting the nightmare behind me. I made the decision that I would also be getting out of the Marine Corps. The last breath of hope of me making a career was destroyed by what happened on the second of December and the days that followed.

My plan for New York was simple: walk around the city, spend time with people who have always loved me and would continue to love me, get some Christmas spirit, and get back to being the person everyone needed to go to for advice, because being the other person was something I was not good at. I just wanted to get better, and I was going to die trying.

It was cold in New York; I arrived early in the morning. I grabbed my bagel with cream cheese and headed to Bryant Park in the city. I got a hot chocolate from a nearby Starbucks and sat down in the freezing weather, taking in the sights and sounds of New York City. Eating a bagel with cream cheese didn't hurt the New York ambience. I had bought a pack of cigarettes for about $9 from a local vendor and had it after my frozen bagel and warm *hot* chocolate. I read the paper, disappointed by the lack of Iraq War coverage. I had family there and so did thousands of others, but that was no longer news. It wasn't interesting to anyone anymore.

I walked around the city in the early morning. I waited for it to be past nine o'clock, so I could make some calls to everyone I knew in town. I wanted to tell them I was in town but didn't say that I wanted to see them. I had tried that before and it just didn't work for me. I wanted to see if they wanted to spend time with me, and if they did, I'd make it happen. One of the people I called was a girl I had a crush on in high school. She had gone with me to a Knicks game a month before and I asked her if she wanted to go to another one. She agreed. Another group of friends I knew from my time in China asked me to meet them Friday night at the "W" hotel. Not bad, so far I was two for two.

My walk took me to a part of the city I had only seen on television growing up. Even though I was raised in Brooklyn, I never got to see the Christmas tree at Rockefeller Center. As I walked further north from Times Square I saw the famous "Radio City Music Hall" sign that I had also only seen in commercials. I turned into the area and found gorgeous lights of angels and snowflakes. The area was festive and then up ahead I saw the tree. I stared at it for at least thirty minutes, ignoring the fourteen-degree weather as stated on an electronic thermometer. There I was, as New Yorker as can be in my New York Giants cap asking someone to take a picture of me in front of the tree. They were probably thinking, "Fucking tourist."

It was beautiful; I was a kid all over again, taking in the atmosphere around me. I don't know why my parents never took any of us there. Maybe it was "too American" or something, but it's a place that surely makes you forget everything.

I walked by a police officer; on his uniform I saw the familiar "Eagle, Globe and Anchor" of the Marine Corps emblem. I stopped him and made conversation as Marines do with each other from time to time. I told him I was still in the Corps, and he told me where he served and how he had just missed out on going to Iraq in 2003. Santa Claus came and joined in on the conversation and everyone walking by stared, wondering why Santa Claus and a police officer were talking to me. I took a picture with the two of them and shook each of their hands, thanking them for their kindness.

On my way home I got a phone call from Napoleon. He informed me that Kelly's brother had tested positive for cocaine and needed to get back to Camp Pendleton immediately. I told him that I was in New York but I would call him to tell him to get on a plane. I was told not to worry about it, that he would call him instead. I could not believe what the hell was going on. As disappointed as I was with him, and as mad as I was about what his sister had done to me, I never wanted this to happen. He'd have to leave his family and go back to Camp Pendleton to receive punishment...Merry Fucking Christmas.

I met with my friends on Friday night. It was good to see people I had known before. We headed downstairs to the basement of the "W" Hotel where there was a nightclub and a bar with drinks begging to be poured into my glass. I was done with the apple martinis, the Jäger, the Smirnoff Ice, and the Miller Lites. I needed something different. "Jack and Coke," I said to the bartender. I'd had Jack and Coke a few times before, but it was never to my liking. I guess after eating sand and shit for the past two years you acquire a different taste for things.

We spent the entire night in the bar. I was double fisting two Jack and Coke drinks while walking around the club mingling with anyone who seemed bored. I checked in with my friends during every walk around, overhearing one of them saying, "Nah, don't worry about him. He's having a great time!" I was having a great time, but I was not supposed to be there. It just wasn't me.

On one of my walks around the club I returned to the spot where my friends were, but they were gone. I finished my drinks and looked around to find them. In the club there was no cell phone reception, so I couldn't receive the calls that were made by them and the texts that came later. They had left; they were tired and saw that I was still alive and walking around. They said goodnight and went home. It was good of them to tell me; I appreciated it. It was time for me to go home now, too.

I called my buddy who was still in California. He hadn't taken Christmas leave like the rest of us. I was drunk but called him to tell him to take care of Kelly's brother. I told him that I knew he fucked up every now and then, but he was still my Marine, and he was still someone I cared about deeply. I said to him that I wanted him to treat him as he would treat me; he promised me that he would. It was 2:00 a.m. now, and I walked around the vacant streets of New York. A few shady characters walked by me making comments and some making threats. I yelled back at them without fear, causing them to back down and to continue walking.

I was trying to get a hold of my thoughts. I imagined the pain both Kelly and her family were going through with having to see her brother leave and I felt awful. I walked through alleys and parts of town I had never seen. I saw the sun begin to rise. Barely able to walk, I hailed a cab. I told him Brooklyn and give him the address. I got home in the early morning, just as my younger brother headed to work. I passed out on the bed in my bedroom.

When I woke up I bought two tickets to the Knicks and Mavericks game at Madison Square Garden. I wanted to make sure I had the tickets before the game was sold out. I cleaned up the apartment and ordered a pizza. I took it easy for the next few days. Kelly's brother and I talked over the phone; once again I was providing guidance to him. When he got back to Camp Pendleton he was told why he was called back.

I asked how his family was handling it. He answered with the obvious; they were sad, scared, and shocked. He said his sisters were heartbroken and crying, and though I thought it would, it didn't make me feel any better because it was only one of his sisters who broke my heart, not the others. I called a lawyer for him and asked if they would be able to provide him with legal advice. The lawyer was out of town with a family of his own. I never did get a response from him.

The day of the Knicks game was also the first day of winter, the shortest day of the year. I called my friend to pick her up. I smiled at how far I had come with her. During the final year of my time in high school, I had a serious crush on her. I would write her letters and stories that she later told me she kept hidden away in a box. My awkwardness and naivety caused me to make rash decisions in that I would tell her I couldn't be her friend anymore. I guess when I was a teenager I was more dramatic. Now nine years later we were going to a Knicks game together.

She had gotten married soon after she graduated college, but when I saw her this time around she was getting divorced. It was something that shocked me, but what shocked me even more was that I didn't try to act upon it. I appreciated our friendship more now than ever before, and I didn't want to ruin it by doing anything thought out with stupidity. When I got to her house, I was holding a plastic bag; in it were two Knicks jerseys that we'd be wearing to the game. I had bought them earlier in the day in a local sporting goods store, the same store where I got my first pair of Nike sneakers fifteen years before. She gave me the biggest hug. It was warm and loving.

We took the train into the city. All the time I had known her I had never known how to act around her. I was always nervous and my words seemed scripted. I had been through too much the past two years to script anything now. I also had no time for bullshit, no time to waste on formalities. I knew that if you didn't say or do what you felt, you'd always look back and wonder if you should have said or done something different. I now had a fear for time—not having enough of it.

When we got to Penn Station we walked underground to get to Madison Square Garden. Before we got there, I felt hungry and asked her if she was as well. She said yes, and we had pizza in the subway. We sat down on the floor of the subway, eating our pizza that was terrible and watched as people walked by. I had a play-by-play for everyone, causing her to laugh hysterically. She asked me to stop making her laugh because she had to pee.

This Knicks game was something I had never seen before. I had been to two Knicks games prior, but the Knicks were competitive in each of them, in fact winning them both. At halftime the Knicks were down to the Mavericks 75-36. I told her, "You don't understand. This has never happened before. Down thirty-nine points with a whole two quarters left? We'll be lucky to lose by fifty." It was a lost game, but I had fun. I had learned to project my voice while in the Marine Corps; I decided to use it during the game. With each three pointer the Mavericks hit to increase the lead I made a sarcastic cheer, "It's okay Knicks, at least you're not losing by a hundred!" My friend and others around me were laughing. I started calling out to the referees; I was high up, but could be heard. My section was following my reaction more than the game. A few tourists from Japan were filming me.

The Knicks had a player by the name of Bruno Sundov; if he played, it meant we were either losing big or winning big. Either way I wanted him on the floor, so I started chanting for "Bruuuuunnnooooooooo!" When he finally came in, I cheered hysterically. My friend was in tears.

Bruno was a giant of a man, but I wanted him to shoot a three pointer, "Bruno, shoot a three!" He took one and missed, drawing an "awww" from the crowd. The next possession down the court he took another one…"THREEEEEEEEEE POINT GOAL…BRUNO SUNDOV!"

Our section, now fully involved with my antics, went berserk. I started making claims that Bruno needed to be our starting point guard and that we'd be NBA champions with him out on the perimeter. My friend lost it, now dehydrated from all the tears of laughter. She said to me, "Khaled, I never knew you were like this!"

"I've always been. I've just been saving it for the right time," I said in response.

At the end of the game, we lost by less than fifty; a few of the patrons came to shake my hand, thanking me for a good time. I thanked them for not wanting me kicked out of their section. My former high school crush had an amazing time; she wanted to do it again, this time she was the one asking me if we could hang out. It was a pleasant surprise. She wanted to be around me and wasn't doing it because she felt sorry for me or wanted something from me. She wanted to be around me because she actually liked it.

"What about against Charlotte?" I asked. "The game is the day after Christmas."

She couldn't make it to that one, but when I told her about the next home game after that, she said yes. The next game would be pitting the Knicks against the Minnesota Timberwolves. On the Timberwolves was one Latrell Sprewell, a former Knick star that helped take us to the finals in 1999. It would be his second game against the Knicks since he'd been traded from the Garden. It would be drama for sure. I got us the tickets later that night.

I was invited by my friend Erin to have Christmas dinner with her and her family. It was the first time I'd seen her since San Francisco. At the dinner, it was nice to be around a family that actually cared about each other. Erin would be coming into town the next day, so she asked if I was free to do something. I said I could take her to a Knicks game against Charlotte. I don't know why, but for some reason I really wanted to go to that game. Erin handed me a small package, DVDs she had bought me for a present. One of the DVDs had a title that suited me best, *Man on Fire*.

This was what I needed. This was what I wanted. I was spending time with people that I had known for years. They were still around because they loved me, and I loved them. I didn't ask much, just for a little love in return.

On the 28th of December, I was in a movie theater about to watch a movie. My high school crush called me and asked if her boyfriend could come with us to watch the game the next day. I told her I didn't know how to get a third ticket, but it sounded like she really wanted him to go to the game. I told her, "Don't worry; I'll take care of it." She asked me not to do anything crazy, and I respond with, "Me crazy? You know me better than that."

Later that evening I found myself in Hell's Kitchen with another friend I had known from my time in China. He said he'd be in town and that if I wanted to meet up, he'd be there with some of his friends. I sat down and had a drink, then another, and then another. I was drinking more than usual, but I was drinking for two. It was my brother Eric's birthday and he was not there to toast his life with me. With each drink I bought a round for everyone at the table and we toasted him. Each drink we honored him. Only I knew who Eric was, but I felt everyone should celebrate the man.

My phone rang. It was my oldest sister. It was the first time she'd heard me drunk, but I wouldn't tell her what I was doing. She asked if I was okay because I sounded overly happy. I wasn't happy, but I couldn't tell her that. Drinking will do that to you. It will make you happy and then you crash and burn. We left the bar, everyone went their separate ways, and I took the subway home, completely obliterated. I asked a girl waiting on the platform, "Do I smell like alcohol?" She nodded and laughed. I then asked her, "How you doin'?" sounding like Joey from *Friends*. I had no idea where it came from.

I got home without an issue; no one would sit next to me on the train, but no bother, more room for me. When I got home I plopped down on the couch, my younger brother back from work smoking a joint looked at me and smiled. He'd never seen me drunk; he'd always known me to be serious and uptight, but no one in my family really saw how I was. They never knew the Khaled others knew.

I thought about what my high school crush asked me and I went to the computer in the other room. Like I had done nine years earlier, I wrote her a letter. In this letter I told her how special she was to me and that if she asked for anything, she'd get it. I needed people like her in my life; she stuck with me through my awkward stage and hadn't discarded me. For someone who was completely drunk, I was quite eloquent.

I put the letter and tickets for the Knicks game in an envelope and shopping bag. I walked outside and to her house. I hung the bag with the tickets and letter on her doorknob. The next morning I received a text from her, saying she needed to talk to me. I didn't want to talk to her for two reasons. The first was I couldn't talk, my throat was sore from all the drinking. The second reason was that I didn't want her to give the tickets back. I wanted her to have a good time with her boyfriend. She later texted before she left for the game, saying that for someone who was drunk I sure wrote well. She thanked me over and over, but I didn't want thanks. She had already given me what I wanted.

My brother was at work, and I was home alone. I put in one of the DVDs Erin had given me for Christmas. I put on *Man on Fire* and watched how a man who was haunted by the things he had done now found something to live for. I watched it with my eyes glued to the screen, taking in every emotional moment. At the end of the movie, I was so overcome I nearly lost it. By lost it, I mean that I nearly lost everything.

Tears streamed down my face, the cigarette in my mouth served no purpose. I dropped it and looked up at the ceiling. It wasn't the movie that made me go into a state of emotional turmoil, it was what it represented in my mind. It was, at that moment, that I had to make a choice. Did I go on, or did I call it quits?

I looked at the walls around me, looking at the emptiness of the apartment. I felt empty, too, empty and alone. Though I had been shown love, I was still haunted by all that had transpired. It was killing me inside, and if it didn't finish the job...I would.

But no, I couldn't do that. My father did not give up everything for us, so I could just take the easy way out. I couldn't be selfish; it was never the way I operated. My older brother would be coming to New York tomorrow, headed to Yemen on the 31st. It wasn't about me and never was about me. It was about everyone else around me.

I picked my brother up from the airport, in the car my father had left behind. It still ran and had his strength. It's what reminded me most about him, because he loved it so much. He spent a month looking for the right car to buy, and on March 28, 1986, he drove the car home. Eighteen years later it was still taking us around, except someone else was behind the wheel. I talked to my brother about how things should be now that Dad had died. "Nothing changes. Everyone is going to try to come at you and get what they want out of you," I said to him.

"Don't worry," he says to me. "I got this."

His confidence showed me something. I told him that I would support him as long as he honored my father's wishes and his name. To go against my father would be to kick dirt on his grave. My brother knew how much I loved Dad; he knew that if he made a mockery of my father, he'd have an enemy in me.

I never knew what it was like to travel on New Year's Eve, but there we were at the airport checking my brother in. I took a taxi in with him; I told him I'd see him off and go to the city for the countdown. They asked for all travelers to go through security, so I wished him well and good luck. He hugged me and thanked me. I asked him for what and he replied, "For being supportive."

I've always been known to be supportive, why would that change now?

The city was packed; everyone was there to see the ball drop signifying the end of the year. It took me thirty minutes to get from one corner to the next. I held onto my wallet and cell phone. I was sure that it was a pickpocket's paradise; I had better keep my stuff close. I found a pizzeria nearby; I was hungry and hadn't eaten all day. As I entered a police officer made eye contact with me and nodded in approval. I don't know why he did, but it felt as if he knew.

I ate two slices and decided to head back home to watch the end of the year from my couch. I found a channel that was coming in somewhat decent. I tuned in alone and watched as the ball began to drop. I leaned forward, my elbows on both knees as each second counted down.

10, 9, 8, 7, 6, 5, 4, 3, 2…

Time stops; every scene in 2004 played over and over, fast forwarding through the clips of my memory. Every word spoken, every dagger twisted into me spun faster and entered me deeper. The words my sister spoke to me over the phone about my dad, the words spoken about Rudy played over and over. Christine…just Christine. The night of the Ball and the days after still fresh in my memory played out again to remind me of what a year it had been. The Red Sox jumping up and down on the Yankee Stadium grass…

1…

I looked down and closed my eyes, the pain in my chest now gone completely. The burden lifted off my shoulders…

Happy New Year.

Epilogue

In the End

A few months after New Year's I left 1st Light Armored Reconnaissance Battalion and my platoon. On my final day with them the acting platoon sergeant asked me if I had anything to say to the Marines one last time. I shook my head, enough had been said and enough had been done. There was no need to talk about what the Corps stood for because if they didn't know by now, they would never know. I did feel a bit sad for some of the Marines that were new. They never got to experience the best of me.

    I went back to the first unit I had been assigned to in the Marine Corps at Camp Lejeune, North Carolina. It was my intention to do my time there and get out a year later. In that time I provided guidance to the Marines, using the chaos that was my life for two years as a mine for knowledge. I was very private this time around, spending more time alone than not. The other staff NCOs in the platoon I was assigned to wanted to do more things with me outside of work, but I just couldn't risk going through what I had gone through again. The walls were built; I was content where I was, so I declined each time.

    In that time I began to write, mostly things sports related, especially about the Yankees. Other times I expressed myself through poetry. On a social networking website called MySpace I joined a Yankees chat group known as "The Yankee Empire," led by great men, which contained a great group of people. I never told them my history, only that I was a Marine and a diehard Yankee fan. They never judged me, nor did they ever try to get me to speak about what I went through. They accepted me for who I was.

    I went on to meet these people. After I drank in honor of Eric I stopped drinking entirely, up until I met with them in a gathering of

Yankee fans at the moderator's apartment. I was nervous. I had never met any of them before, and it would be the first time I would be doing anything with anyone since my time in New York and the time immediately after the Ball. I introduced Jäger Bombs to the group, none of them knowing that each one we did was a salute to Rudy, my dad, and everyone else serving. I also brought them Marine Corps shot glasses. They, in turn, introduced me to Jell-O shots; they smell great, by the way. At the end of the gathering, the Yankees won on a Bernie Williams walk-off homerun. We all celebrated like children do. I fell in love with them immediately.

My older sister was later abducted in Yemen, tricked into running off with someone, causing me to drop everything and fly over there. My brothers and every male in the family were to show up as a show of force, something I laughed at because it looked as if every single one of them wanted to be something they weren't, a warrior. We got my sister back, but not without cost. I found that my older brother was indeed my mother's son, not the son of my father. He contradicted everything my father had done and allowed everyone else to walk over him. I challenged him and told him he was a terrible leader. He threatened to leave and to hand me the family reins of responsibility, but I said to him, "What does that do other than prove my point?"

Eric was back in the United States. He served in Fallujah and other areas in Iraq. He lost brothers-in-arms, his own men, and even came back wounded himself. I saw some of the same things that I had been haunted by and told Eric that he would hold that against many people who just do not understand, including his own family. I was happy to have him back alive and safe; I just hoped he wouldn't walk the same path to recovery I did.

I did give Kelly another chance. I found out that her grandfather died and sent my condolences. I was not heartless; it just wasn't in me. Her brother later went back to Iraq and was also injured. But with Kelly it would never be the same, eventually ending on my terms. She never apologized.

I was a platoon sergeant yet again, this time until I would get out of the Marine Corps. My Marines loved me, and I provided guidance for them as much as I could. Toward the end of my time, I would go to parties they held, building camaraderie with one another. One of the senior Marines admitted that when he heard that I was coming to the battalion, he knew how quickly I had been promoted, he expected me to be a dick, but was pleasantly surprised with my leadership style and respected me greatly. I appreciated it.

My platoon commander on the other hand, once he knew I was set on getting out of the Marine Corps, he treated me different. He began to question me and make comments that were unprofessional in nature. He wasn't respected by the other Marines, but he believed the bars on his collar commanded it. That is never the case. He is still the one and only Marine who ever gave me a special counseling on my performance, which in his eyes was poor performance. He made Napoleon look like a God, even though they were the same height.

I didn't care anymore about the fickle nature of some people I worked with or came across. I didn't care about the petty drama some would try to start so they could feel better about their existence. I had other things to do and worry about in life, such as life itself.

On April 19, 2006, a platoon formation was held. On this day three Marines were getting out of the Corps. The first was announced and received a plaque from the Marines of the platoon. Another Marine was announced and began to speak to the Marines in attendance. I was hiding, a rush of emotions was overcoming me, tears ran down my face and then the third Marine was announced…

"Staff Sergeant Hafid, where is he?" asked one of the Marines.

"I'm here," I said, sounding sad and dejected.

I stood there in front of the Marines, all looking at me with smiles on their faces. I cried as I stood, leaning against a refrigerator behind me as another Marine spoke. The Marine speaking was once a mentor to me. He was a sergeant when I first met him; I was a lance corporal and nineteen years old. Now a gunnery sergeant, he told a story of me that was somewhat doctored, trying to draw laughs from the Marines and then went on to tell the story of a young kid who became the leader standing in front of them today.

He pulled out a plaque that the Marines had gotten for me. They were not required to get any of the staff NCOs a plaque but wanted to get one for me. It read, "Staff Sergeant Khaled 'K' Hafid. From July 15, 2005 to April 19, 2006. Motivated, dedicated Platoon Sergeant, Yankee fan, leader and towel head. Your guidance will be missed. Semper Fidelis…. That was easy."

He handed me the plaque. I looked at it, at him, back at it and then back at him again. He was upset that I was leaving and was angry at me; I could see it in his face, though he knew I was doing what was best for me, finally thinking for myself. For years I had always wondered what I would say to the Marines when it was time for me call it a career, and even as I opened my mouth, I still wondered...

"You think about what you're gonna say for...as long as you've been in or what you're gonna say the day it's your day. I thought about it every day in my car. What am I gonna say to the Marines? What am I gonna say? I didn't know how I was going to react. Honestly, I did not know. Some people who knew me before were like, 'Yeah you're not gonna fucking cry...' I have done ten years in the Marine Corps or close to it...and I've done everything I can to help Marines. Everything I can. I wanted to make sure that everyone of you was, in some shape or form, affected by me somehow. I think that's been the case...But hey, listen. Honestly, hey...everybody here is a Marine. Nobody is going to take that away from you, all right? When I get out today or whatever and EAS in a month, I will always be a Marine. Never forget that shit. Never forget who you are, where you come from, or where you want to be...cause nobody's gonna take this from you, not even God himself. Remember who you are, don't forget what you are okay? And I thank every one of you from the bottom of my heart. I love you all. I seriously mean that shit." – Staff Sergeant Khaled Hafid

When you least expect it, surprises that were actually destined from the start begin to appear before you. The girl named Nicole who said she had to stop talking to me when I first got back to Iraq? She found me years later and became my best friend. I have a daughter now, and like my son, I told everyone what day she would be born on, and I was right. I named her after my mom. In 1975, my father was thirty-three years old; he brought his family to the United States. Fast forward to present day and I, at thirty-three years of age, brought my own children to the United States, "to grow up and live happy in the land of the free..."

Years go by and there is not one day that I haven't missed the Corps. There is not a day that goes by I do not honor those who have fallen or my father. I watch the news and see that there are men and women still thrown to the wolves bearing the name of "Marine" or "soldier" and carrying out their day-to-day mission without the thoughts of the millions they are sworn to protect and serve.

I know that without the Corps and the pride it demands from its Marines, I would not have survived 2004. I know that without the teachings of my father, I would be nowhere near the man I am today.

How many men and women have you come across in uniform and have not thanked them for what they do or have done? I am sure there are countless times this has occurred, but I don't blame anyone. You don't know what we go through or what any of us are fighting inside. Just don't be ignorant to the fact that we are people as well. We hurt, we cry, our hearts get broken, we mourn…but we do so in our own way. We are not like everyone else.

I have found success outside the Corps, and have accomplished things I could only wish for my father to see. He was proud of me as a Marine, and died while I was still a Marine. My father's last memory of me was as a Marine, "the few, the proud," and I can only hope I have done him proud and my son in the future.

I do not wish for things to have gone any other way. The trials we face in life will test us, but it's our overall character that will push us through and help us reach goals once thought unattainable. I am not angry with Christine or Kelly; let it be. I am not sad about Rudy or my dad. Instead, I celebrate their existence and everything they have done for everyone they had come across.

The measure of a hero is not based on actions or deeds. The measure of a hero is based on what he or she is best known for. A hero is nothing without those who he or she wants to be heroic for, and there are people in my life that have given me reason to push forth.

The one thing I learned most about my two-year ordeal is that I am indeed a better man than I was before I set foot on that ship in 2003.

War is hell, and war is shit…

What the fuck can be said to better explain war and its impact on our lives? Though *the silence* in our inner battles *is* indeed *deafening*, it's a statement that comes in louder and clearer than any radio transmission I've ever heard before…*over.*